M000305589

TO THINK
LIKE A
MOUNTAIN

Also by Niels S. Nokkentved

Back Road Daydreams: Reflections on the Great Outdoors

*A Forest of Wormwood: Sagebrush, Water
and Idaho's Twin Falls Canal Company*

Desert Wings: Controversy in the Idaho Desert

TO THINK LIKE A

MOUNTAIN

Environmental Challenges
in the
American West

NIELS SPARRE NOKKENTVED

WSU
PRESS

Washington State University
Pullman, Washington

Washington State University Press
PO Box 645910
Pullman, Washington 99164-5910
Phone: 800-354-7360
Email: wsupress@wsu.edu
Website: wsupress.wsu.edu

© 2019 by the Board of Regents of Washington State University
All rights reserved
First printing 2019

Printed and bound in the United States of America on pH neutral, acid-free paper. Reproduction or transmission of material contained in this publication in excess of that permitted by copyright law is prohibited without permission in writing from the publisher.

Cataloging-in-Publication Data is available from the Library of Congress.

On the cover:
The effects of livestock grazing and the disappearance of beavers show in this creek in the mountains of central Idaho. *Author photo*

For Michael Frome

May 25, 1920–September 4, 2016

teacher, mentor, friend

*"Only the mountain has lived long enough to listen
objectively to the howl of a wolf."*

Aldo Leopold, *A Sand County Almanac*

Contents

Maps

Preface

The charming landscape which I saw this morning is indubitably made up of some twenty or thirty farms. Miller owns this field, Locke that, and Manning the woodland beyond. But none of them owns the landscape.

—Ralph Waldo Emerson

Early one May morning in 2006, I stared into the yellow-green eyes of a wild yearling wolf. It had been caught in the rubber teeth of a leghold trap and tranquilized. Though immobile, it was fully conscious. For a few moments I was transfixed as we stared at each other across the gravel road in the mountains northeast of Boise. Several minutes later, I watched the young male wolf slowly regain control and stagger to his feet as the tranquilizer wore off. He headed upslope, stopped once and looked back, and then melted into the woods. I thought about how we treated that wolf and its fellows in the wilds of the Northern Rockies, barely a decade into reintroduction in Idaho and Yellowstone and still listed as an endangered species at the time. Wildlife biologists tranquilize them, examine them, put radio collars on them, take DNA samples, and fasten numbered plastic tags in their ears. Though their efforts are done with the best intentions and may benefit reintroduced wolves, I could not help but think that the wolves would have been better off in the long run if we had never tried to eradicate them in the first place.

More important is what we do next, and not just as far as the wolves are concerned. This book's title, *To Think Like a Mountain*, is taken from a passage in Aldo Leopold's book, *A Sand County Almanac*, and refers to the idea that when we consider the long-term consequences of our actions, we have clean air and water, salmon spawn naturally, forests thrive, wolves run free, and people find new ways to work and play outdoors. When we do not, we get over-grazed rangelands, sick forests, climate change, and extinct species.

I chose the concept of "thinking like a mountain" because of its implications for those long-term effects of human relationships with the natural landscape. Leopold learned the concept from an encounter with a wolf. He acknowledged that he once thought wiping out wolves would create a hunters' paradise, but the wolf and the mountain taught him otherwise.[1] My own encounter with a wolf also led me to think about our connections with nature. As Ralph Waldo Emerson noted, no one owns the landscape. The resources of the earth itself belong to those who own the land, catch the fish, drill the oil, cut the trees, or extract the minerals. That goes for all lands, public and private.

An articulation of thinking like a mountain was offered by the late Billy Frank Jr., a member of the Nisqually Tribe of Washington and a lifelong activist who went to jail more than fifty times for standing up for the fishing rights granted by the 1854 Medicine Creek Treaty and upheld by the 1974 Boldt Decision. "I don't believe in magic. I believe in the sun and the stars, the water, the tides, the floods, the owls, the hawks flying, the river running, the wind talking. They're measurements. They tell us how healthy things are. How healthy we are. Because we and they are the same. That's what I believe in."[2]

The issues covered in this book primarily involve lands owned in common by the citizens of the United States and administered as property by the government, either federal or state. The United States includes 673 million acres of public lands. Since that land is owned in common, the benefits should go to all of us, but too often they go disproportionately to those who exploit its resources for private gains.

On public lands, individuals benefit by reaping as much as possible, furthering their own wealth, while the cost of overuse is shared equally by all the owners of the land. Limits on individual users help to reduce or prevent such damages. Without limits, all the owners lose, ecologist and philosopher Garrett Hardin argued in a 1968 essay, "The Tragedy of the Commons."[3] The commons he refers to include far more than just the nation's public lands; they also include the rivers, streams, lakes, groundwater, coastal estuaries, and the air we breathe. Since they are all connected, what happens on private land also affects the health of these commons.

Naturalist and author Edward O. Wilson has argued that environmental concerns focus too much on pollution, shortage of fresh water, loss of arable land, and climate change. Those are important issues, but too little attention is paid to what he calls the living environment; that is, the species and ecosystems upon which all life, including humans, depends. Humans have identified about two million species. We know little or nothing, however, about the millions of fungi, algae, and insects that are the foundations of life.[4] The changes we cause through environmental degradation, global climate change, and shortsighted land uses can disrupt species we know nothing about, and could disrupt food chains that have consequences we cannot predict.

The main reason species have disappeared and continue to disappear is the loss of habitat. Wilson argues that the only way to slow the rate of extinction is to save habitat by creating natural refuges wherever possible on public and private lands. In the United States, conservation efforts and the Endangered Species Act have helped slow the loss.[5] (See the end of chapter four for more on the Endangered Species listing process.) In West Texas, for example, the Boise-based Peregrine Fund has been working since the 1990s with local ranchers and other land owners to create protected areas where captive-raised, endangered aplomado falcons have been successfully reintroduced. Worldwide, refuges now cover about 15 percent of the land and 3 percent of the oceans. Wilson contends that there are enough fragments in sufficiently good condition available around the world to protect half the land and half the oceans without disrupting people's lives or infringing on property rights.[6] One example in this country is the land designated as critical habitat for species protected under the Endangered Species Act. Such lands protect ecosystems and can be a buffer against extinction for many more species than the ones for which the land was set aside, including many species whose importance we may know nothing about.

Loss of species can affect us in ways we may not perceive. In 1948 Fairfield Osborn, in his eloquent little book, *Our Plundered Planet*, warned that we humans were more likely to wipe ourselves out by our mistreatment of nature than with wars and advanced weapons.[7] Aldo Leopold put a finer point on that idea when he wrote: "We abuse land because we regard it as a commodity belonging to us. When we see land as a community to which we belong, we may begin to use it with love and respect. There is no other way for land to survive the impact of mechanized man, nor for us to reap from it the esthetic harvest it is capable, under science, of contributing to culture."[8]

In recent years environmental legislation has set some limits on exploitation of resources on public and some private lands and attempted to balance the intrinsic value of public resources against private gain. Setting values on public resources, such as clean air, clean water, or natural aesthetics is difficult. Many have tried. In his book, *A Wilderness Bill of Rights*, naturalist and Supreme Court Justice William O. Douglas quotes Harold E. Alexander of the Arkansas Game and Fish Commission, who in 1960 wrote:

> In assigning values to natural streams, we must emphasize intangible values, the significance of which defies the application of any monetary standards to define their worth. The intangible values we can assign to natural streams are real and are identical with those we attribute to good music, the arts and architecture, which command high prices in the marketplace. They include the concept of our democracy, our family relationships, and spiritual values. These things have not been and cannot be calculated in dollar terms.[9]

Many years later in 1989 a federal appeals court recognized the value to the public of simply knowing that something, such as a free-running river, an old-growth forest, or wild wolves, still exist.[10] The millions of visitors who each year camp, fish, hike, hunt, or otherwise enjoy the great outdoors on our public lands, and the tens of thousands of people who earn a living catering to those visitors, already recognize those values.

For more than a quarter century as a newspaper reporter I wrote about these and issues like them. Inspired by John Mitchell's 1975 book *Losing Ground*, in which he revisits stories he had written in the past, I decided to look again at stories I had covered in my years of writing about natural resources.[11] I wanted to write from a long-term perspective rather than the limited perspective of a daily deadline. The chapters that follow cover issues that reflect our utilitarian relationship to nature and our environment. They include the conflicts between cultures over resource extraction, threats to watersheds by abandoned mines, wolf recovery in the Northern Rocky Mountains, the lingering effects of livestock grazing on western rangelands, and the disappearing sage grouse. They discuss the importance of forest fires, the value of beavers, the failed promises of salmon hatcheries, the reasons behind the decline of the timber industry in the Pacific Northwest, and how unlikely allies learned to set aside their differences to resolve long-standing natural resource issues. My aim is to focus attention on the struggle between those who recognize the importance of thinking like a mountain, and those who do not. To survive, we need to recognize that it profits us most as individuals and as a people if we respect the balance of nature.

The essays that follow are meant for general readers interested in natural resource issues. The chapters are based on my own reporting and observations over the years and expanded by additional research and more recent events. In the course of my research, sadly, I learned that we are still losing ground.

———————◆———————

I would like to thank the people who helped with this project. In particular, Walt Poole for helping me understand the magic of wild salmon, and Dale Toweill for explaining the decline of elk habitat in northern Idaho. Thanks to John Harrison for his help in locating key sources; Craig Collett for his help with salvaging old images; and Janet Jorgenson for the last minute image from the Arctic National Wildlife Refuge. My thanks also to Ed Mitchell, Virgil Moore, and others, for their support, inspiration, comments, and suggestions. Most of all, I want to thank Christian D. Nokkentved for his learned review and critique, editing help and support; without him this book would not have been possible.

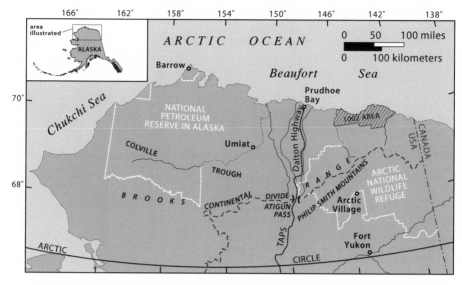

North Slope of Alaska.

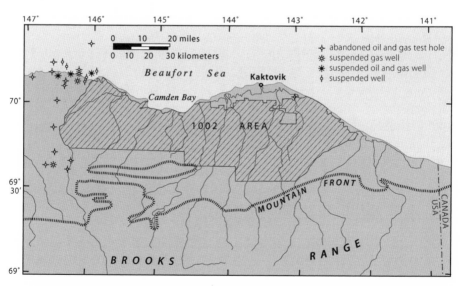

Northeast Alaska with Area 1002 of the Alaskan coastal plain, part of the Arctic National Wildlife Refuge.

Source for both maps: U.S. Department of Interior, *Arctic National Wildlife Refuge, Alaska, Coastal Plain Resource Assessment.* Washington, DC: U.S. Government Printing Office, 1987. *Maps by Chelsea Feeney, cmcfeeney.com.*

CHAPTER 1

Selling Arctic Wilderness

Conservationists call it America's Serengeti for its wildlife migrations. Oil industry officials call it Area 1002, for the section of the 1980 Alaska National Interest Lands Conservation Act that left it open to oil exploration. The native Gwich'in people, who rely on the caribou that give birth in the area, call it "the place where life begins."[1]

Part of northern Alaska's coastal plain, the 1.5-million-acre Area 1002, about the size of Long Island, is the most productive part, in terms of wildlife, of the Arctic National Wildlife Refuge.[2] The refuge was set aside in 1960 specifically to protect this wildlife, and its wilderness and recreational values. Each of the three groups sees Area 1002 from a perspective that reflects their attitude toward the landscape. Conservationists see it for its intrinsic worth and place a value on just knowing it is there and intact. Energy industry officials see it for the value of the oil that it may contain. The Gwich'in see it as part of the community to which they belong. Area 1002 is a place where the most abundant and irreplaceable resource is wilderness; does that not have value greater than any oil it might contain?

Federal officials and Congress certainly seem to have answered the question of worth. In a 1959 Interior Department news release, Interior Secretary Fred Seaton called northeastern Alaska one the world's great wildlife areas and one of America's wildlife and wilderness frontiers. In the 1980 legislation that doubled the size of the Arctic National Wildlife Refuge, President Jimmy Carter said he wanted to restrict "development in areas that are clearly incompatible with oil exploration."[3] A 1987 U.S. Department of the Interior environmental study of the area concluded oil development would threaten or destroy the very values for which the refuge was created, stating, "The wilderness character of the 1002 area would be lost, leaving the designated Arctic Refuge wilderness area east of the Aichillik River to the Canadian border and the three-million-acre

North Yukon National Park in Canada as the only remaining areas of preserved Arctic coastal plain ecosystems in North America."[4]

———————————◆———————————

An American expedition in 1906 discovered clues to the oil potential of the area. Eight explorers landed on the northeast coast of Alaska on the evening of September 17, but they had not come looking for oil. Expedition leader Ernest de Koven Leffingwell and seven others had set out from Victoria, British Columbia, four months earlier in a sixty-five-foot schooner, the *Duchess of Bedford*, to explore the north coast of Alaska and to look for land rumored to be found in the Arctic Ocean north of Alaska.[5]

The group was a mixed lot. Leffingwell, teacher and geologist, was born in Knoxville, Illinois, in 1876 and studied mathematics and physics at the University of Chicago. He organized the expedition with Ejnar Mikkelsen, a polar explorer and author born in Denmark in 1880. Leffingwell had served on two previous polar expeditions; one to East Greenland in 1900, and one to Franz Joseph Land north of Russia in 1900–02. The team also included Boston physician Dr. G. P. Howe, Danish zoologist and artist Ejnar Ditlevsen, and four sailors.[6]

They stepped ashore in the early evening of the long arctic night on Flaxman Island, a spit of sand and gravel where the Canning River runs into the Beaufort Sea. From the island, Leffingwell looked south across the mud flats of the Canning River delta at the featureless terrain of tundra beyond, rising toward the foot of the nine-thousand-foot glacier-clad peaks of the Brooks Range some forty miles to the south.

Leffingwell would eventually explore much of what he saw, and his work would play a key role in the future of Alaska and the arctic wilderness. In his 1919 report for the U.S. Geological Survey, "The Canning River Region: Northern Alaska," he described the area's history, people, animals, geology and the arctic phenomenon now known as permafrost. This frozen layer beneath the surface can be up to two thousand feet thick and is found under most of northern Alaska's coastal plain. He called it "ground ice," and he noted that only the upper two to three feet would freeze and thaw with the seasons.[7] He also identified the Sadlerochit sandstone formation and its oil-bearing potential that would lead to one of the largest oil discoveries in the country. The discovery would change life in Alaska and eventually touch off a long-running controversy over the fate of Alaska's northeastern coastal plain that still simmers a century later.

At stake is an unspoiled arctic ecosystem that stretches east into northwestern Canada and includes the wildlife and native cultures that it supports. It is home to polar bears, wolves, muskoxen, vast herds of caribou, and millions of birds, in addition to two native cultures. To the native residents, the most important animal in the refuge undoubtedly is the caribou (*Rangifer tarandus*) found in much of northern Alaska. Caribou are related to deer, elk, and moose, but unlike the others, both males and females have antlers. Stocky bodies and dense fur keep them warm. Their long legs and snowshoe-like feet help them navigate deep snow.

Leffingwell and his team spent the winter on the ship moored at Flaxman Island, and set out to explore the area. They befriended two Inupiat families who lived on the island and helped them hunt caribou. Over the next nine summers and six winters Leffingwell used as his base a cabin built from parts of the ship, which was damaged by ice that first winter.

Leffingwell's cabin. A party of explorers built this cabin from timbers salvaged from their wrecked ship. *Photo taken in 1949 by Rear Admiral Harley D. Nygren, NOAA Corps (ret.), NOAA Photo Library*

Between 1906 and 1914 Leffingwell explored the region and mapped about 150 miles of the arctic coastal plain between Point Barrow and Herschel Island, off the coast of Canada's Yukon Territory and about forty-two miles east of the U.S. border. Whalers and traders had charted the coastline, but no one had gone inland. Leffingwell did, covering about 4,500 miles by dogsled and small boat. In his U.S. Geological Survey report he described an irregular coastline fringed with islands and barrier reefs of sand and gravel, shallow lagoons, salt marshes, and river delta mud flats with low mud banks. More surface water than land in many places, nearly all of the coastal plain is classified as wetland. The average precipitation is only about ten inches, much of that in snow, but the underlying permafrost keeps the water near the surface. Shallow ponds and lakes dotted the flat and featureless upland. "A bank fifteen feet high is a landmark for many miles, and twenty feet is exceeded in few places," he wrote.[8] Grassy hummocks up to three feet high covered the plain. The highest point in the area, Barter Island, rose up to about fifty feet above sea level.

Bounded by mountains and the sea, the plain rises gently from the marshy coastline to the rolling tundra of the Anaktuvak Plateau at the foot of the Brooks Range, which cuts across northern Alaska from the west at about 163 degrees west longitude to the northeast reaching the coast near the Canadian border at 141 degrees. The part of the coastal plain that would become Area 1002 stretched a little more than one hundred miles from the Canning River to the Aichillik River. The Canning runs north out of the Franklin Mountains and forms the western border of Area 1002. The Aichillik runs north out of the Romanzof Mountains and forms the eastern border. In between, the area spans a little less than forty miles at its widest and about sixteen miles at its narrowest. Along the rivers Leffingwell found patches of cottonwoods up to twenty-five feet tall. He found no evergreens north of the Brooks Range.

Leffingwell also kept track of the weather. The lowest temperature he recorded was minus 61 degrees in February 1907; the warmest was 70 degrees. June through August the average was about 40 degrees. January through March saw an average of minus 20. The combination of darkness, wind, and extreme cold made outdoor work difficult and hazardous during the winter. The area is without sunlight for fifty-six days of the year.[9]

Humans have lived in northeast Alaska for at least 11,000 years. When Leffingwell arrived, he encountered Inupiat Eskimo, a semi-nomadic people who once had lived on what the land provided. The only permanent settlements along the northern coast were at Point Barrow with about 250 to 300 people and Herschel Island across the border in Canada with about 50. In addition, two or three families were scattered along the coast between the two. The 1910 census counted sixty-five people between Point Barrow and the Canadian border.[10] Leffingwell found the remains of thirty to forty ancient homes on a sand and gravel spit on Barter Island, reminders of people who had once lived on the northeast shore of the island, between the Okpilak and Jago rivers facing the Beaufort Sea at a place known as Kaktovik, which means "the seining place." The Inupiat scattered along the coast would meet on the island to trade.

By the time Leffingwell arrived in 1906, whalers and traders had left their influence on the local residents. Barter Island had become a rendezvous for commercial whalers during the 1890s and early 1900s. Flour, sugar, tea, butter, canned fruit, and bacon brought by the whalers had become staples for the local Inupiat; many dressed in European clothing, and they used tents, stoves, and blankets. After the U.S. government purchased Alaska from Russia for $7.2 million in 1867, the native people acquired guns and ammunition from whalers. They hunted the abundant caribou along the coast between Point Barrow and the Mackenzie River in Canada and sold them to whaling ships wintering along the coast, or traded skins for clothing and other items. Caribou as a consequence became scarce on the coast.

In 1923, Tom Gordon, a Scottish whaler and trader, established a trading post on Barter Island overlooking what would become the village of Kaktovik. Then in 1945 the U.S. Coast and Geodetic Survey came to the area while mapping the Beaufort Sea coastline. During the Cold War, the U.S. government chose Barter Island as a site for a Distant Early Warning radar installation. The military moved people in the surrounding area to Kaktovik, and the Bureau of Indian Affairs opened a school there. Government jobs and the school drew more people to the village, as did the 1968 discovery of oil at Prudhoe Bay, about 120 miles to the west. Kaktovik was incorporated in 1971, and the 1980 U.S. Census listed 165 residents.[11] Many of the Inupiat still depend on subsistence practices, and village hunters take an average of twenty-five to seventy-five caribou annually. Today Kaktovik is the only village within the Arctic National Wildlife Refuge.

The Inupiat were not the only people tied to the wildlife refuge. In the foothills south of the Brooks Range, just outside the boundary of the refuge and about seventy-five miles north of the Arctic Circle, forty log cabins overlook the East Fork of the Chandalar River. They comprise Arctic Village, one of fifteen villages in Alaska and Canada that are home to Athabascan Indians called Nets'aii Gwich'in—People of the Caribou.[12] The Gwich'in number about seven thousand people. Their predecessors have lived in the area for as much as 6,500 years, and for thousands of years they have depended for their subsistence on the caribou herd that migrates to the coastal plain. The herd's migration route takes it through two of the Gwich'in villages, Old Crow in the Yukon and Arctic Village. Caribou harvests vary from year to year. Arctic Village residents take up to a thousand caribou annually and Old Crow residents take a similar number.[13] Most are taken between August and April.

Growing up in Arctic Village, Faith Gemmill was taught by village elders to respect the land and the environment, she told a group attending a writers' workshop in 2001. The caribou herd was vital to her culture and made up 80 percent of their diet and provided clothes and tools. She learned how to hunt, how to tan hides, process meat, and how to make tools from antlers, bone, and sinew. Songs, stories, and legends reflected the importance of the caribou in her culture. The Gwich'in believed that at first animals and people were the same, until the Creator separated humans from animals. The Creator, however, left a part of the caribou in the people and a part of the people in caribou. People and caribou still retained a piece of each other. "Whatever happens to the caribou happens to the Gwich'in," Gemmill said.[14]

—◆—

Just as the Gwich'in depended on the caribou, the caribou depended on the coastal plain. The 125,000- to 200,000-member Porcupine herd takes its name from the Porcupine River, which runs from the mountains north of Dawson in the Yukon, and flows through the village of Old Crow and into the Yukon River near Fort Yukon, Alaska. The herd's range covers an area the size of Wyoming, and includes parts of the Yukon and North-west Territories in Canada as well as northeastern Alaska. In the spring the herd migrates about fifteen hundred miles from the interior along the Porcupine River drainage heading north to the calving grounds on the coastal plain of the Arctic National Wildlife Refuge. Feeding on the green shoots of cotton grass in the tussock meadows, the females produce rich milk that helps newborn calves thrive. The herd spends the summer on the coastal plain, wading into the ocean to seek relief from the hordes of mosquitoes. The summer is short here, and the fall migration begins by mid-July. The animals winter at the edge of the boreal forest in the southern portion of their range. The route, both north and south, varies depending on the weather and snow.

Caribou represent only one of the many species that inhabit the Alaskan arctic, some of them year round. An arctic icon, polar bears spend most of their lives hunting seals on the pack ice that covers the sea most of the year. Some females make their dens on land, including the Arctic Refuge coastal plain, sometimes more than thirty miles inland, but most den on the ice. They begin to look for den sites in October or November and give birth to one or two cubs in December or January. They emerge in late March or early April, depending on the weather. If disturbed by human activity, however, the females may abandon their dens prematurely. In 1986 the population was estimated at thirteen hundred to twenty-five hundred.[15] On May 14, 2008, the U.S. Fish and Wildlife Service listed the polar bear as threatened across its range under the Endangered Species Act. The greatest threat was the melting of their sea ice habitat as a result of a warming climate, which climate experts say has affected the Arctic and Antarctic regions disproportionately. As the sea ice they rely on to hunt seals decreases, polar bears come ashore more frequently, especially in Kaktovik, where scientists counted eighty bears in the fall of 2016. Here they resort to feeding on scraps from Inupiat whaling.[16] Some even starve to death.

Other threats include oil and gas operations, subsistence hunting, shipping, and tourism. In 2009, the U.S. Fish and Wildlife Service proposed designating critical habitat for polar bears that would incorporate most of the coastal plain within twenty miles of the coast, including barrier islands and spits along the coast, and sea ice above the continental shelf. Such a designation could add restrictions to oil and gas exploration and offshore drilling. The critical habitat proposal of about 120 million acres was challenged in court, but the Ninth Circuit Court of Appeals in 2016 upheld the designation.[17] The bears and their habitat also get some protection under the U.S. Marine Mammal Protection Act and an international treaty between the United States, Canada, Denmark, Norway, and Russia, which requires protection for bear habitat, including den and feeding sites.[18]

Another arctic denizen in trouble is known to the Inupiat as *omingmak*, or "the shaggy one." Muskoxen live year-round on the flat arctic tundra just south of the coastal plain. Wiped out by hunting in the late 1800s, muskoxen have been reintroduced. In 1969 and 1970, the U.S. Fish and Wildlife Service brought sixty-four muskoxen to the refuge. The population grew to nearly 500 by 1985, and today Fish and Wildlife biologists estimate about four thousand muskoxen live in Alaska.[19] Long guard hairs, thick wool, and square, short-legged bodies help them retain heat. To save energy, they do not move much. They feed along rivers in summer, and find dried grasses in wind-blown areas with little snow in winter.

Gray wolves roam in the mountains and foothills along major rivers on the refuge's north slope east of the Canning River. Numbers vary seasonally and fluctuate from year to year, because of disease or changes in prey migration patterns. Recent estimates vary from five to ten and as many as twenty-five to thirty gray wolves.[20] They prey primarily on caribou, moose, and Dall sheep.

North America's northernmost Dall sheep populations live year-round on ridges above the timberline, on dry meadows, and steep slopes of the Brooks Range. Grizzly bears live in the mountains inland. Ground squirrels and foxes are found over the coastal plain as well. Bowhead whales, seals, and other marine mammals ply the off-shore waters of the Beaufort Sea and were hunted by the Inupiat. "A full-grown whale was worth nearly $10,000 at the prevailing price of $5 a pound for whalebone," Leffingwell wrote.[21] The whales are still hunted by natives. Today Kaktovik residents capture one bowhead whale a year on average.[22] In all, the area is home to thirty-six species of land mammals and nine species of marine mammals. Leffingwell also reported seeing wolverines, golden eagles, ravens, gulls, arctic foxes, and jaegers.

About 195 bird species, including birds that migrate to and from most parts of the United States, can be found here in the spring and summer. Eider ducks migrate in huge numbers, up to fifty thousand per day. Black brandt, white-fronted and snow geese, ducks, ptarmigan, black-billed and yellow-billed loons breed in the refuge. The coastal plain also is a key fall staging area for an annual average of more than a hundred thousand migrating lesser snow geese.[23]

The indigenous inhabitants once used gill-nets and jigged through holes in the ice in the rivers for fish that included trout, whitefish, grayling, and salmon. The area supported a rich diversity of fish and wildlife, to say nothing of the insects, and plant-life including sedges, grasses, mosses, lichens, small flowering plants, and dwarf shrubs. In addition the area is rich in aesthetic, natural, scientific, and cultural values.

The area also exhibited potential for the presence of oil deposits. Oil oozed from the ground in places along the north coast of Alaska, but whether it existed in underground deposits sufficient to be economically viable in the harsh northern climate was unknown. Natives had told Leffingwell of a deposit near the shore between Prudhoe Bay and Point Barrow that resembled axle grease and could be dug easily with a shovel. His 1919 report included notes about oil seeps near Barter Island and oil bearing sands as well as shale outcrops that smelled of oil along the Jago River about ten miles south of Barter Island. Other seeps on the North Slope indicated the possible presence of an oil field. Leffingwell suggested oil bearing rocks might be found elsewhere on the North Slope, but he was uncertain about the potential for development in his report. "Even if an oil pool were found in this northern region, there is serious doubt of its availability under present conditions, though it might be regarded as a part of the ultimate oil reserves that would some time be developed."[24]

Leffingwell's report of the potential oil deposits along the north coast of Alaska caught the interest of government officials. In the early 1900s, the United States had established the Naval Petroleum and Oil Shale Reserves, consisting of three oil fields in California and Wyoming, to secure oil for the U.S. Navy, which was converting its ships from coal to oil in the years before the start of World War I. In 1923, President

Warren G. Harding added twenty-three million acres of the North Slope as Naval Petroleum Reserve No. 4.

As the interest in oil on the North Slope grew in the first half of the twentieth century, so did interest in protecting Alaska's vast arctic wilderness. Just before his death in 1938, Robert Marshall, U.S. Forest Service forester, writer, and wilderness activist, recommended that all of Alaska north of the Yukon River, except Nome, be set aside and protected from industrial development. "In the name of balanced use of American resources, let's keep Alaska largely a wilderness," he said.[25] Already in 1935 Marshall, one of the founders of the Wilderness Society, and future society director Olaus Murie had started a move to establish an arctic preserve in northeastern Alaska. Murie worked as a wildlife biologist for the U.S. Biological Survey from 1914 to 1917, and studied Alaskan caribou between 1920 and 1926, mapping migratory routes and estimating numbers.[26]

With his 1945 appointment as Wilderness Society leader, Murie became an important advocate for the National Park Service, which took an interest in protecting part of northeastern Alaska. Marshall turned out to be the catalyst. While hiking in Minnesota in 1936, Marshall had met and befriended George L. Collins, whom he would influence with his ideas on wilderness. Collins later became a National Park Service planner in Alaska where he eventually would lead the Park Service's efforts in protecting part of northeastern Alaska's arctic wilderness.[27]

During World War II, most of Alaska's North Slope that Marshall had recommended for protection was closed to development, though not immune to oil exploration. In January 1943, President Franklin D. Roosevelt's Public Land Order 82 closed forty-nine million acres—everything north of the crest of the Brooks Range—again for military purposes.[28] After the war, the Bureau of Land Management launched a program of widespread oil and gas exploration in the North Slope reserve to gauge its oil and gas potential. Between 1944 and 1981, government geologists drilled more than 130 wells in the Naval Petroleum Reserve No. 4.[29] In 1976 the reserve was renamed the National Petroleum Reserve-Alaska. In 2017 the USGS estimated that the area held about 8.7 billion barrels of oil, and about 25 trillion cubic feet of natural gas.[30]

In addition to oil and gas reserves, the federal government began to take an interest in the recreation potential of northern Alaska. In 1949 participants in the American Association for the Advancement of Science's Alaska Science Conference recommended the government study areas worthy of protection. The National Park Service took on the lead role in what became the Alaska Recreation Survey and put George Collins in charge.[31] From 1951 to 1953 Collins and biologist Lowell Sumner looked at many parts of Alaska. U.S. Fish and Wildlife regional director Clarence J. Rhode invited Collins and Sumner to tag along on the agency's annual wildlife survey in northern Alaska in 1952. Collins and Sumner found northeast Alaska had the greatest potential as a national park and published an essay in the *Sierra Club Bulletin* of October 1953 titled "Northeast Alaska: The Last Great Wilderness." Describing the area's varied arctic terrain, plants, and animals, they wrote: "It includes perhaps the most completely undisturbed but accessible large wilderness area in North America today with some of the most unusual and inspiring scenery of all arctic scenery."[32] They recommended northeast Alaska be preserved as a field laboratory and for education and recreation in order to "protect one of the most valuable continental wildlife breeding areas and one of the great scenic and historic regions of North America."[33] The article drew attention and support for arctic preservation from conservationists including Olaus and Mardy Murie, Howard Zahniser, Sig Olson, and many others.

Building on his earlier work with Marshall, Murie spearheaded an effort to permanently protect part of northeast Alaska. Oil, gas, and mining interests were pressuring the federal government to open the North Slope lands closed by Roosevelt's Public Land Order 82. Murie and other conservationists recognized that same order also protected some of best areas in northeast Alaska from development, and they opposed the efforts to lift it. In 1956, Murie and his wife, Mardy, began a campaign to protect what would eventually become the Arctic National Wildlife Refuge. After prodding by Murie, Supreme Court Justice William O. Douglas in 1957 visited the Murie's camp in the Sheenjek River Valley, part of the future wildlife refuge. Douglas, an eloquent outdoor writer, wrote of his visit in his book *My Wilderness*, published in 1960.[34] He helped persuade President Dwight Eisenhower to set aside a portion of northeastern Alaska.

In the summer of 1957, the Eisenhower administration urged Congress to establish a wildlife reserve in the area identified by Collins and Sumner. When Congress failed to act, the U.S. Fish and Wildlife Service asked the Interior Department to set aside part of the area closed by Roosevelt's earlier land order as a wildlife refuge.[35] Interior Secretary Fred Seaton proposed modifying Roosevelt's land order, opening access to potential resource development on part of the North Slope and establishing a wildlife refuge in northeast Alaska. The wildlife refuge met with stiff opposition from oil and mining interests as well as Alaska's congressional delegation. Some suggested the area should be turned over to the state instead. In 1960, when another legislative effort failed, the Eisenhower administration resorted to executive action.

A young Alaska attorney would come to play a key role in that executive action to establish the wildlife refuge. Theodore Fulton "Ted" Stevens Sr., born in Indiana in 1923, graduated from Harvard Law School in 1950, and in 1952 went to work as an attorney in Fairbanks. The following year Eisenhower nominated him as U.S. Attorney for Alaska. In 1956, he moved to Washington, DC, to work for the Interior Department, where he first went to work on Alaska statehood.[36] The act that made Alaska the forty-ninth state on January 3, 1959, also allowed it to set aside 104 million acres of federal lands.

The following year, in the waning days of the Eisenhower administration, Stevens wrote Public Land Order 2214, which established the 8.9 million acre Arctic National Wildlife Range. Seaton signed the order on December 6, 1960, creating the range "for the purpose of preserving unique wildlife, wilderness and recreational values."[37] The order was a compromise that also would lift the land order that since World War II had blocked development in Alaska's arctic, while giving the impression that it would grant protection for the northeastern corner from industrial development. The land order Stevens wrote explicitly exempted oil and gas drilling leases, thus leaving the wildlife range open to oil exploration. Years later, in August 1994, Stevens told reporter David Whitney of the *Anchorage Daily News*: "It was a great goal of people, particularly at Interior, who were quite interested in a gas field (near Barrow) at the time."[38] He considered the creation of the Arctic National Wildlife Range a small price to pay for access to Prudhoe Bay's oil. "The order specifically allowed oil and gas exploration in the Arctic range subject to stipulations to protect fish and wildlife," Stevens said. "I think it was a very good deal."[39]

Four years later, Stevens was elected to the Alaska House of Representatives, and in 1968, appointed to a U.S. Senate seat where he served until 2009. Here he would play key roles in the Alaska Native Claims Settlement Act of 1971, Trans-Alaska Pipeline Authorization Act in 1973, and the Alaska National Interest Lands Conservation Act of 1980, discussed below. He died in a plane crash in 2010.

———————◆———————

In 1960, no one had given much thought to the possibility or feasibility of bringing North Slope oil to market. That was about to change. Part of the North Slope opened by the Seaton's public land order included an area just west of the new wildlife range known as Prudhoe Bay, land that Alaska had selected as part of the federal lands granted at statehood. Less than a decade later it would become the site of the biggest oil strike in North America. On the day after Christmas in 1967, in a thirty-knot wind at thirty degrees below zero, noise from underground drew a group of men to an ARCO-Humble drilling rig. The noise grew louder, hinting at an oil strike. Charles G. "Gil" Mull, an oil company geologist at the site recalled the scene: "We could hear the roar of natural gas like four jumbo jets flying right overhead. A flare from a two-inch pipe shot at least thirty feet straight into that wind. It was a mighty encouraging sign that something big was down below."[40]

ARCO began drilling the fateful Prudhoe Bay State No. 1 well in April 1967. Nine months later and a little more than a mile and a quarter down, the drillers hit the marine sediments of the Sadlerochit sandstone formation identified by Leffingwell. Marine sediments are a good place to look for oil. Geologists estimate that nearly all oil the world over was formed in ancient seas. Tiny marine plants and animals sank to the bottom of shallow seas over countless eons, forming thick beds that were buried beneath other sediments. Heat and pressure eventually turned the sediments into stone and the tiny creatures into oil. Geologists estimated that the Prudhoe Bay oil deposit held nearly ten billion barrels of recoverable oil. (A barrel is forty-two gallons.)

One day in 1966, during his own work in northern Alaska, Mull encountered Leffingwell's cabin still standing on Flaxman Island. Mull credited the foundation of the oil industry's understanding of the region's geology and oil potential to Leffingwell's pioneering work in the Arctic. When Mull heard in 1971 that Leffingwell had died at the age of 96, he suggested to the Alaska Division of Parks that the site be protected. Parks officials approved his suggestion, and in the summer of 1971, Mull carried a cedar plaque in a company helicopter to the wind-swept gravel island in the Beaufort Sea. He fastened the plaque to the weather beaten cabin built by Leffingwell and his former shipmates more than half a century earlier: "From this base camp geologist Ernest D.K. Leffingwell almost single-handedly mapped Alaska's Arctic coast during the years 1907–1914. He also identified the Sadlerochit—main reservoir of the Prudhoe Bay field."[41] The cabin and several other buildings still stand on Flaxman Island, about fifty miles east of Prudhoe Bay. On June 2, 1978, the National Park Service designated Leffingwell's camp a National Historic Landmark.

◆

The discovery of oil at Prudhoe Bay changed life in Alaska. Suddenly the settlement of Alaska native land claims and other indigenous rights, unresolved since the United States bought Alaska, took on a new urgency. On December 18, 1971, Congress passed and President Richard Nixon signed the Alaska Native Claims Settlement Act. The act provided money and property titles to settle aboriginal claims of Alaska's indigenous populations to lands where they had lived for generations. The act also organized native people into 220 village and thirteen regional corporations as a framework of ownership that would allow Alaska's indigenous people to become part of the social and economic life of the state and the country. It granted forty-four million acres to the village corporations and twelve regional corporations within Alaska. The thirteenth corporation represented nonresident Alaska natives. The corporations also received more than $962 million, $500 million of that in mineral revenues.[42] The Arctic Slope Regional Corporation, one of the twelve, included the Kaktovik Inupiat Corporation, which represents the economic interests of about eleven thousand native Inupiat from Kaktovik and seven other villages. In addition, the act gave surface rights to more than ninety-two thousand acres of federal land adjacent to the Kaktovik Corporation, which owns twelve or more subsidiaries and pays shareholders annual dividends.

Not all Alaskan native groups accepted the offer, however. The Gwich'in residents of Arctic Village and Venetie to the south rejected the Settlement Act, opting instead to maintain their traditional ways. The 1971 law revoked their aboriginal claims and their 1.8 million-acre reservation set aside under the 1934 Indian Reorganization Act. The Gwich'in instead used a provision of the 1971 Act that allowed them to take title to former reservation lands. They now own the 1.8 million-acre reservation.[43]

The act also called for the protection of eighty million acres of federal lands in Alaska as parks and wildlife refuges. The act gave the government eight years to identify these so called "national interest lands." The deadline, December 18, 1978, would become a key turning point for the Arctic National Wildlife Refuge.

Meanwhile, additional oil discoveries on Alaska's North Slope spurred oil companies to consider how best to get the oil to market. As early as 1924, the U.S. Geological Survey had suggested a thousand-mile pipeline to get oil from the Arctic to the lower 48 states. Oil industry officials took the suggestion to get the crude oil from Prudhoe Bay to a terminal at Valdez on Prince William Sound, the country's northernmost ice-free port. Within weeks of the Prudhoe strike, engineers went to work to design a pipeline for Alaska's harsh environment. Arctic conditions and the physical challenges of transporting 160-degree oil over a frozen landscape without thawing the ground that supported the pipeline, would delay the start of construction. In addition, environmental and legal challenges following the 1969 Santa Barbara oil spill off the California coast resulted in a federal court injunction in 1970 that blocked the pipeline.[44]

The Arab oil embargo of October 1973 sparked a sense of urgency. With help from Senator Stevens, Congress passed the Trans-Alaska Pipeline Authorization Act, which authorized the pipeline construction and blocked all legal challenges. Construction of the pipeline, officially the Trans-Alaska Pipeline System, or TAPS, began in March 1975. It would require eight hundred miles of forty-eight-inch diameter steel pipe, and it would cross three mountain ranges, three major earthquake faults, and more than five hundred rivers and streams. About half of it was elevated to avoid melting the permafrost, and the corridor included more than 550 wildlife crossings. The $8 billion pipeline was completed in June 1977. Its capacity would set the limit of oil production from the North Slope at just over two million barrels per day. Crude oil began flowing in the pipeline on June 20, and the first tanker filled with North Slope crude oil left the port of Valdez on August 1. At last the oil Leffingwell believed was hidden beneath the tundra in the Arctic Refuge had become marketable. The refuge was open to oil exploration, and now the possibility of finding oil there had become more interesting.

The pipeline brought its own troubles along with the oil. Just after midnight March 24, 1989, the tanker Exxon-Valdez ran aground on Bligh Reef in Prince William Sound in the Gulf of Alaska and disgorged at least 11 million gallons of crude oil. The single-hull tanker, about the length of three football fields, had taken on about 62 million gallons of crude at the pipeline terminal in Valdez, Alaska. The spill was the largest to date, contaminating more than a thousand miles of shoreline and killing thousands of birds, marine mammals, and fish.

No one really knows how much oil exists beneath the tundra, said Ken Boyd, a geologist and oil industry consultant and former director of the Alaska Division of Oil and Gas, speaking at a 2001 writers workshop.[45] Nor does anyone know what would happen if the area were opened to oil exploration and extraction. The existence of the Prudhoe Bay field suggested to some the presence of a large field, but estimates vary greatly. Some geologists say there is a 95 percent chance of finding sixteen billion barrels and a 5 percent chance of finding up to forty-two billion barrels. The amount that can be economically extracted, however, depends on technology and the going price of oil. Conservationists cite an earlier U.S. Geological Survey estimate of 3.6 billion barrels. Boyd's middle-of-the-road estimate is ten billion barrels of recoverable oil, about the size of the Prudhoe Bay field. "But nobody knows until you drill," he said.[46]

Meanwhile the 1978 deadline to select national interest lands, set in the 1971 Alaska Native Claims Settlement Act, approached. Conservationists urged Congress to designate the coastal plain as wilderness; oil and gas industry officials and their supporters pushed for opening the area to exploration and extraction. Legislation to settle land ownership issues and designate national interest lands stalled. A proposed Alaska National Interest Lands Conservation Act (ANILCA) would have designated the entire original wildlife range as wilderness, off limits to oil and mining interests. The Senate, however, wanted the Department of Interior to assess the wildlife and petroleum resources and the potential effects of oil and gas development on the 1.5 million-acre coastal plain.

In the waning days of the Carter administration, Interior Secretary Cecil D. Andrus went on the road to generate support for the act, often facing hostile crowds. The energy industry and personal greed were the biggest hurdles, he said. And he proudly noted that he once threw an oil industry representative who opposed any restrictions out of his office. The Carter administration was determined that some areas should be left alone. "We ought to be intelligent enough to say let's save that little chunk," Andrus said. The coastal plain was one of the last places without industrial development. It was like a laboratory, where scientists could study wildlife in its natural state. Some oil industry officials realized that if the legislation did not pass by the deadline, protected status for the national interest lands would be forfeit and all of the Alaska Arctic National Wildlife Range would be open to oil exploration. So they stalled, said Andrus.[47] He persuaded President Jimmy Carter to use the Antiquities Act of 1906 to tie up all the lands of the refuge, including the 1.5 million-acre coastal plain, in a national monument to bring the oil industry back to the table. On November 16, 1978, the Carter administration withdrew 110 million acres of federal land in Alaska. It worked, but it took a couple of years; meanwhile it satisfied the deadline set in the 1971 act.

In 1979 the House passed the same legislation, and again it ran into stiff opposition in the Senate. When Reagan won the November election in 1980, House leaders recognized that attitudes favorable to protecting Alaska lands were waning. With a sense of urgency, the House passed the Senate bill without any changes on November 12. Carter signed the Alaska National Interest Lands Conservation Act on December 2, 1980.[48] Essentially a land use plan for 375 million acres, ANILCA rescinded the 1978 Antiquities Act order and set aside 104 million acres, almost 57 million in wilderness, and required review of wilderness potential on an additional 70 million acres of federal land. It established the 18-million-acre Arctic National Wildlife Refuge, which replaced the Arctic National Wildlife Range, and included about 9 million acres of wilderness. Section 1002 of the act set aside 1.5 million acres of the coastal plain, an area known henceforth as "Area 10-0-2," and required the Interior Department to complete a comprehensive assessment of fish and wildlife resources and the potential effects of oil and gas exploration and extraction on those resources, along with an estimate of the potential petroleum resources. It was a concession to the oil industry, which had been blocking the act. "We didn't shut the door on development, we made it possible," Andrus said.[49] Andrus was instrumental in one more key requirement: opening the Area 1002 to oil or gas exploration and extraction would require the express approval of Congress.

The required report, completed in 1986, identified 26 potential oil deposits with an estimated 4.8 billion to 13.8 billion barrels of oil. It concluded that exploration and development would likely result in widespread, long-term changes in habitat availability or quality that could affect the Porcupine caribou herd. U.S. Fish and Wildlife Service biologists concluded that oil field operations would reduce or displace the herd by 40 percent. Oil operations could also displace reintroduced muskoxen and reduce their numbers, and would affect wolves, wolverines, polar bears, snow geese, seabirds, shore birds, and arctic fish. They also would result in major restrictions on subsistence activities of Kaktovik's native Inupiat residents.

The report acknowledged the effects on wilderness values: "Noise and presence of oil-development facilities would not only eliminate the wilderness character in the 1002 area, but there could also be some visual and sound intrusions in the designated Wilderness by activities and developments in the adjacent 1002 area. The existence of oil facilities and activities would eliminate the opportunity for further scientific study of an undisturbed ecosystem."[50]

Despite the findings of Fish and Wildlife Service scientists, then-Interior Secretary Donald Hodel recommended to Congress that the entire 1002 coastal plain be opened to full exploration. "The Arctic Refuge coastal plain is rated by geologists as the most promising onshore oil and gas exploration area in the United States," he wrote in a letter introducing the Interior Department's assessment of the Arctic National Wildlife Refuge.[51] He expressed concern about the country's increasing reliance on imported oil and how that would affect national security. Hodel also based his recommendation in part on seismic exploration funded by a group of oil companies.

Meanwhile, a controversial land trade would result in the only exploratory well drilled within Area 1002. In 1983 the Arctic Slope Regional

Corporation acquired the subsurface rights to more than ninety thousand acres on Kaktovik Inupiat Corporation lands from the Department of Interior in exchange for surface rights to more than one hundred thousand acres near Chandler Lake in the Gates of the Arctic National Park. The trade allowed the native corporation to drill a test well in the coastal plain of the Arctic National Wildlife Refuge and to retain the exclusive right to any test well data.[52] British Petroleum and Chevron began to drill southeast of Kaktovik in the winter of 1984–85. The well was plugged and the results have not been released, except to the Alaska Oil and Gas Conservation Commission as required by Alaska state law.[53] In April 2019, however, the *New York Times* reported that court documents and recent interviews suggest the test well results were disappointing and revealed nothing significant about the oil potential of the coastal plain.[54] Still, no production of oil or gas could occur anywhere within the refuge unless specifically authorized by Congress. The site of the test well still shows clearly in the tundra more than thirty years later.

The footprint of the KIC-1 test well about 14 miles southeast of Kaktovik is still visible in this 2018 photo. The test well was capped and abandoned in 1986. The Beaufort Sea coast is visible in background. *USFWS photo.*

Interests on both sides of the issue have worked hard to convince Congress of the competing values of oil and of wilderness and an intact arctic ecosystem. The U.S. Fish and Wildlife Service has pointed out that oil development would eliminate the wilderness values of the area and threaten subsistence activities of native arctic cultures. U.S. Senator Frank Murkowski of Alaska, a strong proponent of opening the coastal plain to oil exploration, in a *New York Times* op-ed column in October 2000 wrote that the oil "can be extracted and moved to consumers in the 'lower 48' states without harming the wildlife that inhabits the coastal plain at various times of the year. More than 25 years of experience at nearby Prudhoe Bay...have shown that energy production and environmental protection can coexist."[55]

Prudhoe Bay, however, may not be the best example in support of drilling. The discovery there transformed the better part of six hundred square miles of arctic tundra into an industrial landscape. Three primary oil companies and several smaller ones operate more than eleven hundred production wells in an industrial complex about fifteen by forty miles, with miles of roads, gravel pits, drilling rigs, airstrips, buildings, and thousands of miles of pipeline. Andrus had this to say: "I've been up to Prudhoe Bay, heard the industry dog and pony shows....I have also come away unconvinced. Air and water pollution problems at Prudhoe Bay are more serious than generally believed. Predators have vanished from areas around the pipeline and existing oil developments. Platforms and roads and pipelines might well disrupt migration of the Porcupine herd."[56] The 1986 Fish and Wildlife Service report noted:

> Accidental spills of crude oil and refined petroleum products are an inevitable consequence of oil-field development. Throughout the operation of Prudhoe Bay, the very large spills (on the order of at least 10,000 gallons) have been of crude oil, gasoline, and diesel. Larger spills not only cover a larger area, but they also penetrate deeper into the soil.... According to 1985 records (the first full year of computerized oil-spill data) there were 521 reported spills totaling 82,216 gallons (Alaska Department of Environmental Conservation, Fairbanks, unpublished data). Diesel and crude oil were the most commonly spilled products.[57]

Most spills, however, were small, many less than ten gallons, and the effects have been localized and not significant, the report continued.[58]

On the coastal plain, the importance of caribou has not diminished. Snow machines have replaced dog sleds, and rifles have replaced traps. Despite better hunting techniques, wage jobs, and store-bought food, caribou is still the most important food and cultural resource for the Gwich'in, providing 80 percent of their diet. The Gwich'in people fear oil development would interrupt the cycle of caribou migration and birthing.[59] To get to their calving grounds on the coastal plain, the caribou would have to run a gantlet of haul roads and pipelines, noisy diesel trucks and heavy equipment, drilling rigs and helicopters.

Oil may bring prosperity for some, but when the oil is gone, the wilderness qualities that made the coastal plain important will have vanished. Without the caribou the Gwich'in say their lifestyle would vanish. By then some Inupiat elders fear the people will have forgotten the ancient ways. "We shouldn't be expected to sacrifice our way of life for short term benefit," said Gwich'in Nation spokesperson Faith Gemmill. "It doesn't matter how much oil is there, our way of life would be lost. No amount of money could replace that."[60]

Interior Secretary Hodel's justification for oil exploration in Area 1002 may have been valid in 1987, but not so much today. He cited concerns about our dependence on foreign oil imports, particularly from the Middle East, and the implications for national security as justifications for oil exploration in the coastal plain. Recent discoveries, however, have increased the nation's oil reserves to their highest since 1972. Changes in technology, advances in alternative energy technologies, new discoveries, and improved efficiency already have reduced the nation's dependence on oil imports and taken the urgency out of Hodel's justification. In 2016, an oil deposit was discovered in the Wolfcamp Shale formation in West Texas, part of the energy rich Permian Basin. The U.S. Geological Survey estimated that it held up to twenty billion barrels of oil, twice the size of the initial Prudhoe Bay estimates and three times larger than the Bakken and Three Forks shale formations in the Dakotas and Montana. In addition, experts say there may be even more oil in the West Texas area.[61]

The rate of extraction in West Texas or the Arctic, as with any oil or gas resource, depends on the cost to bring it to market and the going price of oil. The cost for oil from the Arctic was among the highest in the world at nearly $50 per barrel in 2016. By contrast, the cost to get oil in Saudi Arabia to market was less than $10, one of the lowest in the world. The average in the United States was between $20 and $25 per barrel, with oil from shale slightly higher. The price of oil, however, varies with demand and supply, even if manipulated artificially. In 2017 the United States imported about 10 million barrels of petroleum per day. The top source was Canada at 40 percent. The Middle East accounted for about 17 percent.[62]

Though supplies may have increased in recent years, demand may not continue to rise. A February 2017 report predicts the growth in demand for oil will peak in 2020, in part because of the decreasing cost of electric vehicles. The report, "Expect the Unexpected: The Disruptive Power of Low-carbon Technology," predicts that by 2025, electric vehicles could reduce oil demand by two million barrels of oil per day.[63] The report cites the oil price collapse in 2014-2015 as an example of the economic crisis that a two-million-barrel reduction in demand can bring. At the beginning of 2014, world oil production lagged consumption by about 600,000 barrels per day. By the end of 2015, world oil production had risen to more than two million barrels per day higher than demand.[64]

When the price goes down, the first places where oil exploration is halted are those where costs of production are highest, including environmentally sensitive areas, such as the Arctic National Wildlife Refuge. As of this writing, no drilling rigs could be seen in the refuge, no haul roads or pipelines, and no sprawling industrial complexes. For the most part, the area remains in its natural state. In January 2015 President Barack Obama pushed for a wilderness designation for most of the refuge, including the coastal plain. The designation would end the arguments, politics notwithstanding.

In 2017, Congress included in a massive tax cut package authorization for oil exploration in Area 1002. Then in April 2018 the Trump administration opened a sixty-day public comment period on proposed oil drilling leases on the coastal plain. Meanwhile Canadian government officials and native people decried plans to drill for oil in the area where the Porcupine caribou herd goes to calve each summer. The herd spends much of its time the rest of the year in Canada. Canadian officials and the native people who depend on the caribou feared drilling would undermine their efforts to protect the herd. The decision to allow oil exploration threatens the calving ground of the vast Porcupine caribou herd, whether or not oil is found. Thinking like a mountain, however, would preserve the wildlife ecosystem and the native cultures that depend on it, values already well established by the public, federal officials, and an earlier Congress. It behooves us to respect this major arctic wilderness.

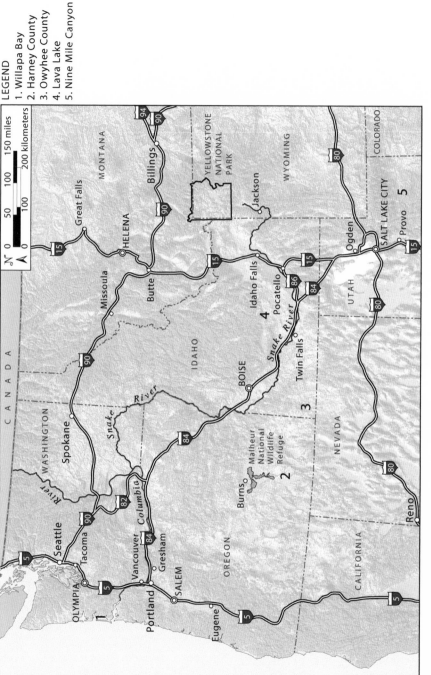

Pacific Northwest region and key sites discussed in this book: 1. Willapa Bay, southwest Washington (Ch. 10: Overcutting Ancient Forests); 2. Harney County, southeast Oregon (Ch. 8: Bringing Back the Beaver); 3. Owyhee County, southwest Idaho (Ch. 11: Saving America's Outback); 4. Lava Lake, Snake River Plain, central Idaho (Ch. 8: Beaver); and 5. Nine Mile Canyon, eastern Utah (Ch. 2: Ancient Art in Nine Mile Canyon). *Map by Chelsea Feeney, mcfeeney.com*

CHAPTER 2

Ancient Art in Nine Mile Canyon

Pecked into a reddish rock face along a dirt road in a remote canyon in eastern Utah, images of four men, bows drawn, face a herd of about two dozen bighorn sheep. Thought by archeologists to be between seven hundred and two thousand years old, the Great Hunt panel is one of an estimated ten thousand petroglyphs and pictographs at more than a thousand sites left by ancient inhabitants, the Fremont and Ute Indians, in Nine Mile Canyon, northeast of Price, Utah. (See #5 on map, page 24.) Petroglyphs are pecked or scratched into the dark patina that forms on the rock surfaces over time; pictographs are made with pigments applied to the rock. Archeologists consider the canyon to be one of the country's richest archeological resources.

Petroglyphs like this six-foot wide panel in Nine Mile Canyon are threatened by natural gas exploration. *Author photo*

The canyon and its ancient and historic rock art stretch back in time, spanning the length of human presence in eastern Utah, from the earliest known American Indians to pioneers who hauled their dreams down this dusty canyon road. For thousands of years, this humble canyon has served humans as a travel, trade, and transportation route. Many have left marks of their passing, some thousands of years old, others more recent. From about 300 CE, the canyon was inhabited by Fremont Indians, scattered groups of hunters and farmers who were part of a diverse culture that lived in western Colorado and the eastern Great Basin. Their farming practices included irrigation, and they lived in mud and timber pit houses with stone granaries built of stacked rocks in areas protected by canyon walls. They hunted the deer and elk that still thrive here. The height of their culture lasted from about 750 to 1250 CE. They disappeared sometime between 1250 and 1500 CE. No one knows exactly why. Some experts say that other people, such as Utes or Shoshone, may have migrated into the region and either displaced or absorbed the Fremont. The stunning collection of ancient rock art in the canyon could be a key to understanding the cultures that created it.

The ancient art, however, faced a modern threat. One of the country's largest natural gas reserves was discovered in 2000 beneath the West Tavaputs Plateau. The deposit was thought to be capable of producing an estimated 250 million cubic feet of natural gas per day. The primary access to the plateau and its gas was the Nine Mile Canyon Road. Both are mostly on public lands managed by the federal Bureau of Land Management. Archeologists said energy exploration and extraction activities in the area could damage or destroy some of the ancient art that had stood for perhaps a millennium or more; others said an energy extraction project here could also compromise areas proposed for wilderness designation. BLM officials had the unenviable job of juggling the push for energy extraction and the protection of natural, historic, and cultural resources. It is an issue common in places where oil and gas are found on public lands. The BLM's job was to find a way to balance publicly owned resources whose values cannot be measured in dollars with the lucrative energy resources that also play an important role in the nation's economy.

BLM officials were well aware of the archeological sites in the canyon, but they were also under political pressure to increase energy production from western public lands. Moreover, measures to protect the art by rerouting some truck traffic, or paving the road, or drilling farther from the canyons would increase the company's costs. Those expenses would become part of the cost of doing business, just like other companies pay to accommodate the needs of the human or natural environment in other places.

Nine Mile Canyon cuts west to east through the remote and rugged West Tavaputs Plateau. The Tavaputs is part of the vast Colorado Plateau, a land of ancient horizontal sedimentary rock layers cut by vertical fault lines and deeply etched by the Colorado River and its myriad tributaries. The Tavaputs rises from the Uinta Valley in the north and drops into the Castle Valley to the south. It reaches from the Wasatch Range in the west and stretches into western Colorado. The Green River's Desolation Canyon cuts the plateau into the West Tavaputs and the East Tavaputs.

Nine Mile Canyon is named after Nine Mile Creek, which runs through part of the forty-mile canyon. While I have heard several versions of how the Nine Mile Creek got its name, it was most likely named for a nine-mile triangulation drawn by topographer Francis M. Bishop, a member of John Wesley Powell's party exploring the Colorado River in 1869. Powell and his party passed through the canyon on a side trip examining the geology of the West Tavaputs Plateau.[1] In 1886, following trails of the ancient inhabitants, the Buffalo Soldiers of the Ninth Cavalry built a road along the creek to supply Fort Duchesne, to the north. The road linked the fort to the railroad in Price, a six-day trip by wagon. It also served as the route for mail, freight, stagecoach, and telegraph in the Uinta Basin of eastern Utah.[2]

Some years ago I explored this area with Troy Scotter, head of the Utah Rock Art Research Foundation. We followed Soldier Creek Road north from U.S. Highway 6 just outside the town of Wellington, east of Price. At the Soldier Canyon Mine, the pavement ended, and the road became Nine Mile Canyon Road. In a few miles the road dropped into the canyon. Down the middle of the canyon, cottonwoods and willows lined Nine Mile Creek. Pines and junipers dotted the higher parts of the canyon walls, and the gravel road, passable most of the time, wound along the creek. Sedimentary rock layers stacked like pancakes formed near-vertical canyon walls more than a thousand layers thick in places.

Along the way Scotter and I saw ancient granaries, pit houses, watchtowers, and some spectacular petroglyphs. We passed an old homestead, and a little farther on, Nine Mile Ranch, which offered the only over-night accommodations in the canyon, including lodgings, food, camping, a country store, and guided tours of the canyon's rock art. Soon after, we came to the first major petroglyph panels. As we continued down the canyon, the road ran through the ghost town of Harper, once a stage stop known as Lee Station. Next we came to a hundred-yard-long rock ledge covered with petroglyphs that included human shapes with headdresses, some with toes and fingers. Across the road on a smooth, black rock face halfway up a hillside, a large snake stood out clearly. Trees, birds, and human figures covered another rock face. Farther along we passed a former stagecoach stop. A stone building against a cliff and a log cabin beside it were once part of a relay station for the telegraph between Fort Duchesne and Price. About three hundred feet up the canyon wall, we saw a large, well preserved granary, and high on the opposite side we could make out a watch tower. A large alcove known as Rasmussen's Cave held several pictographs. Here we also found a worn rock once used to grind corn by hand.

The past, however, was not allowed to rest in peace. Where Daddy Canyon came in from the north, Nine Mile Canyon widened. Here the BLM had built a parking area with toilets and a trail that wound through a self-guided tour of rock art panels. We heard the baritone rumble of heavy industrial engines that drove a natural gas compressor station less than a quarter mile away and drowned out the gurgle of Nine Mile Creek. The compressor ran twenty-four hours a day. About a mile farther down the road, we came to the Great Hunt panel, with its famous hunting scene chipped into a rock outcropping about ten feet above the road. The thousands of petroglyphs and pictographs, some more than a thousand years old, found in Nine Mile Canyon are important to archeologists because the concentration and variety of rock art helps experts interpret all of it in context. "I think this is a place that could help us understand rock art, more than many other places. And by studying rock art, we can understand the culture that created it," Scotter said.[3]

The compressor reminded us that the modern world had intruded in this otherwise peaceful place. In 2003 Denver-based Bill Barrett Corporation had proposed a seismic mapping project on 58,000 acres just south of Nine Mile Canyon and in culturally rich tributary canyons. The three-month project would produce a three-dimensional subsurface map from a series of more than five thousand "source points" consisting of small charges set off in drilled holes and from specially built thirty-ton "thumper" trucks equipped to send vibrations into the ground. The resulting map would help evaluate the area's natural gas potential. The company already had several operating and capped wells in the area and had proposed a separate project to drill sixteen exploratory wells.[4]

Blaine Miller, staff archeologist with the BLM's Price office, warned of potential damages to these ancient rock structures and art from the proposed exploration. For twenty-five years, these canyons and their archeological treasures were Miller's domain. He knew the rock art better than anyone else in the BLM. It was his job to provide information on archeological resources that could be affected by a seismic mapping project. Miller had voiced his concerns that dust raised by heavy truck traffic and by dust-suppressing chemicals, such as magnesium chloride, could damage rock art and cultural artifacts. He also expressed concern that fragile rock structures could be damaged by the vibrations of seismic mapping, huge trucks, drill rigs, bulldozers, and industrial traffic associated with gas exploration and extraction on the West Tavaputs Plateau. As a result, his bosses reassigned him.

Later in 2003, federal officials in the BLM's Price office released an assessment of the potential effects of the proposal on the archeological resources in Nine Mile Canyon. While the agency had characterized the area as the world's longest art gallery, the BLM and Barrett company officials maintained that the exploration project would not affect any historical artifacts in the canyon. They said that any proposed vibration source point closer than three hundred feet to a known historic structure would be moved or abandoned.[5] Yet the person who knew best the location of those historic structures and artifacts had been taken off the job.

Like Miller, the National Trust for Historic Preservation (NTHP) raised questions about the effects of the seismic project on archeological resources in Nine Mile Canyon. The NTHP also argued that the rock art panels within the canyons were susceptible to damage from increased dust and vibrations from the seismic mapping process as well as increased public access and vandalism. In a September 29 letter to the BLM, NTHP maintained that the BLM's assessment of the project was not adequate to conclude that the project would not harm the archeological resources.[6]

BLM officials said they were interested in protecting the historic and cultural resources, but the National Trust and other critics doubted BLM's sincerity. If BLM wanted to protect the canyon's rock art, they asked, why had agency officials reassigned the man who knew the area and the locations of the rock art better than anyone else?[7] Clearly it was the BLM's job to know whether the project would affect the archeological resources. Section 106 of the National Historic Preservation Act of 1966 required the BLM to consider the effects of proposed projects, including oil and gas exploration and extraction, on historic properties that are included or potentially eligible to be included on the National Register of Historic Places.[8] A legal challenge failed to halt the project, but Barrett agreed to revise the proposal, and BLM released a revised environmental assessment in 2004. The seismic mapping survey was conducted over that summer.

Projects like Barrett's are governed by federal law. The Mining Law of 1872 opened public lands to prospecting for "all valuable mineral deposits in lands belonging to the United States, both surveyed and unsurveyed," including prospecting for oil and gas.[9] The law also allowed prospectors to buy for $5 an acre the land on which they had staked a successful claim. Early in the twentieth century this led to a boom in oil prospecting claims, not all of them valid. Federal officials sought a more orderly process, and Congress enacted the Mineral Leasing Act of 1920, which covered coal, oil, oil shale and gas, phosphate, potassium, sodium, and sulfur. The law gave the Interior Department responsibility for oil and gas leasing on public lands and on private lands where the federal government had retained mineral rights.[10] Interior gave the job to its Bureau of Land Management.

The BLM follows an established process to award oil and gas leases on public lands. The agency identifies areas available for oil and gas leasing in land-use plans, and studies potential environmental effects. The BLM awards leases through oral auctions conducted at least quarterly when lands become available. Bidders or their representatives must attend the auction in person and submit a legally binding bid form. Costs include an administrative fee, which rose to $160 in 2016, the first year's advance rental of $1.50 per acre, and at least the $2-per-acre minimum bonus bid. The bidder must also pay a royalty of 12.5 percent of the value of the oil or gas produced from federally administered public lands.[11] Royalties on state lands are higher and range from 16.67 percent in four western states to 25 percent in Texas.[12] Any restrictions, limits, or requirements to reduce or eliminate unacceptable environmental effects of oil and gas extraction can be included in the terms of the lease. Leases are good for ten years but can be renewed.

Before lease holders can start drilling, they must apply for a drilling permit. The application spells out all related activities, including road building, pits to store drilling mud, and pipelines to carry oil and gas to market. After a permit is approved, the company can still submit proposed changes to BLM, such as well locations, additional pipelines, or other equipment. Sometimes those changes require additional review of their potential effects on natural or cultural resources.[13]

In 2005, based on completed seismic mapping, the Barrett company submitted its proposal. It would develop natural gas leases on 137,700 acres of public, state, and private land, about 90 percent of it managed by the BLM. When fully developed, the project was expected to produce up to 250 million cubic feet of natural gas per day. The company already had some wells in the area producing about 25 to 28 million cubic feet per day.[14] Development, driven largely by rising energy prices, was expected to add millions of cubic feet of natural gas to the country's energy market.

Barrett's proposal included drilling up to 807 gas wells from up to 538 well pads spread over 53,250 acres within the leases on the West Tavaputs Plateau south of Nine Mile Canyon. The project would bring 164 miles of new access roads, improve more than forty-six miles of existing roads, and close or reroute six miles of road to avoid sensitive areas. Twenty well pads would be within wilderness study areas and 218 pads in areas with wilderness character and potential to qualify as federally designated wilderness.[15] Under the proposal, nine drilling rigs would operate year-round during the first and peak year of drilling. After the first year, drilling was expected to decline but would continue for about eight years. The estimated life of a well was about twenty years, reclamation would take about five, and the run of the project was expected to be about thirty-three years. An average well produced about 1.4 billion cubic feet of gas over thirty years—some less, some more. The area already had more than seventy wells; nearly half had been drilled in the previous three years, but some dated to the 1950s. Some were capped and some abandoned.

Though no drilling would be done in Nine Mile Canyon itself, it would be affected. Heavy truck traffic would bring drilling equipment and supplies up the road through the canyon. Semi-trucks would make an average of about a dozen round trips, and light trucks about thirty-five trips each day to service a single drilling rig. Some trips would serve more than one rig. The roads through the canyon and up to the plateau are dirt, rough, and steep. They are hard on equipment, a company official said. Alternatives worth exploring included improving the road with gravel or pavement. The dust issue required a long-term solution, and such alternatives would be covered in an environmental impact study. Still, the company's proposal did not contemplate any reconstruction or upgrades of the main access roads. The company could consider other routes, but that would have raised issues with other resources.[16]

Another controversial part of the proposed project involved fifteen of Barrett's leases within designated wilderness study areas—areas proposed as wilderness and that are supposed to be managed as such until a final designation is made by Congress. The proposal included about

The dirt road that once passed close the Hunt Panel has been moved to the far side of the trees at right to protect the ancient art from the vibration and dust of semitruck traffic. *Author photo*

23,000 acres of the 290,845-acre Desolation Canyon Wilderness Study Area and nearly all of the 7,500-acre Jack Canyon Wilderness Study Area. These leases were issued in 1951 and 1952, and a few wells drilled, before the areas were designated as potential wilderness in the 1980s.

Stephen Bloch, of the Southern Utah Wilderness Alliance, contended the company did not have an unqualified right to drill for natural gas in these protected areas. The proposed project would change the wild desert landscape of the plateau. "It's going to be an industrial landscape," Bloch said. The spider web of dirt access roads and pipelines would affect wildlife in the area. The company only had a right to drill somewhere on its lease. He suggested the BLM consider an alternative that would prohibit drilling in wilderness study areas and areas with wilderness characteristics.[17] In addition, the Utah Division of Wildlife Resources expressed concerns about the effects of the project on mule deer and elk winter range. Roads and activity on the drill pads would disturb the animals and drive them to poorer winter range. Wildlife officials also were concerned about sage grouse.

The BLM was required to consider all of these issues in evaluating Barrett's proposal. On behalf of all Americans, the BLM manages lands leased for oil and gas exploration and extraction through field offices that answer to district and state offices under guidance from BLM headquarters in Washington, DC. Of its 127 field offices, only about thirty handle oil and gas leases, mostly in the West. Despite frequently significant pressure from the energy industry and its friends in Congress, the federal government is not legally obligated to open sensitive lands for mineral leases.

On August 26, 2005, the BLM launched a study of the environmental effects of Barrett's proposal, known as the West Tavaputs Natural Gas Full Field Development Plan. The process was expected to take two to three years. Just weeks earlier on August 8, President George W. Bush had signed the Energy Policy Act of 2005 adopted by Congress in July. Section 390 of the new law would streamline the permitting process by allowing BLM officials to approve permits for some projects without a separate environmental review under certain conditions, a process known as an administrative categorical exclusion. Before the new law was enacted, all drilling permits or changes that would include surface disturbance would require BLM officials to assess their environmental and cultural impacts and to ensure that they conform to federal laws, such as the Endangered Species Act and the National Historic Preservation Act. BLM could add restrictions or conditions of approval to protect those resources.

Under Section 390 of the new Energy Policy Act, the BLM was allowed to skip the environmental review for oil and gas projects if:

- The likely disturbance was less than five acres on a lease where total disturbance was less than 150 acres and where an environmental analysis had been completed.

- A well was to be drilled where drilling had occurred within the previous five years.

- A well was to be drilled within a developed field for which a land use plan or any environmental review within the previous five years had analyzed such drilling.

- A pipeline was to be placed in a right-of-way corridor approved within the previous five years.

- Maintenance was for a minor activity.[18]

In such cases, BLM could approve a project using a categorical exclusion instead of preparing a traditional environmental assessment or an environmental impact statement. Officials are required to document their decisions, and must screen proposed projects against a checklist of extraordinary circumstances that would preclude using the exclusion. BLM officials could not approve a drilling permit unless the requirements of the National Historic Preservation Act and the Endangered Species Act had been met.[19]

The Government Accountability Office in 2009 reported that between 2006 and 2008, BLM approved more than 22,000 new oil and gas drilling permits across twenty states, largely in the West. Of those, BLM officials used categorical exclusions to approve almost seven thousand oil-and-gas-related activities, including about six thousand drilling permits—more than one fourth of those permits. Critics accused the BLM of short-cutting requirements to assess the effects of any drilling project on endangered or threatened species and historical or cultural resources. BLM defended the exclusions as a way to promote drilling for gas and oil in the West.[20]

On February 1, 2008, after two and a half years of analysis, the BLM released a draft of the environmental impact statement for the West Tavaputs project for ninety days of public comment. The BLM's preferred alternative differed only slightly from the proposal submitted by Barrett, reducing the number of well pads to 488, down from 538.[21] The BLM received about 58,000 comment letters from other federal agencies, state and local governments, Indian tribes, and the public. Most comments voiced opposition to the project from people across the country. Critics included the state of Utah, the Hopi Tribe, the National Trust for Historic Preservation, and the Theodore Roosevelt Conservation Partnership. The Environmental Protection Agency called the draft environmental impact statement inadequate and wanted BLM to do further analysis to consider impacts to air quality.[22]

BLM disregarded this opposition. Just as the public comment period was winding down, the BLM between April and June 2008 approved drilling permits for twenty-five new wells near Nine Mile Canyon under the categorical exclusion loophole. The wells were in addition to the more than eight hundred wells proposed as part of the West Tavaputs Project. On August 6, the Nine Mile Canyon Coalition, the Southern Utah Wilderness Alliance, and The Wilderness Society sued the BLM. The coalition of environmental and historic preservation groups argued that the approval of the twenty-five new wells violated federal laws. By applying categorical exclusions, the BLM did not analyze the full range of environmental effects of natural gas drilling and extraction before approving the project, as required by environmental and historic preservation laws. The lawsuit argued that BLM was wrong in its interpretation that the use of categorical exclusions was not subject to screening for extraordinary circumstances.

The lawsuit also argued that the BLM's Price field office had failed to analyze properly the cumulative effects of the additional drilling permits. The BLM should have considered the indirect, as well as the direct, cumulative impacts of drilling, such as corrosive dust released into the air and onto neighboring rock art panels in Nine Mile Canyon. The groups accused the BLM of using the exemptions to allow more drilling on the plateau above Nine Mile Canyon without properly analyzing the cumulative effects on the rock art in the canyon. Their concerns were the potential damage from drilling in proposed wilderness or areas with rich cultural resources, such as Nine Mile Canyon, or when adequate measures are not required to protect other public land values. The West Tavaputs project would industrialize an area that has received global recognition for its cultural resources and would permanently alter its unspoiled and wild nature, the Southern Utah Wilderness Alliance, Nine Mile Canyon Coalition, and The Wilderness Society said in a joint news release.[23]

In addition to the threats to cultural artifacts in Nine Mile Canyon, the proposal also would have placed drill pads in BLM wilderness study areas in Jack Canyon and Desolation Canyon, along with two adjacent areas that BLM recognized as having wilderness characteristics. Under the preferred alternative in the BLM's environmental impact statement, 230 wells, more than a quarter of the total number of proposed wells, would be in these wild areas. The Desolation Canyon portion of the Green River, one of the West's most iconic and remote stretches of river, was designated a National Historic Landmark in 1969. That designation required the BLM to preserve the canyon's remote and natural setting.

The lawsuit was settled on March 31, 2010. The BLM agreed that it would not issue categorical exclusions in the Nine Mile Canyon area until an environmental impact statement for the entire project was completed, and it would continue to study the effects of dust on rock art in the canyon. The agency also agreed to clarify that extraordinary circumstances identified in the National Environmental Policy Act apply to categorical exclusions.

Meanwhile a negotiated agreement signed January 5, 2010, reduced the scope of the proposed West Tavaputs project. The coalition of environmental and historic preservation groups and the Barrett company agreed to measures that would protect cultural resources from the dust raised by increased vehicle traffic and noise associated with energy development. The agreement also called for enhancing and interpreting key archaeological sites in Nine Mile Canyon. The BLM approved the agreement with minor changes, and included it in the final approval of the project, signed July 2, 2010, and released to the public on July 29.

The amended project permit included drilling 626 wells from 85 new and 57 existing well pads spread over 18,000 acres; it called for 79 miles of new road, 47 miles of improved roads, and six miles of road closures and rerouting to avoid sensitive areas. No well pads would be in proposed wilderness areas, but seven new well pads would be in areas with wilderness character. It included 1,323 acres of temporary disturbance, with 711 acres of long-term disturbance.[24]

In addition, Barrett consented to several mitigation measures. The company agreed to relinquish leases in the Desolation Canyon and Jack Canyon wilderness study areas, to develop only six sites with wilderness characteristics, and place well heads at those sites underground. In addition, the company reduced the number of wells by a quarter, and agreed to create a dust mitigation plan to protect rock art panels, and to construct information kiosks in Nine Mile Canyon. It also would set up a $250,000 grant pool to preserve archaeological resources and an additional $5,000 more for each well drilled, and it would put up gates on several remote dirt roads to protect fragile archaeological sites, wildlife, and wilderness resources.[25]

Parties on both sides of this issue praised the agreement. In a July 2010 news release, Interior Secretary Ken Salazar said it "clearly provides for the orderly and balanced development of our nation's energy supply while, at the same time, serving as an outstanding example of the fresh look of how we can better manage our energy resources. It improves protections for air, land, water, and cultural resources, while reducing potential conflicts that can lead to costly and time-consuming litigation." Fred Barrett, CEO and chairman of the Barrett Corporation, said the agreement would make the project "the most environmentally progressive natural gas development in Utah." He called the agreement good business. By working with the Barrett Corporation, the Southern Utah Wilderness Alliance was able to protect the Desolation Canyon proposed wilderness area, "one of the most remarkable, remote landscapes in the lower 48 states...while allowing the company to achieve its goal of developing the natural gas resource," Bloch said.[26]

Barrett did the right thing in scaling back its project and taking measures to protect the ancient artifacts, funding archeological research, and saving a chunk of important wilderness. With dropping gas prices, however, Barrett stopped drilling in 2012. It had completed about three hundred wells, with more than five hundred left to drill on about twenty thousand acres.[27] In 2013 the company sold its interests in the West Tavaputs project for $369 million to Houston-based EnerVest Ltd.

Public pressure had succeeded in scaling back an ambitious energy project with conditions that protected potential wilderness and a lot of valuable ancient artifacts. The public, along with a couple of lawsuits, forced BLM to do more to protect natural, historic, and cultural resources in Utah's Nine Mile Canyon, which it was supposed to protect. More recently, BLM has gotten better at holding energy companies to the terms of their permits meant to protect other resources.

At the same time, the agency and its parent, the Department of Interior, also were subject to political pressure from the powerful energy industry and its supporters in Congress to increase production of energy resources on public lands in the western states. Some of that pressure came in the form of a national energy policy developed behind closed doors during the George W. Bush administration by government officials and energy industry representatives. Taxpayers, who ultimately own the resources and who may prefer other values from public lands than energy extraction, were not included.

Granted, drilling for oil or gas is a risky business. The cost to drill a gas well is the same whether the driller comes up empty or hits a high producing well. Seismic studies can show the most likely places to find gas, but eventually wells have to be drilled to find out how much gas is there, if any. If gas is found, the company has to consider the cost to get it to market; that means pipelines, roads, and compressor stations. When officials in the energy business talk about the amount of recoverable gas or oil in a given deposit, they are usually referring to the amount that can be economically extracted, and that depends on technology and the going price of gas or oil. Other factors affecting the cost of extraction include terrain, weather, and remoteness. Sometimes not all these costs are borne by the drillers. Some ultimately are borne by taxpayers in damaged and polluted lands and waters, lost or degraded wildlife habitat, and sometimes in the loss of priceless historical and cultural resources, some of them thousands of years old.

Resource extraction is by nature destructive, some methods more so than others. When the gas is gone, and the drilling rigs have moved to other fields the land is returned to the public. Equipment and machinery may be removed and roads re-graded, but the land may remain scarred long after the resource is gone. Wildlife may have been driven off by three or four decades of human disturbance and by the destruction and fragmentation of its habitat by roads and pipelines. It is one of the intangible costs of energy extraction on public lands, as is the loss of potential wilderness values. The energy company's drilling and extraction permits may include requirements to reclaim the land when leases are closed. Sometimes, however, companies go bankrupt when the energy market drops. Even if it remains solvent, the company cannot replace lost wilderness characteristics, or restore petroglyphs eroded by thirty years of dust-suppressing chemicals, or ancient structures brought down by the vibrations of heavy truck traffic. The best intentions notwithstanding, when resource values on public land conflict, when one of the country's richest archeological sites sits right next to one of the richest natural gas deposits, the public interest in archeological treasures must outweigh private economic gain. Protecting the rock art in Nine Mile Canyon is important, but in the end, is the gas worth more than the ancient rock art or potential wilderness?

New finds in other places may increase the supply, new technology and alternative energy sources may drive down demand, affecting the value of natural gas in the future. The Associated Press recently reported a newly discovered oil and natural gas deposit in the Wolfcamp Shale formation in west Texas, part of the energy rich Permian Basin. The U.S. Geological Survey estimated that the deposit included sixteen trillion cubic feet of natural gas.[28] In addition, a February 2017 report, discussed in the preceding chapter, predicts a decrease in the growth of demand for natural gas by 2020. The report "Expect the Unexpected: The Disruptive Power of Low-carbon Technology" predicts that the growth of solar power means it could provide about one fourth of world-wide energy production by mid-century, "entirely phasing out coal and leaving natural gas with just a 1 percent market share."[29]

Other factors affect the demand for natural gas. In addition to its use to generate electricity, gas also is widely used to heat homes. In homes and buildings heated by gas, modern, energy-efficient furnaces and buildings reduce the amount of fuel consumed. Another, underutilized, way to heat a building is passive solar energy. By simply orienting a new home to face the winter sun, solar energy can cut the heating costs by up to 50 percent without adding to the cost of home construction. Buildings designed to capture as much solar heat as possible may be more expensive to build, but they can be comfortable without additional heat sources, even in cold climates, such as Edinburg, Scotland, or Snowmass, Colorado. Using other energy sources, such as methane from landfills to generate electricity, will lower the demand for natural gas, reducing the need to drill in sensitive areas. That means in places like Desolation Canyon and Jack Canyon wilderness areas in eastern Utah people would not see drilling rigs or natural gas pipelines as they float down the otherwise stunning Green River. Today the road through Nine Mile Canyon is paved, giving ancient art a reprieve from potentially damaging road dust. The treasures in this canyon seem to be worth the extra expense of making sure they survive the short term quest for energy.

CHAPTER 3

Abandoned Mines, Tainted Water

The narrow washboard road rumbles up along the American Fork River past dusty pine trees and around house-sized boulders, worming into the heart of the Wasatch Mountains about fifty miles southeast of Salt Lake City. Up here, miles from civilization, water gurgles from a pair of pipes leading from an old mine adit, blasted shut years ago. The brown-orange deposit on the rocks hints at the contamination in the otherwise gin-clear water. Miners once extracted gold, silver, and lead at the Pacific Mine, one of eleven abandoned mines in Mineral Basin at the upper end of Utah's American Fork Canyon, which rises above the densely populated cities along the Wasatch Front. The first mining claims were filed here in 1870, and the miners formed the American Fork Mining District in July of that year. The mine and mill buildings are long gone. Only some eroded concrete foundations and old sunburned wooden structures, where milled ore once was loaded into wagons, have survived. Piles of contaminated mine waste also remain.

Those early miners might not have thought much about the effects their mining would have on the nearby river over the years. Though most mining had stopped by the end of the 1920s, the water running from the Pacific Mine nearly a century later still carried lead at levels ten times the federal Clean Water Act standard of fifteen parts per billion. The mill at the mine once pumped tailings into a pond that sat on what became national forest land. Water from the mine ran through those tailings, and by the time it reached the American Fork River it carried more than one thousand times the lead allowed by current regulations. A spring arising in the tailings carried more than four thousand times Clean Water Act standards, contamination that also once ran into the American Fork River, which empties into Utah Lake and eventually the Great Salt Lake.[1] Two abandoned mines on a nearby tributary also leaked heavy metals into the river. Both are on private land in steep terrain, but the contamination reached the stream below the mines and thus violated federal water quality standards.

Government officials acknowledge that the value of minerals extracted from public lands over the years is unknown, but the costs of mining are clearly written in the thousands of abandoned and poorly reclaimed mines across the West, a legacy of the country's archaic mining law of 1872. Abandoned hard-rock mines, such as those in the American Fork Canyon and in thousands of other locations throughout the West, constitute a serious threat to western watersheds. They are the long-term consequences of shortsighted mining practices that put other public values at risk. The U.S. Forest Service estimates 38,000 abandoned mines remain on national forest lands alone. Other federal officials estimate the number of abandoned mines across the western states may be as high as half a million. No one knows exactly how many. The miners and mining companies who worked and abandoned them paid nothing for the minerals they extracted from the public lands, leaving others to pay for cleaning up contaminated sites. The federal Environmental Protection Agency estimates that acid mine drainage and heavy metals from abandoned mines have contaminated 40 percent of headwater streams in the West, and more than sixteen thousand miles of streams.

When mining operations stop, the natural processes set in motion by the disturbance inherent in mining continue. Sulfuric acid forms when sulfide minerals, such as pyrite, common in hard-rock mining, come in contact with air and water. It is a natural function of weathering. In undisturbed rock the formation and release of acid is slow and poses little risk to the environment. Mining and milling operations, however, expose large amounts of such rock to air and water. Acid forms in the waste rock and tailings piles, in the walls of open pit mines, and in the tunnels of underground ones. It can be a long-term process, and the environmental effects can increase over time even at long abandoned sites.

Ore piles, former processing facilities, and spills in chemical storage areas also are sources of acid drainage. In some places byproducts of ore processing left in tailings ponds behind earthen dams continue to seep through or under dams, the failure of which can release tailings to nearby waterways. Storm water and snowmelt also carry pollutants from abandoned mines. Water fills open pits or underground workings of former mines that provide direct connections to groundwater. The acid in turn leaches lead, copper, silver, manganese, cadmium, iron, arsenic, zinc, and other pollutants from the rock and makes cleaning up abandoned mines more expensive. Acid drainage from abandoned or poorly reclaimed mines often requires ongoing water treatment—sometimes in perpetuity.[2] U.S. Environmental Protection Agency experts say acid drainage and the contamination it carries is still the most serious environmental issue facing the mining industry today.[3]

Abandoned mines present physical hazards as well. Remaining structures are often unsafe as a result of the ravages of time, weather, and exposure to mining chemicals, and in places contain chemicals in deteriorating containers. Some mine openings hide hazards that can injure or kill curious explorers, including unstable ground, bad air, insufficient oxygen, or poisonous gases, such as carbon monoxide. Some openings are hidden by vegetation or collapsed buildings. Vertical shafts, some of them hundreds of feet deep, are particularly dangerous to any unsuspecting person or animal. Nothing in the nation's mining law, however, addresses these issues.

No one is more closely associated with the General Mining Act of 1872 than William Morris Stewart, the Nevada mining lawyer and senator variously known as the Silver Senator or Big Bill Stewart. The mining law he pushed through Congress grew out of the chaos of the California Gold Rush when most mining was done by individuals with picks and shovels, and some wielding hydraulic jets and floating dredges. Stewart was born in Galen, New York, on August 9, 1827, attended Yale College from 1849 to 1850, then headed West.[4]

Stewart came late to the Gold Rush. Two years earlier, on January 24, 1848, James W. Marshall had discovered gold in the tailrace of John A. Sutter's sawmill on the South Fork of the American River east of Sacramento in the western foothills of the Sierra Nevada. Though California was still part of Mexico, the discovery changed the course of history in the West. On February 2, 1848, nine days after the discovery at Sutter's mill, the war with Mexico ended with the signing of the Treaty of Guadalupe Hidalgo, which made California a U.S. territory. Marshall's discovery and the consequent influx of people spurred the rush to statehood for the new territory. The California constitution was written in Monterey and completed in October 1849. California became the thirty-first state on September 9, 1850. That same year, William Stewart arrived in San Francisco. He had little success as a miner, and in 1852 he turned to mining law instead. He practiced in California and Nevada and earned a fortune in mining litigation.[5] A prominent lawyer, he entered politics and served on the Nevada territorial council in 1861 and at the state constitutional convention in 1863. When Nevada was admitted as a state on October 31, 1864, Stewart was elected as the state's first senator and took office in 1865.[6]

Meanwhile, two principles with roots in English common law took shape in the chaos of the gold rush. One was the first-in-time, first-in-right principle of water rights, also known as the principle of prior appropriation. A person who first diverts water and puts it to a recognized beneficial use has a right to continue to divert and use that water, so long as he or she is not affecting another's existing water right. The second is similar in its practicality: a person who files a mining claim has the right to explore and develop that claim. Both principles spread through the mining country of California and Nevada and eventually throughout the West. The water right principle was adopted as the basis of water law in most arid western states. The mining principle, however, ran headlong into a legal tangle.

The end of the war with Mexico had abolished all Mexican laws in California, including mining claims. At that time, U.S. federal and state policies reserved mineral wealth for the government and leased or sold mineral claims, and Congress required one third of the profits from mines on federal public land. Uncertainty quickly came to a head with hordes of would-be gold seekers arriving in California. Under existing law, Gold Rush miners had no real legal authority to mine public lands in the West, even in the newly acquired territories of California and Nevada. In the absence of clear federal rules, however, the forty-niners organized themselves and operated under an informal system of mining districts that eventually became common law.

The Gold Rush also sparked the interest of Congress, and the debates were lively. Some considered charging miners a royalty fee, thinking miners should pay for the minerals they dug up from public lands, which had been public policy until the Gold Rush. Others proposed selling mining land in hopes ownership would promote stability in mining country. Still others thought the settlement of the West was more important than revenue, and mining should be encouraged with free access to the land and its mineral wealth. Most, however, agreed on selling the land. The debate continued until 1865 when Stewart was elected to the Senate and wrangled a seat on the Senate mines and mining committee. He supported free access to public lands in the interest of settlement.[7]

Stewart essentially wrote the Mining Law of 1866. It standardized the already informal rules in various mining districts in the West that had been used by miners in California and Nevada since the late 1840s. Despite some strident opposition, he pushed the mining act through the Senate and got it tacked onto other legislation. Passed and signed into law, it gave miners on public land legal status. In 1870 the Placer Act, an amendment to the 1866 law, allowed miners who worked ore-bearing sand and gravel deposits, known as "placer mining," to buy the land they were working.[8]

In 1872 Stewart helped push another amendment through Congress. It kept in place the concept from the 1866 law that local mining practices constituted common law.[9] The amendment also cleared up some uncertainties in the 1866 law, including the requirements for making a legal mining claim and specifying the amount of work required annually to keep the claim active. Today miners are required to complete at least $100 worth of work annually to keep a claim valid. The 1872 amendment also established the process of patenting a mining claim to make it private property and set the fee at five dollars per acre, where it remains today. Once a claim was patented, the land and the mineral riches it holds became private property free and clear. Miners could work without permits or regulation, though today they have to abide by state and federal water and air quality rules.[10]

Not all claims were patented for mining purposes. Some were patented only to obtain title to the land for remote home sites, subdivisions, resorts, or real estate speculation. To prevent such abuses, the federal Bureau of Land Management, which today oversees surface mining on most federal public lands, examine patent applications to determine whether they have economically viable mineral deposits.[11] A BLM moratorium on patenting mineral lands was enacted October 1, 1994, and remains in effect today.

————◆————

The 1872 mining law was meant as an incentive to settle the West and to develop the mineral resources of the United States.[12] It gave miners free access to the public domain and its minerals and a statutory right to mine a commercially viable deposit. To mine on public lands today, claim holders must file a permit application and a plan of operation with the BLM. Federal land managers can add restriction and cleanup requirements in the permit to operate the mine, but they are all but powerless to stop a mining company from mining a legal claim. The public has no effective way to hold mining companies accountable short of legal action. Other federal and state laws require environmental reviews of mining operations, and may require mitigation measures and reclamation plans before a mining permit is issued. That, however, is only on public lands.

State and federal land managers have no authority over mines on private land, unless contamination leaves the site. Mines on private lands still must abide by environmental laws; the Clean Water Act restricts discharges to streams and lakes, the Clean Air Act limits air emissions, and the Antiquities and National Historic Preservation acts protect historic structures and archeological sites. These laws, however, cannot protect groundwater and streams and other resources from ongoing pollution from abandoned mines. The mining law does not require environmental review of the potential effects of a proposed mining claim on private land. No environmental law specifically covers hard-rock mining, nor does the mining law require reclamation once the mine shuts down.

Most western states now require operators to submit reclamation plans before mining permits are issued and operations can begin. States also have the authority to require mine operators to post a bond or financial guarantee to ensure reclamation when the mine closes. Some states require only proof that the company has the money to clean up when the mining permit is issued. A few states do not require reclamation bonds.

Sometimes companies run into trouble after paying comparatively little or nothing for the minerals they remove from public land or from patented land. Costs to develop and operate a mine may turn out to be greater than what the mineral is worth, or the ore plays out, or the company files for bankruptcy and shuts down the operation. Some companies simply walk away. All of those eventualities leave only reclamation bonds, if any, to pay for cleanup at abandoned mines. As events have shown, most such bonds fall short of the actual cost of reclamation.[13] That leaves the state and federal agencies, that is to say taxpayers, to make up the difference.

In 1998, one such instance involved the Canadian mining company Pegasus Gold Inc. Pegasus operated seven gold mines in Montana, Idaho, and Nevada. In the early 1970s, the company had bet its future on a process that used cyanide to leach microscopic gold deposits from ores too poor to be profitable using ordinary methods. In the 1970s and '80s, gold prices rose steadily and the company flourished. In January 1980, gold prices were about $668 per troy ounce or more, but when gold prices dropped to a low of about $282 in December 1997, Pegasus declared bankruptcy. A new company emerged from that bankruptcy to operate three of the former company's still profitable mines, while four unprofitable mines were abandoned.[14]

The Zortman-Landusky mine, one of the four abandoned mines, is located in north-central Montana, where mining began in 1880s. Things did not go so well here. The Zortman-Landusky, two mines really, used cyanide leaching and operated between 1979 and 1998. Pegasus removed about 137 million tons of ore from about twelve hundred acres, about half of it public land managed by the BLM. Though acid drainage was noticed at the mine in 1992, the company made plans to expand mining. In 1998, the expansion plans were scrapped, and Pegasus abandoned the mines when it filed for bankruptcy. The $40 million reclamation bonds posted by Pegasus were not enough to cover the clean-up costs. The state of Montana and the BLM worked together to clean up the abandoned operation, leaving state and federal taxpayers with additional costs. While some sources estimate that those costs amounted to more than $30 million, others contend only a small portion of the additional costs were paid by federal and state taxpayers. In response, Montana voters in 1998 banned any new cyanide heap leaching operations.

Cyanide leaching has been used in mining for more than a hundred years, and it can make some low-grade ores profitable. It started with Prussian blue, a dye created in 1704 by a paint maker in Berlin. It was later renamed cyanide after the Greek word for blue. Cyanide is made up of carbon and nitrogen and is formed in several ways, including by lightning in the atmosphere. It can also combine with other elements to form basic amino acids, the building blocks of life. Sodium cyanide, also a deadly poison, could dissolve gold, and was used in electroplating in England. Around 1840 someone discovered that a cyanide solution would dissolve gold without the use of electricity. It was first used successfully to recover gold from mine tailings in 1890 in Johannesburg, South Africa.[15] This useful characteristic has made it vital to modern gold mining operations.

Improvements in cyanide leaching technology and in large-scale earthmoving equipment allowed industrial-scale processing of gold ore. In the late 1970s and '80s when gold prices climbed, cyanide use increased as further improvements in leaching technology allowed even lower grade gold ores to be mined economically. As a result some large mining companies like Pegasus became little more than earth-moving operations that created huge holes—some visible from space—or removed entire mountain tops. Huge dump trucks hauled out a hundred tons of low-grade ore per load, which would yield only an ounce or two of gold.[16]

Typically, a cyanide leaching operation excavates ore from an ever-growing pit. Explosives break lose the rock, giant shovels scoop up the ore that is then hauled away and dumped on a "leach pad," hence the name heap leaching. Layers of clay and plastic sheeting line the pad. Overhead sprinklers spray a weak solution of sodium cyanide over the huge quantities of ore to dissolve minute quantities of gold as it trickles down through the ore and collects at the downhill end of the pad. The "pregnant" solution is piped through a recovery plant where the gold is removed. Ore varies in richness; at an average of .022 troy ounces per ton, it would take about forty-five tons of ore to yield an ounce of gold.[17]

Because of the need for large quantities of low-grade ore, the immense scale of cyanide mining operations raised concerns over the potential environmental hazards. Critics noted that liners leak, pipes break, operators make mistakes or use improper practices. Even so, cyanide is not the main long-term concern at abandoned mines since it breaks down quickly, especially in sunlight. The biggest concerns at abandoned open-pit cyanide leach operations are the large piles of spent ore and waste rock, and the large pits from which the ore was removed. Acid mine drainage typical of hard-rock mining forms in the spent ore, the pits, and waste rock piles, and any residual cyanide may increase the potential for heavy metals to dissolve. Some such piles cover hundreds of acres,

This fenced pond at a gold mine in Idaho near the Nevada border contains a solution of cyanide used to dissolve minute particles of gold from low grade ore. *Author photo*

and may rise several hundred feet and contain tens of millions of tons of spent ore.

The trouble with open pits of abandoned or closed mines was not limited to gold mines. The mines may be hundreds of feet deep, and when they were blasted beneath the level of the local water table they became especially troublesome. One of the most notable cases is the Berkeley Pit, a large open-pit copper mine near Butte, Montana, in the headwaters of the Clark Fork River, an area with about twenty-four hundred abandoned mines. Officials estimate more than eight thousand exist in Montana.[18] The area was a center of mining long before 1955 when the Anaconda Copper Mining Company began operating there. In 1977 Atlantic Richfield Company bought the Anaconda Company and continued mining the Berkeley Pit until 1982. The pit is about one mile long, half a mile wide, and about a third of a mile deep. Over the years, mining companies excavated more than one billion tons of ore and waste rock.[19]

To make mining below the groundwater level feasible, the water table must be lowered by pumping. The pumping station for the Berkeley Pit sat 3,600 feet below the surface in a nearby underground mine. When mining stopped in 1982, the pumps were shut off. Water began to rise in the pit and nearby interconnected underground mine shafts. The acidic water in the pit contained high concentrations of arsenic, copper, cadmium, cobalt, iron, manganese, zinc, and sulfate. In 2015 the water level was still about a hundred feet below the level at which water would have to be pumped out and treated to prevent it from seeping into shallow local aquifers.[20] Officials estimate the critical level would be reached by about 2023. By then, federal and state government officials hoped to have a plan for treating the water. No one knows how long the treatment would have to continue; perhaps forever. A recent incident, however, pointed to the hazard the pit presents. In the fall of 2016, a snowstorm blew a flock of migrating snow geese off course and they landed on the contaminated water of the Berkeley Pit. About three thousand geese died.[21]

Today the pit is a Superfund site administered by the U.S. Environmental Protection Agency, under the federal Comprehensive Environmental Response, Compensation, and Liability Act of 1980 (CERCLA). Funded primarily by a tax on chemical and petroleum industries, the act authorized direct federal responses to releases or potential releases of hazardous chemicals that threatened public health or the environment. The tax revenue goes into a trust fund used the pay for cleanup of abandoned or uncontrolled hazardous waste sites.[22]

Flooding is also common at abandoned underground mines, and can have long term and sometimes disastrous effects. On August 5, 2015, three million gallons of accumulated water and mine waste spilled from the mouth of the Gold King Mine in the Cement Creek drainage above Silverton, a town of just over six hundred in southern Colorado. Workers for the Environmental Protection Agency were trying to insert a pipe to drain and treat the accumulated waste water in the mine when they accidently broke the plug of rocks and dirt holding back polluted water and tailings that subsequently flowed into Cement Creek.[23] About ten miles downstream from the mines, Cement Creek joins the Animas River in the town of Silverton, which then runs south through Durango and into New Mexico. The leak turned the Animas River mustard yellow.

Mining in San Juan County began with several mines in the late nineteenth century. In 1887, the Gold King Mine was started by a miner working at a nearby mine who noticed a mineral outcropping and filed a claim. He died before he could develop it, but his widow sold the claim in 1894. The resulting mine tapped into a vein of ore that lived up to the mine's optimistic name.[24] The new owners patented the claim and expanded mining.

The Gold King was abandoned in 1923. Water filled its open tunnels and formed acid drainage. The mouth of the mine had been bulldozed shut with rocks and dirt, but polluted water leaked into Cement Creek. All the water, however, did not originate in Gold King. When a new access tunnel in a nearby mine intercepted the groundwater flow, the drainage from the Gold King and a couple of other nearby abandoned mines all but dried up. Later when the access tunnel was plugged, water trapped in the tunnel began leaking out through the Gold King and other mines. The U.S. Environmental Protection Agency became involved in the 1990s because of the concern over the increasing contamination in Cement Creek and the Animas River. Cleanup efforts, however, pose their own risk. Workers wanted to keep the large volume of toxic liquid secured inside the Gold King mine and remove it at a controlled rate to be treated. Four water treatment ponds were built nearby. The ponds are functioning, but such structures have failed in other places.[25] The spill at the Gold King mine was a stark reminder of what could happen at any of the thousands of abandoned and inadequately reclaimed mines across the West. These sites pose serious health, safety, and environmental hazards, and cleaning up the disasters waiting to happen is not cheap or easy.

At some abandoned mines, including the ones in the American Fork Canyon, cleanup has been delayed by cost and federal environmental law. Many individuals, groups, and government agencies want to help, but they could be liable for any remaining pollution under federal environmental and hazardous waste laws that do not allow partial cleanups. The EPA's Good Samaritan Initiative, however, brought some relief. The initiative allows volunteering groups that do not own the property and are not responsible for its environmental conditions to clean up watersheds and fisheries threatened by runoff from abandoned hard-rock mines.[26] By removing the liability and legal roadblocks, third parties, such as private companies, nonprofit groups, and state and local governments, could take on the cleanup without assuming any liabilities.

Since 1999, the Forest Service has spent more than one million dollars to clean up several abandoned mines in the American Fork Canyon. The federal Clean Water Act required the U.S. Forest Service to clean up the runoff because of the high lead levels. "If it hadn't been for the water standards, we probably never would have cleaned any of this out," said Ted Fitzgerald, a retired Forest Service engineer who has worked on several mine cleanup projects on national forest land in the American Fork Canyon.[27] The tailings from the Pacific Mine were dug up and moved a few miles downstream to Dutchman Flat, another former mining site in the canyon. Here the tailings joined about a hundred thousand cubic yards of waste from other area mines, all of it covered with an impervious plastic liner and three feet of soil. The cover keeps water from seeping in and leaching contaminants out of the waste. A nearby groundwater monitoring well lets officials check whether it is working. The former tailings pond at the Pacific Mine became a series of oxidation ponds where lead, arsenic, and other metals settled out. By the time the water ran through the ponds the lead level had dropped significantly.

Other concerns besides water quality drove continued cleanup of the remaining waste in the canyon, Fitzgerald said. People, birds, and animals were at risk from contact with the piles of contaminated mine waste. More than a million people visit the American Fork Canyon every year, many of them on motorcycles and all-terrain-vehicles. Before parts of the site were fenced, people would race up the contaminated waste piles and jump from the tops. The dust they kicked up contained enough lead to be dangerous for children.[28] Wind can carry dust from dumps and spoil piles, roads, tailings, and other disturbed areas. Dust and soils contaminated with chemicals or heavy metals continued to pollute surface water and degrade stream habitat, and posed health risks to anyone who drank the water or ate fish or shellfish from the stream. The clean-up project included fencing and warning signs to keep people off the now-covered waste piles, and interpretive signs explain the area's mining history and the reasons behind the reclamation effort.[29]

Fitzgerald, who once headed the Uinta National Forest's clean-up efforts, estimated that there were about 150 patented mining claims in the American Fork Canyon. Most of them were too far from the river or too small to contribute to water quality problems.[30] Complicating cleanup of those that do was the inconsistent ownership. Early mining claims resulted in a checkerboard of public and private property in the canyon. Ownership of some properties dated back a hundred years or more and included dozens of private and public entities, making it difficult to hold any one individual accountable for the pollution. The Forest Service has no authority to clean up contaminated areas on private land. The Pacific Mine and the ten other sites in the canyon sit on property now owned by Snowbird Ski and Summer Resort. They are among the more than ten thousand sites in all of Utah where miners and mining companies have simply walked away.

When Fitzgerald retired from the Forest Service he went to work for the environmental group Trout Unlimited and became involved in a cooperative effort to clean up the abandoned mines in the American Fork watershed. Though the Snowbird Resort owns eleven of the abandoned mines, it did not create the contamination and was not responsible for its cleanup under federal law. Nevertheless Snowbird has helped with the $1.5 million cleanup.[31] An agreement between the EPA and Trout Unlimited, with donations from the Tiffany and Company Foundation and some taxpayer money, launched the cleanup. The EPA's Good Samaritan waiver allowed the cleanup to proceed without the risk of liability.

Many reclamation projects are simply too large for even the most generous volunteer groups, and estimated costs to clean up abandoned sites are mounting. From 1997 to 2008, four federal agencies—BLM, the Forest Service, EPA, and Office of Surface Mining—together spent at least $2.6 billion to reclaim abandoned hard-rock mines on federal, state, private, and Indian lands. The EPA alone spent about $2.2 billion.[32] That's an average of about $260 million per year. Some estimate that the price tag will be at least $20 billion, according to the Pew Campaign for Responsible Mining.[33] Others put the cost at 50 to 70 billion dollars.

Such estimates are anything but certain because the government does not really know how many abandoned mines exist on public lands. In a 2011 report, the Government Accountability Office, the investigative arm of Congress, acknowledged that the number was unknown partly because no consistent definition of what constitutes an abandoned mine existed.[34] So the GAO in 2008 developed its own definition: "a site that includes all associated facilities, structures, improvements, and disturbances at a distinct location associated with activities to support a past operation, including prospecting, exploration, uncovering, drilling, discovery, mine development, excavation, extraction, or processing of mineral deposits locatable under the general mining laws."[35] Using that definition, GAO investigators asked officials in twelve western states and Alaska to determine the number of abandoned hard-rock mines and the number of sites with safety hazards and environmental issues. They came up with an estimated total of 161,000 abandoned mines, 332,000 physical safety hazards, and at least 33,000 sites with environmental contamination or degradation, according to the 2011 report.[36]

Some say the mining law needs to be changed to resolve the contamination issues at abandoned and poorly reclaimed mines. Repeated efforts have been made to repeal the law, so far unsuccessfully. In 1973 President Richard Nixon in his State of the Union Address urged Congress to replace the mining law.[37] Critics say it is outdated and no longer serves its original purpose to encourage settlement with free access to minerals and low-cost patents to foster stability through private ownership. In 1920 Congress removed coal, natural gas, and oil from the 1872 law, and the federal government now charges royalties of 8 to 12.5 percent for their extraction on federal lands. The 1920 Mineral Leasing Act also holds the coal miners and oil and gas drillers responsible for reclaiming the land when mining or drilling is done.

Changing the mining law will not fix the problems of abandoned mines. It might prevent some future problems, but that still leaves the question of who is going to pay to clean up these sites. Some have suggested that federal royalties should be imposed on hard-rock minerals and the revenue used to help cover the cost of reclaiming abandoned mines. Western states charge mining companies royalties or functional royalties in the form of taxes on hard-rock mineral mining on state lands. The rates and structures vary from state to state, some base royalties on net income or gross value of mineral produced, with rates ranging from 2 percent to as high as 10 percent. Some states have different rates for different minerals. Colorado, for instance, charges 7 percent royalty on placer mining, 5 percent on the gross or 10 percent of the net proceeds for gold or silver, and 2.25 percent for raw uranium ore.

Efforts to impose royalties on hard-rock mining on federal public lands have so far failed. In 2007 a failed legislative proposal called for a 4 percent royalty on existing mines and an 8 percent royalty on new mines on federal lands. It might have raised as much as $40 million per year based on a 1993 estimate that put the value of hard-rock mineral extracted from federal public lands each year at about $1.2 billion. No one really knows. Because mining companies pay no royalties, the federal government has no reason to collect data on the amount or value of gold, silver, or other hard-rock minerals being extracted from public lands each year.

Even so, federal royalties might not cover the cost of cleaning up abandoned mines in the West. In 2012 the U.S. Interior Department estimated, based on the earlier 1993 figures and a 2011 survey, that the value of minerals taken from public lands was about $6.4 billion.[38] A 4 percent royalty on that amount would average about $256 million a year, not quite enough to cover what the federal government spent annually in the first decade of the twenty-first century to clean up abandoned mines. Proposed federal legislation in 2009 would have imposed a royalty on minerals and provided money to help clean up abandoned mines, and it would have strengthened environmental protection and given federal officials the authority to block mines that would have posed a clear danger to the environment. So far it has not become law.[39]

Meanwhile, thousands of abandoned mines still bleed acid drainage like so many open wounds. The 1872 Mining Law remains in effect. It contains no provisions for dealing with abandoned mines, nor does it impose any royalties on hard-rock minerals, such as gold and silver, extracted from federal public lands. It does not seem unreasonable, however, that American taxpayers should get something for the minerals they own. Royalties alone would not be enough to cover the cost of cleaning up abandoned mines, but they could contribute to the efforts of Trout Unlimited, Tiffany and Company Foundation, the Snowbird Resort, and so many others, to clean up a toxic legacy and restore tainted watersheds. It would mean clean water running in more western streams as long as the Wasatch Mountains stand.

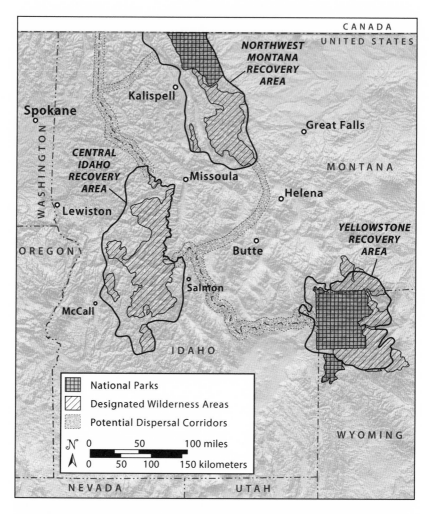

Wolf recovery areas in the Northern Rockies. Wolves captured in Canada were reintroduced in Idaho and Wyoming. Wolves in northwestern Montana had moved down from Canada on their own. *Source: Northern Rocky Mountain Wolf Recovery Plan, courtesy of US Fish and Wildlife Service, August 3, 1987. Map by Chelsea M. Feeney, www.cmcfeeney.com*

CHAPTER 4

Lurching Toward Wolf Recovery

The shallow, freshly disturbed hole, maybe eighteen inches across, barely showed in the gravel alongside the narrow dirt road. Two biologists stopped their government pickup truck. Something had sprung one of eight wolf traps they had set the day before in the mountains an hour or so northeast of Boise. The mountainside rises sharply to the right of the road and drops abruptly on the left. Beaver Creek runs through deep shadows far below. Even as the early morning sun peeked through the trees, shadows lingered among the ponderosa pines that dominate the forest here, along with a scattering of firs and occasional stands of aspen. The area is popular with anglers and hunters, backcountry skiers and snowmobilers, hikers and campers. It is also home to a growing number of gray wolves. Idaho Fish and Game wildlife biologists Michael Lucid and Steve Nadeau had come this May morning in 2006 to put radio collars on any wolves they caught. They had set several leg-hold traps buried just under the dirt and baited with dog food and wolf scat.

The previous fall, Lucid had picked up a mortality signal from the only radio-collared wolf in the Timberline Pack. He figured it might be an illegal kill, but when he tracked it down, instead of the expected dead wolf, he found a collar that appeared to have been chewed off, perhaps by other animals in the pack. As part of the wolf recovery effort in the Northern Rocky Mountains, Idaho wildlife managers tried to keep a radio collar on at least one wolf in every pack in the state. The Timberline Pack had been off the air for about six or seven months. The pack members were descendants of wolves reintroduced in the Northern Rockies in the mid-1990s.

Controversy preceded their arrival. Nearly exterminated in the United States by the 1930s, wolves were listed as endangered in the late 1960s. The federal government decided to reintroduce them in the Northern Rockies despite strident opposition from hunters, ranchers, and others.

Hunters feared wolves would deplete elk and deer herds. Ranchers believed wolves would stand in their way of wresting a living from public grazing lands. A few feared for their personal safety. As wildlife ecologist Aldo Leopold might say, however, those notions have been disputed by the wolf.[1] Others contend that wolves provide more benefits to Rocky Mountain ecosystems than the economic and recreational interests of those who want them eliminated.

Since their reintroduction, wolves have been at the center of contention. Anti-government and states' rights sentiments have been galvanized, and ranchers who rely on public grazing lands have made wolves scapegoats for losses caused by weather, disease, rustling, poor animal husbandry, fluctuating beef prices, and the hazards of grazing in places where farm animals probably do not belong. Wolves have also become a scapegoat for hunters and wildlife managers who blame them for decreases in big game numbers that in reality are often caused by changes in habitat. Biologists and state wildlife managers are caught in this political crossfire that has forced them to do things that are not necessarily in the best interests of the wolves or the ecosystem. Most are serious about

The rubber teeth of leghold traps like this are less likely to injure the paw of a trapped wolf. *IDFG photo by N. S. Nokkentved*

wolf recovery and recognize that a few wolves will be lost in the process of restoring the population. Their bosses, state wildlife officials, rely on these capable and well educated biologists, but they are also subject to the pressures of politics.

On that May morning in 2006, an animal had stepped in one of the traps, pulled it up and dragged it into the woods. Nadeau and Lucid followed the trail made by the hook at the end of the eight-foot drag chain attached to the trap. The trail led them up an embankment and into the trees. About a quarter mile up the road, they found the trapped wolf hunkered down behind a stump just off the road. Pleased at finding a wolf so soon and eager to start their work, the two biologists headed back toward the truck to get their gear. On their way, however, they were nearly run down by a pair of male elk at a full gallop. They wondered what might have spooked the elk. Had they caught wind of the wolf in the trap, or were other wolves in the area? They would find out later that day.

Armed with capture equipment and a dose of tranquilizer, they returned to the trapped wolf. Caught by the left front foot, the animal strained against the trap as Lucid distracted it with a metal catch-pole.

The effects of a tranquilizer are wearing off in this young male wolf, trapped in the central Idaho mountains. *IDFG photo by N. S. Nokkentved*

Nadeau jabbed its hindquarter with a syringe on the end of a six-foot fiberglass pole. Once the tranquilizer took effect, they freed the wolf, carried it down to the road and laid it on a canvas tarp. Just over a year old, it weighed about eighty pounds. They tied on a blindfold, covering its eyes to keep it calm and to protect its eyes. They measured its temperature, counted its pulse, examined its physical condition, attached a numbered tag in its ear, and fitted the sedated wolf with a new radio collar. The front paw showed a little swelling from the trap. After administering an antidote to the tranquilizer, they waited as the animal woke up to ensure it was not injured. It staggered drunkenly before getting its legs under control and disappearing in the timber on the hillside above the road.

A short time later, I watched the two biologists free a second tranquilized wolf from a trap. This one too was a young male, and it got the same treatment. On that May morning as I watched the two young wolves struggle in the leghold traps, one nearly dislocating a shoulder as it resisted the trap, I could not help but wonder what drives us to treat these animals like this, barely a decade into their reintroduction in Idaho and Yellowstone, and in 2006 still listed as an endangered species. The wolf biologists I accompanied were both sincere and showed respect and concern for the animals. We capture and put radio-collars on them and track their moves. I reluctantly accept that the data gathered help us understand the wolves and ensure their continued existence but regret the necessity. The two newly radio-collared wolves would help Idaho Fish and Game biologists track wolf packs in the area with regular aerial surveys. The radio signals would lead biologists to the pack's den or to a rendezvous site where they could count the year's pups to help generate annual population estimates, as required by the Endangered Species Act.

On their way back down the road, their work done, Nadeau and Lucid learned what had spooked the elk they had encountered earlier. The story was written clearly in the surface of the dirt road. Two sets of elk tracks, deep imprints of splayed hooves, ran parallel to a set of clear paw prints of a wolf in apparent pursuit, claws digging in, evidently chasing the two elk. About fifty feet short of where the two elk passed the biologists, the wolf tracks veered off into the woods.

The gray wolves, *Canis lupus,* were once more widespread than any other mammal except humans. They roamed most of North America from the Arctic reaches of Alaska and Canada to the central mountains and the high interior plateau of southern Mexico. Some estimates put the wolf population as high as 350,000 in the contiguous United States at the time Europeans arrived on the east coast.

The wolf is the largest wild member of the dog family. In the Northern Rocky Mountains, the average weight of an adult male is just over a hundred pounds. Most wolves are a grizzled gray, but they can vary from white to black. Though similar to coyotes and some domestic dogs, wolves have longer legs, bigger feet, a wider head and snout, and straight tails. They kill and eat deer, moose, elk, caribou, bighorn sheep, mountain goats, and smaller mammals. Some packs will also tackle bison. Wolves do not select their prey by age, sex, or health. They take whatever they can catch, most often the old, sick, or injured, the slow and unwary. Even a young elk if healthy can outrun a wolf. Adolph Murie, as a field biologist in Mount McKinley National Park, was the first biologist to conduct intensive and objective ecological study of wolves, including their feeding habits. In his landmark study from 1939 to 1941, Murie noted that of the Dall sheep skulls he found most were less than two years old or older than eight. Most of the few in between showed signs of disease. Wolf predation was one among several causes of death.[2]

Wolves live in packs. These family groups consist of two to twelve animals, including an alpha male and female, pups from the current year, juveniles from the previous year, and occasionally an unrelated wolf. Normally, only the alpha male and female breed. The pups are born from early April into May, and litters can vary from a single pup to a dozen. Pack members defend their territory from other packs and individual wolves, and from domestic dogs. Many young wolves, especially males, disperse from their packs. They often travel long distances looking for a mate or suitable habitat to establish their own pack. One of the two young wolves trapped in the Boise Mountains that May morning disappeared shortly after being released. It showed up about two years later near Missoula, Montana, nearly three hundred miles from Boise, apparently now the alpha male of his own pack.

When European settlers arrived in North America, they brought their culture and superstitions, and their fear of wolves. In Europe, wolves had long been associated with the forces of evil, and on this continent settlers started trying to kill them off almost as soon as they arrived. Some historians say New England set the first government bounty on wolves in 1622. Peter Matthiessen, in his book *Wildlife in America*, put the date at 1630, when the Massachusetts Bay Company offered a bounty of a penny per wolf.[3] Farther south, Jamestown in Virginia established a bounty in 1632, and New Jersey established a bounty in 1697.[4] By 1800 wolves had been all but wiped out in New England and eastern Canada. The last wolf in New England was killed in Maine in 1860. They hung on in eastern Pennsylvania and upper New York State until the beginning of the twentieth century. New York paid out bounties as late as 1897. Many settlers saw killing wolves as a sign of progress, extending civilization into the wilderness.

Miners, trappers, and settlers brought similar attitudes to the West. When market hunting depleted the nearby wildlife, livestock was required to feed the mining crews. Wolves, too, turned to eating livestock once their natural prey disappeared. Ranchers launched a concerted eradication effort by hunting, trapping, and poisoning wolves, eventually with help from the federal government.

In 1895 political pressure from western ranchers launched the U.S. Department of Agriculture's Animal Damage Control, now known simply as Wildlife Services. Its primary function was, and still is, to control rodents and predators. On July 1, 1915, Congress appropriated $125,000 to kill wolves, coyotes, and other predators on public lands throughout the West. The money, which became available in March of 1916, went to hire hunters who shot, trapped, and poisoned predators. That year, they killed 424 wolves, 9 mountain lions, 11,890 coyotes, 1,564 bobcats, and 2,086 other animals. These numbers, however, do not include most of the animals that were poisoned since few of them were recovered.[5] At first government trappers targeted primarily bears, bobcats, coyotes, mountain lions, badgers, beavers, ferrets, foxes, and wolves. Over the years, however, the program has expanded to include other animals and resulted in the unintentional killing of millions of non-target species. In 2014, for example, Wildlife Services spent more than $127 million and killed more than four million animals, of which only 66,600 some were predators.[6]

By the 1930s, government and private hunters, miners, and ranchers, spurred by federal and state bounties, had effectively exterminated wolves in most of the country. Wolf control in Yellowstone stopped in 1926, and by 1927 annual superintendent reports noted few signs or sightings of wolves within the park.[7] Human animosity drove wolves to the edge of extinction. "We deliberately killed them," said Ed Bangs, wolf recovery coordinator with the U.S. Fish and Wildlife Service in Helena, Montana.[8] By the 1960s, however, public attitudes toward wolves and other predators had begun to change. Wolves were listed as endangered in 1967 under the Endangered Species Conservation Act of 1966. The act provided limited protection for native animals considered endangered and authorized federal agencies to protect listed species, and when practical to preserve the habitats of such species. The act also authorized the U.S. Fish and Wildlife Service to acquire land as habitat for endangered species.

In 1973 Congress replaced the earlier act with the Endangered Species Act we know today. At the time, only a few hundred wolves remained in northeastern Minnesota and on Isle Royale in Lake Superior off the coast of Michigan. It is possible that a few scattered wolves roamed the Upper Peninsula of Michigan, northwestern Montana, and the American Southwest. Only rumors and occasional sightings of single wolves were reported anywhere else in the lower forty-eight states.

The U.S. Fish and Wildlife Service in 1974 added the gray wolf to the endangered species list as four subspecies—one each in the Northeast, Southeast, Northern Rocky Mountains, and in the Southwest. Studies of wolf skulls in the early 1970s, however, showed little significant difference between the subspecies. As a result of the taxonomic uncertainty, Fish and Wildlife in 1978 listed the entire species as endangered throughout its historic range in the contiguous forty-eight states, except Minnesota, where it was classified as threatened. "This rulemaking clearly indicates that the gray wolf is listed everywhere to the south of the Canadian border," the Fish and Wildlife listing document says.[9] That same year, the U.S. Department of Interior's National Park Service recommended wolves be transplanted from British Columbia or Alberta, or perhaps Minnesota, to restore a viable population in Yellowstone National Park.

The Endangered Species Act requires the Fish and Wildlife Service to develop recovery plans for listed species in suitable habitat. In 1980 Fish and Wildlife's wolf recovery plan for the Northern Rocky Mountains proposed reintroducing wolves in Yellowstone National Park and central Idaho. Ranchers and other critics protested loudly, claiming the skilled predator would kill domestic livestock and wipe out big game herds. When the plan was updated in 1987, wolves already were making their way back into the Northern Rockies, wandering south out of Alberta and recolonizing northwestern Montana.

Government agencies at the time were ill equipped to handle the problem. Ranchers wanted the wolves moved. The U.S. Fish and Wildlife Service did not want them killed because they were protected under the Endangered Species Act. No one at the agency, however, had experience with wolves, and no one had traps or equipment for dealing with them. Officials turned to the U.S. Department of Agriculture's Wildlife Services. They tapped wildlife biologist Carter Niemeyer, the Western Montana District Supervisor for Wildlife Services in Helena. Niemeyer grew up in northern Iowa and held a master's degree in wildlife biology from Iowa State University. He was an expert trapper and hunter, and thus the logical choice as the local government wolf manager. When Niemeyer got the call in 1990, he refused at first. He liked being district supervisor dealing with a variety of problems. A year later he relented and took over as the federal government's wolf management specialist. The federal wolf recovery program gave Niemeyer the opportunity to use his trapping skills to catch wolves. He mastered the art of shooting wolves with tranquilizer darts from a helicopter and has probably darted more wolves from a helicopter than anyone else outside of Alaska. It was a costly but quick and effective way to catch wolves, and doing it quickly often diffused potential conflicts.

Meanwhile, efforts at reintroducing wolves in the Northern Rockies progressed. In May 1990 U.S. Senator Jim McClure, an Idaho Republican, introduced legislation mandating the return of wolves to Yellowstone National Park and creating protected recovery areas in Glacier National Park and in wilderness areas of central Idaho where limited numbers of wolves would be reintroduced. Outside the recovery areas, wolves would be considered pests or game animals. The bill did not pass. Instead, in November Congress established a ten-member national wolf management committee to develop a gray wolf reintroduction and management plan for Yellowstone and central Idaho. The following year, the Fish and Wildlife Service began working on an environmental evaluation of the proposal to reintroduce wolves into those two areas. The environmental impact statement was released in May 1994. In it, Fish and Wildlife proposed to reintroduce wolves as a non-essential experimental population, giving wildlife managers more flexibility with the wolves. If Idaho and Wyoming and indigenous peoples developed acceptable wolf management plans, they could take the lead in managing the listed wolves.

In 1995 and 1996 the process of reintroducing wolves in the Northern Rockies began. Because of his expertise, Niemeyer would lead efforts to capture and collar wolves in Alberta and British Columbia, for the reintroduction efforts that would follow in Idaho and Yellowstone. Six wolf packs already were well established in northwestern Montana. The U.S. Fish and Wildlife Service and Canadian wildlife biologists captured thirty-five wolves in Alberta and British Columbia and shipped them to central Idaho. On January 14, 1995, the first four wolves were released at Corn Creek on the edge of the 2.4-million-acre Frank Church-River of No Return Wilderness in central Idaho. Two young males and two females loped into the woods from the metal transport crates that had held them while legal disputes and bad weather delayed their release. The weather changed plans to helicopter the wolves deep into the Frank Church Wilderness. Instead the crated wolves rode down the Salmon River Road in the back of a truck. A week later, eleven wolves were released at Indian Creek and Thomas Creek along the Middle Fork Salmon River, also in central Idaho. The following January twenty wolves were released near Dagger Falls at the edge of the Frank Church-River of No Return Wilderness, some of the wildest country in the West.

The Fish and Wildlife Service handled reintroduction in Yellowstone a little differently. Biologists put fourteen wolves in pens in northern Yellowstone, one at Soda Butte, one at Rose Creek, and one at Crystal Creek. The following year, seventeen wolves from British Columbia were put in two pens in the park's northern range, and in pens at Nez Perce Creek and on southeast arm of Yellowstone Lake. Park biologists kept the wolves in the pens for about ten weeks and fed them on road killed deer, elk, moose, and bison until they were released to roam the park.

Shortly after they were released, a pair of wolves and their pups made it from Yellowstone to Red Lodge, Montana, where they attacked livestock. The male was shot. Niemeyer led an effort to trap the female and her pups. The team set six traps then went to wait in a nearby motel room. The traps were rigged with radio collars to signal when they were sprung. Early in the morning one trap caught the adult female, whose pups were found in a nearby rock pile. It was not Niemeyer's first encounter with wolf No. 9, which he had previously trapped in Canada. He recalled riding in a pickup truck with two wolves in his lap—she was one of them. The female and her pups became the foundation of the Rose Creek pack, which eventually became the most productive pack in Yellowstone. "That effort got wolf recovery off and running in Yellowstone," he said.[10]

———————◆———————

Today about six thousand wolves roam the lower forty-eight states over about 5 percent of their former historic range. At the end of 2014, most of them lived in Minnesota and Wisconsin, while nearly seventeen hundred gray wolves roamed the Northern Rockies of Idaho, Montana, and Wyoming, according to reports compiled by the states and released by the Fish and Wildlife Service. Idaho had the most with at least 770, Montana was next with 554, and Wyoming reported 333. Packs also have been confirmed in Oregon and Washington. Many game managers, hunters, and ranchers say that is too many; population biologists say it is not enough.

Trouble followed close on the heels of the reintroduction. Two weeks after the wolves were released in central Idaho in 1995, a rancher shot a female wolf on his Lemhi County ranch. The wolf apparently had killed a newborn calf. Federal officials, however, determined the calf was already dead when the wolf reached it. The incident seemed to foreshadow the wolf issue in the West. Wolves would be killed for crimes they did not commit in the furor over federal wolf recovery efforts. Some say wolf reintroduction has been a success, but changes in the attitudes that led to them being listed as an endangered species still have a long way to go.

Not all local residents opposed the reintroduction. As day broke on August 7, 2000, eight people standing abreast blocked Pole Creek Road in the White Cloud Mountains of central Idaho, trying to keep out a government trapper. The group blamed livestock conflicts that threatened the lives of a local wolf pack on the unwillingness or inability of the rancher and the U.S. Forest Service to change grazing patterns and schedules. The Wildlife Services trapper gunned his Dodge pick-up truck through sagebrush and lodgepole pines to get around the group. Lynne Stone, head of the wilderness and wolf advocacy group, the Boulder-White Cloud Council, blocked his way. The trapper's truck came to a halt as she planted her hands on the vehicle's hood. He had no interest in talking to the protesters, and referred them to the U.S. Fish and Wildlife Service in Boise, which at the time was responsible for wolf management in Idaho. Stone and the other group members already had spent much of that summer trying to keep sheep flocks and wolves separate. Their offers of help had fallen on deaf ears.[11]

In the summer of 2000 rancher William Brailsford of Buhl, Idaho, and his sheep became the problem. Brailsford had moved his flock of about two thousand onto a grazing allotment in the Pole Creek drainage in the Sawtooth National Recreation Area, knowing the wolves of the Stanley pack were there. He also moved sheep up Fourth of July Creek, north of Pole Creek, where wolves also were known to gather. The results were predictable; sheep died and wolves were blamed. Stone contended it would have made more sense to move the sheep to safer ground.[12] Officials of the U.S. Fish and Wildlife Service in Boise, the Nez Perce tribe of north Idaho, and Wildlife Services planned to trap and remove as many of the fourteen-member Stanley wolf pack as they could. Sawtooth National Forest Supervisor Bill LeVere said the Forest Service had no option but to move the sheep by the schedule set out in Brailsford's grazing plan, despite the presence of wolves.[13] No other grazing allotment was available. Moreover, Stone noted, Brailsford's herders had aggravated the problem. They had killed two sheep at their camp on Pole Creek. One was lying with its throat cut, stomach split open and entrails exposed, and it had been fed on by the herding dogs. Another slaughtered lamb hung in a tree. The smell of dead sheep can attract wolves from miles away.

When gray wolves were reintroduced in 1995, federal officials pledged to "control" wolves that preyed on livestock. The federal government, however, typically spent more money trapping, relocating, or killing wolves that attack or kill livestock on public lands than the grazing fees can cover. In August 2000, federal officials spent $2,000 to $3,000 to trap and relocate a single wolf. The previous year Wildlife Services spent about $70,000 on wolf control, and in 2000 the agency spent about $100,000.[14] Brailsford paid about $540 per month to graze his flock of two thousand sheep on public land near Pole Creek Road. For the grazing season from July 15 through October 15, that totaled $1,620. Stone's group argued that it would be simpler and cheaper to move the sheep, rather than track and kill the wolves. The group had even offered to help guard the flock and to obtain guard dogs for the flock's owner. Brailsford rejected the offer.

Brailsford was convinced that wolf reintroduction would prove to be a "horrible mistake."[15] His sheep and lambs, however, were more likely to be killed by coyotes than wolves. National Agricultural Statistics Service statistics show that coyotes kill about five to ten times as many sheep and lambs as wolves. Overall, predators account for about a third of lamb deaths and a little more than a fourth of sheep deaths. Other causes include weather, disease, lambing complications, and old age.

In general, wolves get blamed for more damage than they actually do. Nationwide, predators kill less than a fraction of a percent of grazing cattle and sheep. Typically, ranchers turn their cattle out in the spring. Many roam freely for more than three months before the cowboys come back to round up their herds and bring them back to the home pasture. Any missing animals from the spring count, unless the dead are found and a cause can be determined, are often simply attributed to wolves. Ranchers consider such losses intolerable. In fact, the number killed by wolves fades to insignificance when the total number of cattle is considered. By far the biggest killers of calves on Western public lands are digestive and respiratory problems. The numbers lost to predators are only a fraction of the numbers lost to other causes. Most of those killed by predators are killed by something other than wolves, including bears, mountain lions, and domestic dogs. Like other predators, wolves sometimes feed on already dead animals.

The average running total number of cattle in the three states in any one year, including public and private land, is about 6.3 million, and the total number of sheep is about 845,000. Granted, the numbers are not evenly distributed, and some ranchers are hit harder than others. The numbers vary from year to year and not all of them graze on public lands.[16] The total deaths over the 18 years following reintroduction amounted to .03 percent of the average number of cattle and .4 percent of the average number of sheep in a single year in the three states.[17] Overall the number of livestock deaths attributed to wolves, when compared the total number of livestock in the states, is less than one in 10,000 cattle and about 5 in 10,000 sheep. Across the country—not including Alaska—cattle losses from all causes totaled about 4 percent of 96 million head. Losses to predators amounted to about two-tenths of a percent. Coyotes accounted for most of those with 97,000 deaths, while wolves accounted for 4,400 deaths.[18]

Statistics mean little when one's own livestock are killed. Individual ranchers may lose more than a few animals and can be hurt financially. But ranchers are compensated at market value for the animals lost to verified wolf kills. They are also compensated in the low grazing fee of about $1.50 for a cow and calf or five sheep per month. The rate includes a small discount as compensation for the increased risk of losses to predators on public lands. Help is also available to deter wolves from killing livestock. Compensating livestock owners for losses to confirmed wolf kills may be counterproductive, though, since it removes the incentive to change grazing practices to accommodate wolves.

In September 2000, Niemeyer took over the U.S. Fish and Wildlife Service's wolf reintroduction program in Idaho. He moved to his new position in Boise during the furor over wolves killing sheep in the central Idaho mountains. Niemeyer approached wolf recovery as a social and political issue that pitted the western tradition of livestock grazing against wolf advocates and conservationists. The most important thing to know in managing wolves was how to deal with people, he said.[19] Niemeyer hates to kill wolves. Yet he knows that sometimes a few will have to be killed so the rest can survive.

Niemeyer learned that compensating ranchers for losses to wolves can bring its own problems. He described one encounter with a rancher in Big Timber, Montana. Ralph Weller and his son lost seven calves. A neighbor out riding said he saw the wolf. A game warden and a local trapper said the calves were killed by wolves. Niemeyer investigated the incident and found no evidence of wolves having killed the calves nor did he find sign of wolves in the area. He told the Wellers the calves died from disease. The rancher was not happy. "He's all for the wolf, not the rancher," Weller said. "I think he's a dirty son of a bitch," he said of Niemeyer.[20] The loss amounted to about $5,000. In many cases it was easier for inexpert federal officials to simply agree with the rancher that, yes indeed, it looked like the cow had been killed by wolves. The official avoids political heat, and the rancher gets his compensation for a cow that in most cases, as statistics indicate, died of something else.

A few years ago, I heard about a rancher who said he was short twenty-four cows and fourteen calves when he rounded up his animals in the fall. He blamed wolves. Wildlife Services investigated the livestock deaths, but the animals, reported by hunters, had been dead too long to determine the cause of death. Wolf signs—howling, tracks, and scat—were found nearby. Some deaths could have been natural or caused by mountain lions. The area also was known lupine country, a plant notorious for poisoning livestock. The animals were not monitored, and the rancher had no way to prove his contention that wolves had killed his cattle.

◆

The return of wolves to the Northern Rocky Mountains has also frustrated hunters—in particular, elk hunters. Folks in the region began to complain that they could no longer kill elk in the places they or their grandfathers once did. In recent years, elk numbers have been declining, hunters are going elsewhere, and outfitters are idle. Many see wolves as the culprits. Local residents and hunters scoff at biologists' reassurances that the problem is with the habitat.

Elk habitat has changed significantly. Nowhere is that more clear than in two sprawling game management units in northern Idaho. Covering more than 1.5 million acres on the Idaho side of the continental divide and straddling the upper Lochsa River, the terrain rises toward the crest of the Bitterroot Mountains and the Montana border. Douglas-fir and ponderosa forests give way to western hemlock, western redcedar stands, and Engelmann spruce and subalpine fir at the higher elevations. In 1910, 1919, and 1934, large wildfires burned more than a million acres of these forests. The newly reduced canopy where mature forests had once stood now provided prime elk habitat.

For a time elk thrived there. Once a plains animal, elk have adapted to the mountains and favor semi-open forests and meadows in summers and sheltered valleys in the winter. They find shelter from the weather and places to hide from predators in heavy stands of timber and among tall brush in old clearings. They eat grasses and small leafy plants, seedlings and twigs, and when times are tough, dried grass and even bark. From late May to mid-June, pregnant females find some cover in brush, old clear cuts, and open timber as they go off by themselves to give birth.

In 1939 a long cold winter killed off hundreds of elk, but in the excellent habitat the population recovered quickly. Because of the area's remoteness, hunting pressure was light and elk numbers rose. In 1984 the area boasted about 17,000 elk. Numbers reached their peak in 1986 south of the Lochsa River and in 1989 north of the river, making them among the largest elk herds in the nation. For years hunters came to these rugged mountains for some of the best backcountry elk hunting in the country. Rural residents, hunting guides, and outfitters came to depend on the animals to fill their freezers for the winter, or they paid their bills by guiding big-city hunters into the backwoods.

Following the fires earlier in the twentieth century, aggressive fire policies and effective firefighting eliminated most large-scale fires. The number of acres burned annually dropped dramatically, dead and downed timber accumulated, and brush grew taller. Elk habitat became older, denser, and less productive. Open areas filled in with thick brush and trees. The changes meant fewer open areas and older shrubs that were less appealing to elk. While brush that is twenty feet high provides some security from predators, it provides little forage. Habitat managers consider good elk summer habitat to be about 60 percent open areas and 40 percent canopy cover.

There is no question that elk habitat deteriorated. Over-hunting, changing vegetation, human developments, logging, and domestic live-stock grazing on elk winter range all contributed to habitat changes and declining elk numbers. In 1962 U.S. Highway 12 was completed across Lolo Pass, opening previously inaccessible parts of the Clearwater National Forest to timber harvest. While logging opened the forest and provided additional elk forage, it also increased the number of logging roads that provided easier access for hunters. Prescribed fire was introduced in the region to maintain and improve elk habitat, but on a small scale with limited success. In addition, by 1973, rising waters behind the Dworshak Dam had flooded thousands of acres of prime elk winter range along the North Fork of the Clearwater River.

The first signs of trouble emerged in the early 1970s. This was long before 1995, when wolves were reintroduced to central Idaho. Wildlife managers suspected increasing hunting pressure was responsible for a population decline. In 1975, Idaho changed to a bulls-only elk season, halting and then reversing the decline for some years, but it did not last. In the winter of 1996–97, severe weather killed many elk in the upper Lochsa River drainage—up to 50 percent in some areas. Biologists expected the elk numbers to bounce back as they had in 1939, but they did not. Biologists were uncertain why. In good habitat, a healthy herd can absorb such losses.

Contrary to the evidence, some blamed predators for the decline. Habitat clearly affects the physical condition and pregnancy rates of female elk and consequently, calf condition and vulnerability to predators. Research in Idaho shows calf survival was chronically low or declining in many important elk hunting areas. Not enough elk calves survived to replace the adults that die each year, including losses to predators and hunting. The cause may be related to low levels of some key forage nutrients that result in lower pregnancy rates and poor calf survival. Research also found a relationship between predation rates and birth weights of elk calves. Poor nutrition can lead to delayed breeding in elk, and late-born and low birth-weight young are more vulnerable to predation.[21]

Wolves too often have been the scapegoat for elk hunters' lack of success. Wolves began showing up in the upper Lochsa area in 1998, but by then elk numbers already had dropped to just under eight thousand, down from more than sixteen thousand a decade earlier. Since then the decline has continued. With deteriorating habitat, predators can hold down a struggling population. There is no evidence, however, that removing wolves from the area would bring the elk back.

No doubt wolves have affected game numbers in the Northern Rockies, but wolves also help to keep wildlife diseases in check. When a population is in trouble, biologists find that diseases, such as brucellosis and chronic wasting disease, and habitat are the problems. A number of factors contribute, but fundamental is the change in forest structure, invasion of noxious weeds, loss of winter range to development and domestic livestock grazers, increased road access, human disturbance, and habitat fragmentation. Prey species rely on good habitat to survive, and that means ample forage, shelter from weather, places to give birth and rear young, and places to hide or escape from predators. Without any one of those, prey animals become more vulnerable to predators, weather, disease, and over-hunting; as a consequence animal populations do not rebound.

Wolves are not the only predators affecting elk numbers. Black bears and mountain lions in some areas account for the deaths of two-thirds of newborn elk. A 2005 study by Idaho Fish and Game biologists in the upper Clearwater River drainage found that bears and mountain lions, not wolves, killed more than 80 percent of the radio-collared elk calves that died.[22] A study of Yellowstone radio-collared elk from 2003 to 2005 found that grizzly and black bears there were responsible for about 60 percent of elk calf predator deaths. On the other hand, wolves killed 14 to 17 percent, and coyotes killed up to 11 percent. When radio collars send out a mortality signal, biologists determine the cause of death by examining the animal carcass for the distinctive marks various predators leave on their prey.

Research has also raised questions about the long-term effectiveness of killing predators to benefit game herds. When the southeast Idaho mule deer herd failed to recover from a particularly harsh winter in 1992, Idaho Fish and Game launched a ten-year study of predator-prey relationships among mule deer, coyotes, and mountain lions. They found no significant long-term effect on the total deer population trend. Removing predators cannot bring back game herds where habitat is the problem.[23]

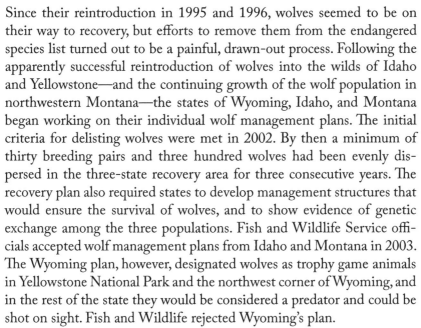

Since their reintroduction in 1995 and 1996, wolves seemed to be on their way to recovery, but efforts to remove them from the endangered species list turned out to be a painful, drawn-out process. Following the apparently successful reintroduction of wolves into the wilds of Idaho and Yellowstone—and the continuing growth of the wolf population in northwestern Montana—the states of Wyoming, Idaho, and Montana began working on their individual wolf management plans. The initial criteria for delisting wolves were met in 2002. By then a minimum of thirty breeding pairs and three hundred wolves had been evenly dispersed in the three-state recovery area for three consecutive years. The recovery plan also required states to develop management structures that would ensure the survival of wolves, and to show evidence of genetic exchange among the three populations. Fish and Wildlife Service officials accepted wolf management plans from Idaho and Montana in 2003. The Wyoming plan, however, designated wolves as trophy game animals in Yellowstone National Park and the northwest corner of Wyoming, and in the rest of the state they would be considered a predator and could be shot on sight. Fish and Wildlife rejected Wyoming's plan.

In February 2007, despite the shortcomings of Wyoming's wolf management plan, the Fish and Wildlife Service proposed removing wolves from the endangered species list. Critics argued that despite the assertions of some wildlife managers, the species by definition was not recovered. Some said delisting the wolf was premature, driven by politics and a violation of the Endangered Species Act. In February 2008 the Natural Resources Defense Council and Defenders of Wildlife submitted a petition to the U.S. Fish and Wildlife Service asking the agency to consider developing a nationwide recovery plan for gray wolves, as required by the Endangered Species Act.[24] Fish and Wildlife had written three regional recovery plans for three disjointed populations in the Upper Midwest, the Southwest, and the Northern Rockies. The regional plans were a start, but they should be part of a national recovery effort of the entire species, the petition said. Gray wolves were listed as a species in 1978 throughout its range in the lower 48 states. In the face of the legal challenge, Fish and Wildlife withdrew its proposed delisting of wolves later in 2008.

The following year Fish and Wildlife tried again after submitting its delisting proposal to additional public comment. On April 2, 2009, wolves in Idaho and Montana, but not Wyoming, were removed from the endangered species list. On April 6, the Idaho Fish and Game Commission set wolf hunting seasons for the fall and winter of 2009. That June conservation groups filed legal challenges arguing that the Fish and Wildlife Service could not delist a portion of a distinct population segment. The wolves in Idaho, Montana, and Wyoming were all part of the same distinct population segment and could not be split. The groups also sought to halt wolf hunts in Idaho and Montana until their lawsuit could be heard.

On September 8, 2009, U.S. District Judge Donald Molloy in Missoula issued his ruling. He denied the injunction that would have halted the wolf hunts, but he also ruled that plaintiffs were likely to succeed in their lawsuit. He added that the Fish and Wildlife Service's decision to delist the predator in those states, but not Wyoming, may have violated its own rules. Politics, rather than nature, are driving decisions, Molloy noted. "The [U.S Fish and Wildlife] Service has distinguished a natural population of wolves based on a political line, not the best available science. That, by definition, seems arbitrary and capricious," he wrote.[25] Over the winter hunters killed 188 wolves in Idaho.

On August 5, 2010, wolves were back on the endangered species list. Molloy had overturned the 2009 federal rule that had removed gray wolves in the Northern Rockies from the list. He ruled that the

Endangered Species Act did not allow the Fish and Wildlife Service to list only part of a species as endangered. As Molloy noted in his ruling, "The Endangered Species Act does not allow a distinct population segment to be subdivided."[26] He noted that the Fish and Wildlife Service had tried to find a simple solution to a legal problem that arose when Wyoming refused to participate in the delisting by submitting an inadequate wolf management plan, but that amounted to a political solution that did not comply with the Endangered Species Act. The Northern Rocky Mountain population segment had to be delisted as a distinct population, Molloy wrote.[27]

Montana and Idaho officials disparaged the ruling as a major setback for state management of wolves. In the end a political maneuver, not science, removed wolves from the endangered species list. On April 15, 2011, Congress passed the federal budget that included a rider sponsored by Senator Jon Tester, a Montana Democrat, and Representative Mike Simpson, an Idaho Republican, reinstating the Fish and Wildlife Service's 2009 delisting rule, removing wolves in Montana, Idaho, eastern Washington, eastern Oregon, and north-central Utah from the endangered species list. Critics called it an overreach by Congress that set a dangerous precedent. In a May 5, 2011, news release Noah Greenwald of the Center for Biological Diversity said, "The rider is not only a disaster for wolves but for any endangered species that a politician doesn't like."[28]

Meanwhile, Idaho, Montana, and Wyoming officials agreed to maintain a minimum of fifteen breeding pairs and at least 150 wolves in each state at the midwinter count. Because wolf numbers are typically at their lowest then, the average wolf population was expected to be much higher than the minimum. Officials expected the number would be well over the combined total of forty-five breeding pairs and 450 wolves. Yet some state officials and residents say they felt deceived when the number of wolves rose above 450. They were incensed when some claimed that wolves were not recovered and recovery would require far more animals. The 450 number, however, was a threshold for delisting, not the ultimate goal. The goal was a viable sustainable population, and some biologists argued that a viable population would take more than 450 wolves in the three states.

Conservation biologists who reviewed the recovery plan felt it was inadequate. They argued that 300 wolves as a minimum was too low, and would be marginal at best. In their comments in the 1994 environmental impact statement on wolf reintroduction, they wrote, "a few hundred wolves in each state cannot be defended as a biologically viable population." The full recovery of wolves in the region "requires not hundreds, but thousands of animals."[29] Some scientists put the number in the low thousands; some put the numbers from two to five thousand. The Fish and Wildlife Service's wolf recovery coordinator, Ed Bangs said, "I, personally, think [300] is too low."[30]

Gray wolves were once spread throughout most of the country. Today wolves can be found in about 5 percent of their former range. That raises the question of how delisting wolves in two parts of their former range would affect the recovery throughout the rest of the wolf's range where suitable habitat still exists. In 2013 Fish and Wildlife proposed delisting the gray wolf throughout its range, except for the Mexican wolf in the Southwest.

Wolves meanwhile took no account of the political wrangling. In the spring of 2007 a hiker reported finding the carcass of a gray wolf with a radio-collar along a tributary to the Salmon River in central Idaho. It had probably died in summer or fall of 2006. According to Idaho's records, the collar was placed in 1995 on wolf B16, a sub-adult female from the Obed Lake pack in Alberta. It was one of fifteen captured and released in central Idaho that year. B16 became the breeding female paired with B9, captured near Hinton, Alberta, and also released in Idaho. They formed the Chamberlain Basin pack, which roamed some of the most rugged, remote country in the heart of the Frank Church-River of No Return Wilderness in central Idaho. Their pack was among the first of the reintroduced packs to produce pups. B16 would have been just over thirteen years old when she died. She was among the oldest of the original thirty-five wolves brought to Idaho. Probably the last and oldest member of those wolves was B7, killed along a highway north of Salmon in January 2007. He would have been about fourteen, making him among the oldest wolves in the wild.

Although some assume the wolf populations in the Northern Rockies and the Upper Midwest will continue to grow, as they fill the available habitat their numbers will level off and most growth will be seen in dispersal into unoccupied habitat. In Yellowstone the numbers of wolves rose to about a hundred in the years after reintroduction, but by 2010 had dropped to fewer than forty.[31]

When wolves were reintroduced in the Northern Rockies they added another factor into the dynamics of animal population. The carrying capacity of the habitat, the vagaries of the weather, the toll of other predators, and the hunting regimes of state game managers dictated prey numbers. When they returned, wolves taught the elk speed and endurance; the elk in turn taught wolves to work together. Eventually wolf and elk numbers will stabilize at levels that will rise and fall with the cycles of weather and fire. Natural cycles are often long, sometimes longer than a human generation.

As a top predator, wolves play a key role in the ecological balance that has been missing in many parts of the Northern Rockies. In the long term, wolves will thin herds, reduce overgrazing by elk and deer, and allow greater plant and animal diversity. They keep elk and deer on the move and prevent them from overgrazing the streamside vegetation that provides shade and food to fish that eat the bugs that fall from the overhanging brush. That may mean fewer elk, but it also may mean better habitat for those that remain. Other animals and plants benefit as well.

Maintaining the balance of nature requires enough of the right predators. The presence of wolves helps promote biological diversity in the ecosystems they inhabit, ecologist Christina Eisenberg told the *Missoulian*.[32] Eisenberg, who has a doctorate in forestry and wildlife, serves as chief scientist for the Earthwatch Institute. In the Northern Rockies meadows she has studied, she found aspens a hundred years old and aspens twenty years old, but few in between. When wolves returned, elk began to move around more and browsed less on young aspens. The older trees grew up before wolves were wiped out, and the number of younger trees has increased since wolves have returned. The declining aspen populations in the American West are a concern among ecologists in part because they form some of the best songbird habitat; without them, songbirds disappear. After wolves were removed, elk browsed more on young aspens, and that has contributed to the trees' decline and thus a decline in songbird numbers and diversity. It is a process Eisenberg calls a trophic cascade, which describes the effects of changes that flow through a food web when a predator is removed or returned.[33]

Other scientists report similar results. Aspens and willows have grown taller in many places were wolves have retuned, said researchers William J. Ripple and Robert L. Beschta. They found that while elk numbers have declined, beaver colonies and bison numbers have increased. In northern Yellowstone National Park, beaver colonies increased from one in 1996 to twelve in 2009. The number of bison counted rose from fewer than a thousand in 1990 to more than two thousand in 2010. Meanwhile elk numbers dropped from about nineteen thousand in 1995 to about five thousand in 2010. The return of wolves has not just helped to reduce the browsing pressure on young aspens and willows, but wolves also have changed elk grazing patterns, how they use the habitat, the size of groups, how they move, and their level of vigilance.[34]

Wolves also have brought secondary effects. Scavenger species, including ravens, bald eagles, and bears, benefit from feeding on wolf-killed carcasses. Wolves have also led to a significant reduction in coyote numbers. Soon after their reintroduction in Yellowstone, wolves began to kill coyotes. By 1998 coyote densities had decreased by 50 percent—up to 90 percent in some areas.[35] As coyote numbers decreased, the numbers of the small mammals they preyed on apparently began increasing. Those small mammals in turn are prey for raptors and smaller predators, including foxes and badgers.

The increase in beaver colonies has had secondary benefits as well. Ripple and Beschta noted that Wyoming streams with beaver ponds have seventy-five times the number of waterfowl than streams without ponds. Beaver ponds also reduce stream bank erosion, trap sediments, raise water tables, recycle nutrients, and affect the number and diversity of plant and animal species.[36] Fish thrive in such an environment.

Scientists caution that ascribing changes in wildlife numbers or in an ecosystem to a single species or event is seldom justified. Weather, fire, and disease also have far reaching effects on wildlife populations. A 2003 *BioScience* article, "Yellowstone after Wolves," argued that changes in the Yellowstone ecosystem cannot be attributed to the return of wolves alone. The researchers maintained that the long-term effects of returning wolves to Yellowstone will not show up for decades, and will take ongoing research and monitoring.[37]

What that all means for the future of the wolf is difficult to say. Wildlife managers and the public generally value wildlife and most accept hunting. Western politics are heavily influenced by livestock interests and hunter groups that put domestic livestock and deer and elk herds over predators. Wildlife officials say they rely on the best science to make their decisions, but many factors that affect wildlife are beyond their control. Ultimately, the fate of wolves depends on human tolerance and policies engendered by that tolerance.

The decision to remove wolves from the endangered species list was political, enacted by the U.S. Congress. State and federal policies that seek to reduce wolf numbers in the backcountry while allowing domestic livestock grazing are driven by politics. Wildlife science comes in second. Game managers can set hunting seasons and limits based on science and research and set out in ten- or fifteen-year plans, but they have little control over the habitat that wildlife depends on or the changing climate, for that matter. They can only advise land owners and land managers who must juggle competing interests and land uses that may conflict with the best interests of wildlife. In the end, however, when it comes to declining big game numbers, science says habitat, politics says wolves.

Wolves are neither warm and fuzzy, nor evil. They are wild animals and predators just like mountain lions. To live, they must kill. That is their nature. They once were part of the Northwest as much as the salmon, or as buffalo were part of the Great Plains. Some people revere them, others revile them, but their continued presence means that natural systems, at least in northern Minnesota and Wisconsin, and now also in the Northern Rocky Mountains, remain wild enough for wolves. Wolves add a complexity to the landscape that in the long run benefits those wild ecosystems.

The Endangered Species Listing Process in Brief

The Endangered Species Act of 1973 seeks to conserve endangered and threatened species and the ecosystems on which they depend. Two federal agencies implement the act. The U.S. Fish and Wildlife Service covers terrestrial animals and plants, and the National Marine Fisheries Service covers marine species.

Endangered means a species is in danger of becoming extinct, and threatened means it is likely to become endangered. Agency biologists identify species that meet the criteria and assign a priority according to the degree of threat. They are known as candidate species, and their status is published in the Federal Register. Any interested individual or entity also may petition to have a species listed. The agencies then determine whether the petitioned species meets the criteria and warrants a proposed listing. A listing may be precluded by higher priorities.

For candidate or petitioned species that warrant listing, a proposed rule is published and submitted for public comment. A final rule is then either issued or the proposal withdrawn. A listing may also include protection of habitat deemed critical for the species' survival.

Source: U.S. Fish & Wildlife Service, "Listing a Species as a Threatened or Endangered Species." www.fws.gov/endangered/esa-library/pdf/listing.pdf.

CHAPTER 5

Private Livestock, Public Lands

On a fall day in 2000 we had come to the northern foothills of the Jarbidge Mountains in Nevada near the Idaho border to look at the impact of cattle grazing on western range land. As we hiked through scenic landscape three mule deer moved across the meadow and into the willows along the creek. In the air over the rocky ridge above us a red-tailed hawk circled looking for prey. A fire several years earlier had left dead trees, probably junipers, along the waterway. Rain clouds threatened in the west. Rancher Chet Brackett, owner of the cattle in question; Jon Marvel, a vocal critic of public lands grazing; and I hiked to a grazing allotment on public lands. We saw the banks of Spring Creek

A public land grazing critic and a rancher (barely visible in upper right), discuss the effects of the rancher's cattle grazing in Spring Creek in northern Nevada. *Author photo*

grazed to bare dirt, and the spring that gives the creek its name churned to mud and fouled with manure. Brackett acknowledged the problems caused at Spring Creek by overgrazing over many years, but the area had looked worse in the past, he said.[1] Brackett suggested Marvel return in the spring before the cows are turned out, because the area looks its worst at the end of the grazing season. Marvel, at the time head of the anti-public-lands-grazing group Western Watersheds Project, countered that after the cows had been through was the time to see the effects of grazing.

Grazing has been hard on arid public lands in the West. In the 1978 Public Rangeland Improvement Act, Congress noted the unsatisfactory condition of public rangelands.[2] The long-term health of arid sagebrush grasslands, its plants and wildlife species, and the ever-shrinking habitat continues to be degraded by a land-use practice that does not pay for itself. At the time of my visit to Spring Creek, ranchers like Brackett paid $1.35 per month for one cow and its calf to graze on public land, while the U.S. Forest Service spent almost $6 per cow per month.[3] Federal subsidies in the form of low grazing fees in some cases are all that makes public land grazing profitable. Yet few dare to question whether domestic livestock belong on public lands, especially in wilderness areas and at the expense of native fish and wildlife and their habitats. Ecologist and writer George Wuerthner calls it the "bovine curtain."[4] It is a question that should be raised by hunters and anglers, hikers and bikers and taxpayers, and anyone who enjoys the outdoors and nature, or who values the integrity of the native sagebrush grassland ecosystem and the wild lands of the western United States.

Spring Creek was part of a U.S. Forest Service grazing allotment and part of about seventy thousand acres of public land and another five thousand acres of private land where Brackett grazed about a thousand cows. Brackett and other ranchers on public grazing lands are required to comply with conditions specified in their grazing permits. Forest Service officials, in response to the damage, considered reducing the number of cattle Brackett would be permitted to run on the allotment, and that could have strained his relationship with his bank, which holds the grazing permit as loan collateral.[5]

Not everyone abides by the conditions of their grazing permits. Just about 150 miles to the north of Spring Creek, Frog Lake, a picture-postcard mountain lake, lies tucked into the high country of the White Cloud Mountains in central Idaho. One summer day several years ago, Don Wiseman rode with a group of friends on mountain bikes to the Frog Lake Basin in the Sawtooth National Recreation Area. They stopped at some horse tie-downs, and across the lake they saw about twenty cows standing in shallow water under some trees, mooing and defecating. "It was pretty gross," Wiseman said.[6] It was apparent that cattle had been up and down the trail Wiseman and his friends had just ridden, but cows were not supposed to be in the area until later in the summer. Forest Service officials knew the cattle had been there for most of the grazing season, a violation of grazing permit conditions that had been recurring over the previous ten years.[7]

Frog Lake is in the headwaters of the East Fork of Idaho's storied Salmon River, where endangered Chinook salmon and steelhead trout return to spawn. The lake also is part of a 131,000-acre grazing allotment leased to the Baker Ranch Partnership of Clayton, Idaho. It is steep, rocky, and timbered terrain, and Forest Service officials estimate about 23,700 acres are suitable for livestock grazing. The area's high mountain lakes and alpine streams, including Frog Lake, are popular with hikers, backpackers, and mountain bikers. Campers are required to camp well away from the lake and to pack out everything they bring in. They are not allowed to leave any human waste near the lake. The area has been proposed as wilderness, which would protect the area from development and from mountain bikers like Wiseman, but not from domestic livestock. Though the area is beautiful, Wiseman was discouraged by the effect of livestock. The damage they do is unbelievable, he said.[8]

Livestock grazing and ranching evoke a pioneer ethic and visions of a time gone by. Though times have changed, some still live like ranchers of the nineteenth century, a time of tough and independent people. Many have learned to care for the land their livestock graze. Livestock grazing on most public lands, however, is not economically defensible. It is subsidized by taxpayers and has damaged public lands, including important fish and wildlife habitat. Many public land policy decisions favor private livestock operations and their bankers over other interests, including those of other people, native wildlife, or the health of the land.

Livestock grazing has a long history. Humans in the Middle East domesticated sheep about nine thousand years ago, goats about a few hundred years later, and cattle about eight thousand years ago.[9] They have been herding these animals ever since, and livestock grazing has become the most widely spread agricultural practice in the world. It is also among the most destructive land uses in arid regions.[10] One dramatic example of the effects of excessive grazing can be found in the arid mountains of Lebanon, where almost two thousand square miles of cedar forest failed to regenerate after extensive logging in ancient times. In 1939 only four groves of the famous cedars remained. One of the groves was surrounded by a stone fence, and has grown from forty-three scattered old trees into a dense, close-growing stand of about four hundred trees. The fence allowed the grove to recover by keeping out the goats that grazed the mountains and all but denuded the lands outside the fence.[11]

In the Unites States, domestic livestock graze about 840 million acres, or 44 percent, of the total land area of nearly two billion acres (not including Alaska).[12] In eleven western states, which cover a total of 750 million acres, grazing—primarily by sheep and cattle—is the dominant land use on 525 million acres of private and public lands. Of those acres, more than 300 million are public lands that include wildlife refuges, national parks, and wilderness areas, as well as some city, county, and state lands, but most grazing occurs on lands managed by the Forest Service and the federal Bureau of Land Management.[13] Public lands untouched by grazing are rare. The BLM administers grazing leases on 163 million acres, and the Forest Service administers grazing on about 97 million acres.[14] For all that, public lands account for less than 3 percent of the nation's beef.

In the early and mid-1800s, immigrants on the Oregon Trail brought their livestock west. The discovery of gold in the Northern Rockies in the 1860s brought prospectors, and close behind came herds of cattle to feed the miners. With the availability of free grass, livestock grazing soon became an unrestricted free-for-all on the unclaimed lands of the West, a vast, unmanaged commons from Texas to Canada, from Oregon to Wyoming. The grass belonged to the rancher whose livestock got there first. Fierce competition resulted in severe overgrazing in many places. Most of the arid lands west of the Rocky Mountains had never supported large numbers of herbivores until Europeans' livestock arrived, and many native plants were particularly vulnerable to heavy grazing.

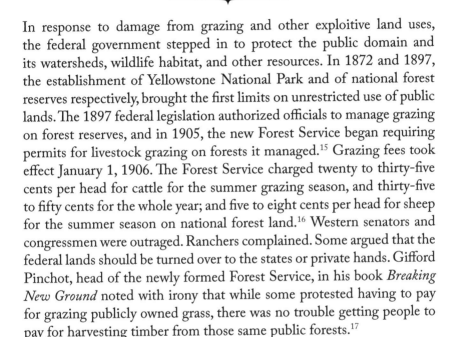

In response to damage from grazing and other exploitive land uses, the federal government stepped in to protect the public domain and its watersheds, wildlife habitat, and other resources. In 1872 and 1897, the establishment of Yellowstone National Park and of national forest reserves respectively, brought the first limits on unrestricted use of public lands. The 1897 federal legislation authorized officials to manage grazing on forest reserves, and in 1905, the new Forest Service began requiring permits for livestock grazing on forests it managed.[15] Grazing fees took effect January 1, 1906. The Forest Service charged twenty to thirty-five cents per head for cattle for the summer grazing season, and thirty-five to fifty cents for the whole year; and five to eight cents per head for sheep for the summer season on national forest land.[16] Western senators and congressmen were outraged. Ranchers complained. Some argued that the federal lands should be turned over to the states or private hands. Gifford Pinchot, head of the newly formed Forest Service, in his book *Breaking New Ground* noted with irony that while some protested having to pay for grazing publicly owned grass, there was no trouble getting people to pay for harvesting timber from those same public forests.[17]

Meanwhile, the rest of the public domain remained open to unsupervised and unrestricted grazing. Some land managers and ranchers expressed concerns about soil erosion and other effects of unrestricted livestock use. In 1930 legislative attempts were launched to halt the damage from livestock with regulations and fees. Edward T. Taylor, a rancher and U.S. representative from Colorado, in 1933 reintroduced a bill that set up the Grazing Service in the Department of Interior to administer the public range lands. The Taylor Grazing Act of 1934 established grazing regulations, ostensibly to improve rangeland conditions. The act's stated purpose was "to stop injury to the public grazing lands by preventing overgrazing and soil deterioration, to provide for the orderly use, improvement, and development, to stabilize the livestock industry dependent on the public range, and for other purposes."[18] It reined in the chaos engendered by unregulated grazing on public rangelands.

The act set up 162 million acres of public land in grazing allotments organized in grazing districts and administered by the Grazing Service.[19] Permit holders were required to pay a fee of five cents per head per month; the grazing permits could not exceed ten years, but they were renewable. Permits could be revoked when drought, fire, or natural disasters degraded grazing lands or for chronic permit violations. Permits also could be issued to build fences, reservoirs, and other developments.

In 1946 the Grazing Service merged with the General Land Office to form the Bureau of Land Management to manage public rangelands deemed "chiefly valuable for grazing."[20] Many ranchers opposed the restrictions and fees imposed by the new legislation. Large established ranches with a land base or home ranch, however, retained preferred grazing "rights" to the public lands they had been using. The U.S. Supreme Court has ruled on several occasions that grazing on public lands is a privilege, not a right, and permits are subject to changes or cancellation. The U.S. Constitution, Article IV, Section 3 clearly states that Congress has the authority to manage public lands and to adopt such regulations as it deems necessary to protect public resources.

The BLM and the Forest Service manage grazing in units known as Animal Unit Months. An AUM represents the amount a cow and her calf or five sheep eat in one month—about eight hundred pounds of dry forage. The number of acres it takes to produce that much forage varies with the land. Some places it is less than an acre, other places it is more than ten. Grazing fees were assessed by the AUM, but fees varied from one agency to another.

Unified grazing fees on all federal public lands were a long time coming. A grazing fee technical committee in the 1970s developed a formula that would represent the fair market value of the forage and account for the differences in the cost of grazing on public land from private land. Some ranchers argued that predator losses were greater on public land because the federal government had failed to control coyote numbers and because of the landscape. As a result, the cost difference was set at twenty-three cents more per AUM on public lands. That difference became part of the base grazing fee formula.[21] The fee also would be adjusted annually with a multiplier that would account for changes in forage value and beef prices. Many complained that they could not afford the new fee.

In 1976 Congress recognized the value of public lands as a national resource in the Federal Land Policy and Management Act. The legislation clearly stated that public lands should remain in public ownership, and it provided the BLM with direction for managing 175 million acres of public land. It further noted that grazing and mining were only part of the BLM's responsibilities. The act also mandated a study of grazing fees on federal lands. It stated that grazing fees were not an appropriate subsidy for livestock grazing because they applied to only a small percentage of livestock producers. The country, however, should get a fair market value for the use of public land and its resources. Ranchers and officials have been arguing ever since over just what constitutes fair market value. Some responded with demands that the federal lands be turned over to the states, a recurring theme.[22]

Grazing fees remain an issue throughout the West. Based on the Interior Department's 1977 grazing fees study, the 1978 Public Rangeland Improvement Act set the base grazing fee at $1.23 multiplied by the value of forage, the price of beef, and a price-paid index divided by 100. The act set the minimum at $1.35 per AUM, and called for a review of grazing fees in 1986. An appraisal of the value of grazing on public lands in 1983, updated in 1992, found values that ranged from $4.68 per AUM in the Southwest to a high of $10.26 in the northern plains.[23] Nearly forty years later, ranchers still lease public rangeland for about $1.35, sometimes a little more. Some states lease their grazing lands through a competitive bidding process, which results in most state lands being leased for considerably more than neighboring federal lands, which are not subject to competitive bidding.[24] Fees on state lands in the arid West range from $1.35 to $80, and private land rates range from $8 to $23 per AUM.[25]

Meanwhile critics argue that the low fees on federal public rangelands encourage overgrazing. Ranchers can afford to put more cows on the land, and the low fees amount to a federal subsidy. Many ranchers pride themselves on being independent and defend their "custom and culture"; they bristle at the suggestion that their operations are subsidized. They argue that the low grazing fees are fair and should not be considered a subsidy. The costs of livestock grazing on public lands are higher than on some private lands, they argue, because they have to share the resource with wildlife; cattle and elk both prefer grasses, and deer and sheep both like succulent plants. This competition affects grazing capacity for livestock; there is only so much forage on the land. Other uses of public lands, they argue, also create higher costs for the rancher.

The real issue is that grazing fees, whatever the rate, do not cover the government's costs to manage grazing on public lands. Federal agencies spend nearly seven times as much managing grazing programs as they take in, according to a 2005 Government Accountability Office report. Ten federal agencies spent $144 million but collected only $21 million in grazing fees. Of those, the BLM spent $58.3 million and collected $11.8 million; the Forest Service spent $74.2 million and collected $5.7 million.[26] Granted, some of the money spent may not have been necessary, but the report did not include money spent by other federal agencies to repair the damage from livestock grazing. Some estimate that other direct and indirect costs to taxpayers have been as high as $120 million in a single year, and others say the total cost could be as high as $1 billion.[27] In addition, federal land management agencies pay for fencing that ranchers put up and for the pipe they lay for water systems used to manage livestock use. The federal government also spends several million annually killing native carnivores to protect private livestock grazing on public land, and millions more on fighting range fires and subsequent rangeland rehabilitation.

Aside from grazing, federal public lands support many other less destructive uses, including watershed protection, wildlife habitat, big game winter range, outdoor recreation, timber production, and even just leaving it as wilderness. In 1977, the Interior Department's *Study of Fees for Grazing Livestock on Federal Lands* noted that, "if grazing is low in economic value, then other uses may be more appropriate."[28] Some economists estimate that outdoor recreation produces more than twice the value of grazing, with much less resource damage. The U.S. Fish and Wildlife Service's 2011 National Survey of Fishing, Hunting, and Wildlife-Related Recreation reported that people across the country spent about $145 billion annually on hunting, fishing, and observing nature and wildlife.[29] As much as $30 billion of that total was spent in local economies of the western states and many of those activities occurred on public lands.

———————◆———————

All is not well on those public lands, however. Sage grouse numbers are dropping. Many native fish are threatened, endangered, or extinct. Streams coming out of remote backcountry violate water quality standards because of silt, high temperatures, and fecal bacteria associated with livestock. Over the past century and a half or more, grazing practices and management on public lands have destroyed millions of acres of wildlife habitat, helped spread invasive weeds, and contributed to an increase in wildfires, soil erosion, and water pollution.

Efforts to improve livestock forage have damaged public rangelands. Past overgrazing in some areas had removed most native bunchgrasses, eliminating competition for sagebrush and allowing the proliferation of other plants considered unpalatable to livestock. To improve livestock forage, BLM and the Forest Service rangeland managers eradicated millions of acres of sagebrush and wildlife habitat starting as early as the 1930s. Some areas were burned, others sprayed with 2,4-D, a World War II defoliant. Sagebrush and encroaching junipers were uprooted with plows, or with pairs of bulldozers dragging lengths of anchor chain across the land. From 1940 to 1994, the BLM treated an estimated forty-six million to one hundred million acres.[30] Much of it was reseeded with crested wheatgrass, a dependable livestock forage plant not prone to fire. Good for livestock, but not so good for many wildlife species, especially sage grouse.

Two bulldozers linked by an anchor chain uproot juniper trees and sagebrush as part of an effort to improve livestock forage on public land. *Author photo*

Unwittingly, livestock have contributed to the introduction and spread of cheatgrass one of the worst invasive plants to western rangelands. Cheatgrass (*bromus tectorum*) arrived in the West in the late 1890s, a stowaway in a grain shipment from Europe. A native of the steppes of central Asia, it evolved over thousands of years with heavy grazing in a climate similar to the arid intermountain West.[31] Railroads helped spread cheatgrass, which readily sprouted along the tracks and in places burned in fires started by locomotives. Cheatgrass hitchhiked on the livestock transported by trains and in grain shipments.[32] It earned its name by invading wheat fields sowed with contaminated seed and taking over, cheating the farmer of his crop.[33] Cheatgrass quickly moved in where livestock had removed the native bunchgrasses and broken up the soil and soil crust.[34] Moving livestock in the spring from home pastures to public grazing lands contributes to the continued spread. Moreover, it readily invades areas where soil has been disturbed including by fire and vehicles, and it out-competes native grasses. By about 1930, cheatgrass had spread over more than sixty million acres in the arid western states.

This invasive grass is a bane to livestock and wildlife. It is found from fifteen hundred to nine thousand feet in elevation where average annual precipitation ranges from as little as six inches to more than twenty inches. After a brief period in the spring and early summer, its nutritional value quickly drops. It stands four to thirty inches tall and produces seeds that germinate in the fall or early spring, giving it a jump on many native species.[35] The seeds stay viable in the soil for up to five years, helping cheatgrass survive periodic drought. It ripens early, burns readily, and carries fire far better than the native bunchgrasses. In areas dominated by native bunchgrasses, fires typically occur once every thirty to seventy years or longer. Cheatgrass, on the other hand, brought more frequent and larger wildfires, on average returning in less than ten years, and in as little as three in some areas. Most native plants are not adapted to such frequent and more intense fires, which in addition have increased fire-fighting costs and fire rehabilitation.[36] Most federal land managers consider the loss of such native plants and the animals that depend on them a threat to the long-term health of entire sagebrush ecosystems.

Livestock grazing also has been one of the factors that contribute to large, catastrophic forest fires in western arid regions. Long before the Forest Service began aggressive fire suppression, the frequency of fire had dropped following introduction of livestock. Grazing reduced or removed the grasses that once carried frequent light, naturally-started ground fires, especially in dry ponderosa forests. Regular fires cleared forest litter and killed most competing seedlings. Without enough grass to carry fires in grazed areas, thickets of fire-prone tree seedlings not palatable to livestock could flourish, eventually increasing the potential for less frequent but more catastrophic fires.

The removal of beavers in the 1820s and 1830s also contributed to the deterioration of public lands in the West. Riparian areas make up only about 2 percent of rangelands in the arid West, but those narrow strips of streamside vegetation are critical to most desert wildlife, small mammals, birds, and fish. It is also here that grazing livestock get more than 80 percent of their forage. Like other animals, cows need water every day and prefer the shade and cool water of these streamside oases. Unlike most other animals, cattle tend to congregate in riparian areas in late summer. As beavers were trapped out, their dams deteriorated and eventually gave out. Floods and runoff that had been slowed by the beaver ponds and dams eroded stream channels.

Furthermore, cattle hooves break down already compromised stream banks, and cows nibble down the shrubs, grasses, tender young willow shoots, and cottonwood seedlings that provide shade and help keep the water cool enough for native fish. With little left to hold stream banks together, slow the current and trap sediments, spring floods added to the damage, resulting in increased erosion and stream-bed downcutting. With resulting lowered water tables, some perennial streams became intermittent or dry most of the year in some areas. Gullies are all that remain in some places that once were beaver ponds, wetlands, and wet meadows and are reminders of the damage that resulted from the eradication of beavers compounded by overgrazing.

Grazing cattle can keep beavers from reestablishing their colonies. Livestock leave the beavers little food or materials they need for building and maintaining their lodges and dams. The result has been the large scale destruction of riparian areas across the West. Since Europeans settled the West an estimated 80 percent of streams on federal lands in Idaho have been damaged by poor grazing management, Arizona estimates it has lost 97 percent of its original riparian habitat, and New Mexico reports a 90 percent loss. The figures are similar for other states. Some estimates for the entire United States put the loss of riparian habitat at about 70 percent. Millions of acres have been affected.[37] The most serious damage to riparian areas throughout the West still results from poorly managed livestock grazing on federal rangelands.

In some areas the mere presence of cattle can degrade an arid area. On a trip through southern Idaho around the beginning of the twentieth century, naturalist John Burroughs noted the lack of sod in sagebrush grasslands.[38] Bunch grasses grew in tufts with the ground showing around them. Had he looked closer, he would have seen that it was not all bare dirt. Down on the ground beneath the sagebrush, a fragile gray mat of cryptogamic crust covered the soil. This natural crust is made up of a mixture of cyanobacteria, green algae, micro fungi, mosses, liverworts, and lichens, depending on location, and it holds moisture and stabilizes the soil. It also keeps the seeds of many invasive plants from taking root. Where it remains undisturbed it stops all but the worst erosion by wind and water on most arid lands. Livestock hooves, vehicles, and fires break up and damage this fragile crust, exposing the underlying soil. Small areas may recover in a few years, but large scale damage can take more than a hundred years to recover. Meanwhile the damage leaves the soil vulnerable to erosion and invasion by cheatgrass and other nonnative plants.

A 2009 report by the Arizona-based conservation group WildEarth Guardians sought to show how livestock grazing has contributed to the decline of native wildlife. The report, "Western Wildlife Under Hoof: Public Lands Livestock Grazing Threatens Iconic Species," is based on GIS analysis of more than 260 million acres of public land grazed by domestic livestock, overlapped with current and historic ranges of selected species. The report concluded that grazing is permitted on 91 percent of sage grouse habitat on federal land, about 80 percent of public land in the historic range of six species of native trout, on 61 to 93 percent of public land in the historic range of four prairie dog species, and about half of the Sonoran desert tortoise's historic range on public land.[39]

Grazing affects ground-nesting birds like sage grouse directly. Reducing tall vegetation makes the birds more vulnerable to predators, and livestock sometimes trample the nests. Livestock grazing also may contribute to a decline in game animals in some hunting units where livestock have overgrazed key wildlife winter ranges, leaving little for deer and elk and other animals to survive harsh winters. Fences that keep livestock within the appropriate grazing areas and out of sensitive areas, such as streams and lakes, also take their toll by entangling birds and animals.

As long as humans have grazed their livestock on open lands, they have had trouble with predators, and herders have defended their herds. In the United States, especially on the vast public lands of the West, livestock owners, herders, or hired trappers once dealt with predators. Today agents of the U.S. Department of Agriculture's Wildlife Services kill predators on behalf of ranchers who run livestock on public lands. Wolves and other predators are as much a part of the West as the terrain and the weather, and livestock losses to predators are part of grazing on public land.

Few ranchers make a living grazing livestock on public lands. Many hold other jobs or a family member has a job outside the ranch, or they graze their livestock on private lands part of the time. Most grazing permits are not held by family ranchers. In the western states, the BLM administers about eighteen thousand grazing permits, and the U.S. Forest Service administers more than eight thousand permits. More than half of those permits are held by about 2 percent of permit holders, mostly large corporations or wealthy individuals.[40] According to a report by Vickery Eckhoff of AlterNet, the largest holders of public land grazing permits include Koch Industries, J. R. Simplot Corporation, Barrick Gold, Barron Hilton, and the Southern Nevada Water Authority.[41] The economic powerhouses behind some of the largest grazing outfits can influence management decisions that affect the health of public lands.

Another important group of players are bankers. Many ranchers consider their public land grazing permits as private property rights that can be bought and sold as part of the ranch.[42] Because federal grazing fees are lower than most private and state grazing leases, the permits take on an artificial value. Though the lands belong to the American people, some ranchers like Chet Brackett use the value of their grazing permits as collateral for private bank loans. Though not all banks will loan money on grazing permits directly, most recognize that permits add value to ranch property. The bank takes a risk if the permit is canceled or expires. The deeded real estate of most ranches provides sufficient collateral, and some lenders may be more interested in the permit as a way to ensure the rancher can repay the loan. If a rancher defaults on a loan, the bank may take possession of the ranch and try to sell it. Bankers argue it would be harder to sell, or to get full value, if the grazing permit is lost.

The trouble starts when changes in grazing permits affect the perceived value of the ranch. Reductions in animal numbers as a result of reduced forage on public rangelands from drought, fire, or overgrazing become an economic consideration for the rancher and the bank that holds the rancher's mortgage. That can lead to land use decisions that favor the value and the marketability of the ranch rather than the long-term health of the land. It is a questionable practice, but officially sanctioned. In the mid-1990s, for example, the Forest Service proposed cutting cattle numbers from 1,188 to 833 head on the Diamond Bar Ranch in New Mexico. The proposal was appealed, not by the rancher, but by the Federal Intermediate Credit Bank of Texas, which held a mortgage on the ranch. The bank, which had acquired the ranch in a foreclosure, balked, saying the 30 percent reduction would cost them $500,000.[43] The bank said it was interested in the ranch's marketability.

More than ten years later, on the same ranch, the Forest Service asked the rancher to take some cows off the allotment early to prevent "unacceptable resource damage," following several years of drought. Farm Credit of Texas, successor to the Federal Intermediate Credit Bank, appealed what it considered a permit modification. The bank held the mortgage on the Diamond Bar and the federal grazing permit for a loan of $560,000. In a March 30, 1995, letter to the Forest Service, Michael J. Cadigan, attorney for Farm Credit Bank, wrote that, "If the permit is modified as anticipated, the value of the base property will decline greatly, and the permittees repayment capacity will be damaged or destroyed. Farm Credit's security and ability to collect its loan will be severely damaged as a result."[44] No one mentioned the condition of the public resource. Forest Service officials denied the appeal. They had not modified the permit, they said. They had simply asked the rancher to remove some cattle from the land because of a shortage of available grass, a condition of the permit agreed to by the rancher.

The Diamond Bar Ranch was not alone. According to the 2009 report by WildEarth Guardians, liens on grazing permits in eleven states totaled more than $1.1 billion, and three hundred ranching operations had used Forest Service grazing permits as collateral against about $450 million in loans. In 2000 a Utah bank confirmed that that financial institution held about $10 billion in ranching loans and other credit transactions, with grazing permits of about $1 billion in collateral.[45] Bankers and lawyers notwithstanding, cows cannot eat grass that is not there, whether the reason is overgrazing, fire, or drought.

Most ranchers do their best to treat public land with respect; after all they depend on it to raise their livestock. They measure the health of the land in the weight gain of their calves at roundup time in the fall, not necessarily in the biodiversity of native plants and animals or the integrity of watersheds. Some, like Chet Brackett, recognize the damage their animals have done, though they contend that such problems are mostly isolated incidents. Other experts, including state and federal wildlife biologists, say that the ecological effects of livestock grazing on public lands are more widespread than any other human activity in the West. Trouble spots, past and ongoing, have been documented across the arid western states. A former Idaho Fish and Game regional manager once quipped that "one man's isolated incident, is another man's widespread problem."[46]

Despite arguments to the contrary, livestock grazing on semiarid public lands has been both uneconomic and deleterious to wildlife habitat and wildlife. Some argue that livestock grazing has brought benefits to wildlife with water troughs or small reservoirs in remote locations. Others argue that grazing can benefit natural ecosystems or function as a vegetation management tool. Experts, including BLM scientists, however, say livestock grazing has contributed directly or indirectly to the spread of cheatgrass, to the decrease in sage grouse numbers and other sensitive species, to changes in fire intensity and frequency, to the spread of desert-like conditions with little plant diversity, and to the destruction of vital riparian areas. Yet grazing is subsidized by taxpayers, and it has led to land use decisions that favor private livestock operations over the health of public land resources and native wildlife.

When wildlife species are in trouble, such as sage grouse, Sonoran desert tortoise or Chinook salmon, biologists look first at the habitat. When there is trouble with the habitat, the trouble is often with land uses. Some contend the solution is removing livestock from public land in areas where the average annual rainfall is less than twelve inches. A just resolution should certainly consider those who make their living from the land, many of whom have built livelihoods that depended in part on public lands and who abide by the conditions of their grazing leases. It does not seem fair to expect them to just walk away, even though a condition of those leases is that they can be cancelled. On the other hand, the solution should also consider the taxpayers, who pay a significant part of the cost of grazing on public land. Most of all, however, it should consider the condition of public resources, land productivity, water quality, and wildlife habitat. Few ranchers in the West depend solely on public lands. Some rural communities rely economically on livestock grazing, but most of the grazing is on private land or involves large corporate livestock operations. More often grazing operations are economically tied to rural communities. Western public lands provide about 3 percent of livestock forage in the country, though some individual ranchers depend more heavily on public lands.[47]

Alternatives exist for ranchers who do not want to give up ranching or their rural lives. Some have discovered that moving their livestock to private land is less costly with fewer headaches. One southern Idaho rancher a few years ago found that his bottom line improved when he gave up his Forest Service grazing allotment in the hills along the Utah border. He lost fewer animals and spent less time rounding them up when it came time to sell the calves. The allotment has since become a state wildlife management area that is home to California bighorn sheep, mule deer, upland birds, native Yellowstone cutthroat trout, wild turkeys, bobcat, and many other wildlife species. In eastern Utah, the owners of the once functioning Nile Mile Ranch offer tourists a place to sleep, food, camping, showers, a country store, and guided tours of the canyon's famous rock art.

Some ranchers have turned their operations into dude ranches with fewer cattle and paying guests who help with the chores, urban residents who come to get a taste of the rural life. Some have given up ranching and turned to outfitting, taking hunters, hikers, and others on horseback into the backcountry. Others have accepted permit retirement, under which they give up grazing permits in exchange for a payment. Such reductions in livestock numbers have reduced the effects of grazing and eased the pressure on many wildlife species.

Some conservation groups have bought out allotments that have greater value for uses other than livestock grazing, such as watersheds, wildlife habitat, and aesthetics. In some areas where livestock were removed, riparian areas recovered; streams ran colder and cleaner; sage grouse, pronghorn, and songbird numbers increased; bighorn sheep survival improved; and improved winter ranges supported healthy populations of elk and deer. Livestock grazing threatens species diversity in the West about as much as mining and logging combined, contributes to desertification, spreads invasive weeds, and contributes the most nonpoint source water pollution in the West.[48] In the end, livestock grazing on most public lands in the arid West is a losing proposition. No one expects the government to subsidize money-losing steel mills so they can stay in business; yet taxpayers are expected without question to subsidize money-losing livestock grazing that threatens western public lands, watersheds, fish and wildlife and the landscape that supports us all. In the long term the money might be better spent supporting land uses and efforts that help restore degraded ecosystems.

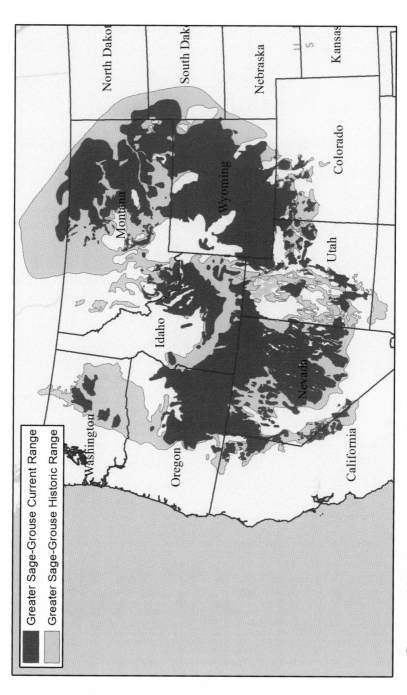

Current and historic greater sage-grouse distribution. *Map courtesy of U.S. Fish and Wildlife Service, Wyoming ES, August 15, 2014. www.fws.gov/greatersagegrouse/maps.php*

CHAPTER 6

Vanishing Sage Grouse

The night crew was on a mission. Loud rock and roll blared from a loudspeaker lashed with baling wire to the grill of the four-wheel-drive pickup, growling in low gear and crashing through the sagebrush. Bright lights groped the dark southern Idaho night. Bouncing over rocks just a few miles north of the Nevada border, I had accompanied two Idaho Fish and Game biologists and a helper for a story about the agency's efforts to learn more about the sage grouse. With wildlife biologist Randy Smith, Conservation Officer Rich Holman, and graduate student Tom Maeder, I helped search the midnight desert for sage grouse. The music echoing across the desert apparently covered the noise of the approaching night stalkers, keeping the birds from flushing. Bob Seger's "Night Moves" seemed to work best. Holman stood in the pickup truck bed, bracing against the roof of the cab, peered through his own version of night vision goggles—a spotlight in one hand and binoculars in the other. Smith drove the truck while Holman probed the sagebrush for the tell-tale greenish glint reflecting from a sage grouse retina.[1] That night, I participated in the capture of eight sage grouse. As I cradled one frightened bird in my hands, I could feel its heart beating.

A likely suspect was caught in the light beam. Holman signaled Smith, who steered toward the lighted spot and turned up the music. Maeder and I, armed with nets on four-foot poles like big fish landing nets, jumped off the tailgate and stumbled in the dark alongside the truck. Holman , standing upright in the bouncing pickup bed, tried to keep the bright light on the hunkering bird. The truck stopped about thirty feet from it. We rushed forward, oblivious of the rocks and brush that threatened to trip us. Maeder slapped his round net over the bewildered bird transfixed in the spotlight. He held the bird firmly to keep it from struggling as he freed it from the net. Dark brown eyes blinked in the glare, as nimble fingers affixed a numbered metal band to one leg and

An Idaho Fish and Game biologist holds a captured male sage grouse to be fitted with a miniature radio transmitter before being released again. *Author photo*

With Randy Smith at the wheel and Rich Holman holding the spotlight, net man Tom Maeder is ready to slap his net over a cowering sage grouse. *Author photo*

strapped a tiny radio transmitter, smaller than my thumb, on its back. Moments later they released the female sage grouse. They watched the bird fly off to make sure the transmitter did not hamper its flight.

Biologists hoped to learn where sage grouse nested, raised their young, spent the winter, and what they ate. They would continue to track the birds for about a year and a half or until the radios stopped transmitting. The data, among other things, helped land managers in the early 1990s to decide where to locate planned burns to control sagebrush and improve livestock grazing and to learn more about the long-term effects of fire on sage grouse habitat.[2] In recent years especially, large, extensive fires in sagebrush grasslands have become more frequent, and today fire, both wild and intentional, is considered one of the primary threats to sage grouse habitat. The other has been the invasion and spread of cheatgrass in part as both a cause and a result of those fires. The irony is that the fires federal land managers once set to improve livestock forage, along with other methods of wholesale sagebrush eradication, have had much to do with the spread of cheatgrass, the loss of habitat, and the decline of sage grouse that once numbered about sixteen million across the West.

Aldo Leopold, in *Sand County Almanac*, dubbed the ruffed grouse "the numenon of the north wood" because it represented the essential spirit of that environment. In the same light, sage grouse can rightly be considered the numenon of the West. The greater sage grouse is the largest grouse in North America at about two feet tall and up to thirty inches from its beak to the tip of its long, pointed tail. It tips the scale at two to seven pounds. Its plumage is mottled gray-brown, with some black and white, and the male sports a white ruff. No other creature better represents the essential spirit of the western high desert sagebrush landscape.[3] Today sage grouse are in serious trouble.

On June 6, 1805, Meriwether Lewis, on his way west, saw his first sage grouse near the mouth of the Marias River in Montana. Members of his expedition learned from local American Indians and their own subsequent observations that the birds were common in the western United States. They found them in abundance, as Lewis noted, from central Montana, along the Clearwater River in Idaho, along the Snake River in Washington and at the confluence of the Snake and Columbia Rivers, where William Clark shot one on October 17, 1805. The two expedition leaders each wrote a description of the birds in their March 2,

1806, journal entries while encamped at Fort Clatsop in Oregon near the mouth of the Columbia River. Lewis called it "cock of the plains;" Clark called it a "heath cock." They described it as a pheasant-like bird nearly as large as a turkey, subsisting on grasshoppers and mostly on sagebrush.[4]

In the two hundred years since, settlement has altered what had been the birds' habitat, range, and numbers. Today sage grouse are gone from about half the area they once inhabited, and their numbers have dropped by an estimated 90 percent. Biologists have been concerned about their decline since the early 1900s. They estimate sage grouse numbered about sixteen million at the time of the Lewis and Clark expedition. They could be found in sagebrush habitats at elevations up to about nine thousand feet in Washington, Oregon, California, Nevada, Idaho, Montana, Wyoming, Colorado, Utah, South Dakota, North Dakota, Kansas, Oklahoma, Nebraska, New Mexico, Arizona, and the Canadian provinces of British Columbia, Alberta, and Saskatchewan. Today it is estimated that the birds number fewer than half a million, and they have disappeared from Nebraska, Kansas, Oklahoma, New Mexico, Arizona, British Columbia, and Saskatchewan.

Not just fire and cheatgrass put sage grouse in jeopardy. More than a century and a half of political maneuvering and land-use policies that favored livestock grazing and other uses have degraded and destroyed sage grouse habitat. In response to past overgrazing, the Bureau of Land Management and the U.S. Forest Service eradicated as much as 100 million acres of sagebrush and replanted them with non-native grasses to improve forage for domestic livestock, eliminating large areas of sage grouse habitat in the process.

Other factors have led to degraded rangeland as well. Overgrazing on many arid western lands, public and private, opened the door to the invasion of non-native species in addition to cheatgrass, resulting in habitat changes. Other land uses, including residential development, growth of industrial scale agriculture, energy exploration, motorized recreation, as well as power transmission lines, roads, and wind power projects have all contributed to the increasing fragmentation and reduced carrying capacity of sage grouse habitat.

———————◆———————

In one place, however, the ritual spring dance of the numenon of the West was about to begin. On a cool March morning in the early 1990s I had joined wildlife biologist Randy Smith to witness the elaborate mating dance of sage grouse. The sun had not yet risen when we pulled off U.S. Highway 93, just north of the Nevada border. We drove up a gravel road in the Shoshone Basin and parked where we found a good spot to wait for the sage grouse males. Mostly hidden in some low brush, we set up spotting scopes and a camera tripod where we had a clear view of the lek, the bare, open area where the birds would gather for their characteristic mating ritual. Leks vary in size from a couple of acres to as much as forty acres. The sage grouse typically return to their breeding grounds in late winter or early spring, often to the same area every year. By the end of February, male sage grouse begin to show up at the leks. The females do not arrive until about the end of March.

Most of the activity happened at first light. The birds began to gather as the sky over the hills to the east grew lighter. We watched as the males walked out of the surrounding sagebrush and began sizing each other up. The morning mist gave the scene a mysterious air, but it also ruled out any decent photos. The lek that morning was not so different from a singles bar as the males gathered in hopes of finding willing females. Like their human counterparts, the male sage grouse puffed themselves up and strutted around. When the females arrived, the males raised their spiked tails, pumped up two large, yellow-green skin sacs, hidden by the white ruff on their breast, and produced a strange "plooping" noise while bobbing and weaving. The dominant males kept other males out of the center of the lek. The younger ones waited at a respectful distance in the nearby sagebrush. When a brazen young male ventured onto the lek, the older males rushed to head off the interloper. Intimidated by the strutting of a dominant male, the younger bird slinked away.[5] Only rarely did these encounters result in a fight to establish dominance. When it did, the competing males would slap each other with their wings, or one might hop up and smack the other on the head. It appeared largely ceremonial as they tried to intimidate competing males and impress the females.

Activity at the lek intensified and then abated slowly. At first the females appeared aloof, and seemed more interested in finding tender morsels to eat than in the antics of the males. Worn down by the wooing of the persistent males, the females finally succumbed. A few dominant males mate with most of the females, and after they have performed their reproductive obligations, they continue to hang around the lek. The females move off to look for nesting sites. With the females gone, the males continue to gather for a few weeks. They strut around as if bragging about their romantic exploits. The dominant males eventually relent and let the younger males onto the lek to practice their moves.[6]

The subsequent part of their life-cycle has been studied and clearly delineated. A female sage grouse makes her nest in a shallow bowl lined with grasses and feathers under sagebrush. She lays an average of six to seven olive to greenish eggs with small brown spots. The eggs hatch about four weeks later. Newly hatched chicks begin eating almost right away, feeding on soft plant parts and high-protein insects through their first month. In a few weeks, when the young are old enough to leave the nest, they move to rearing habitat along streams or wet meadows near springs where they spend the summer. In late summer and early fall they begin to gather for their migration to lower elevation wintering grounds, and have been known to migrate up to a hundred miles between winter and summer ranges. Biologists note that they range over a thousand or more square miles through the year. Sage grouse are found only where sagebrush grows in unbroken expanses in company with other plants. They seem to prefer a density of 15 to 25 percent sagebrush cover for breeding and rearing habitat and up to 30 percent sagebrush cover in winter. Sage grouse are picky eaters. Unlike most other birds, sage grouse have no gizzard to grind their food, and exist almost entirely on soft plant parts. They favor several species and subspecies of sagebrush, and while it is their primary food, they also need the bunchgrasses and small flowering plants that grow among the sagebrush. In winter, however, sagebrush makes up their total diet.

The most common species is big sagebrush (*Artemisia tridentata*) including the Wyoming and mountain varieties, all members of the aster family. Its sharp, sweet smell is characteristic of western rangeland; some refer to it as cowboy perfume. This perennial reproduces from seeds, which ripen in the fall and are shed from September through December. It grows from three to more than twelve feet tall and can live 150 years or more. Their one-inch-long, gray-green wedge-shaped leaves have three distinctive lobes at the ends. Sagebrush send tap roots as far as twelve feet deep to sip from the water table; they also spread a web of shallow roots to soak up moisture from the surface. The leaves and flowers are nutritious, high in protein, fats, and carbohydrates.[7]

Healthy sagebrush habitat provides shelter and forage for about 350 species, including songbirds, pygmy rabbits, sagebrush lizards, mule deer, elk, and pronghorn. The Western sagebrush landscape has also supported humans for more than 11,000 years. Indians made tea from the leaves and drank it as a tonic, and they used it as an antiseptic, as a treatment for colds and diarrhea, and against ticks. They used the tough, stringy bark to make baskets, blankets, ropes, and sandals.[8] Settlers used it as firewood as they cleared the land for farming. While sagebrush covers more land in western North America than any other vegetation, dominating more than 190,000 square miles within sage grouse range, good sagebrush habitat is getting harder to find. In a typical sagebrush landscape, the sagebrush is the tallest, bunchgrasses and flowering plants make up the next layer, beneath that are low-growing grasses and plants, and on the ground a microbiotic crust protects arid lands from wind and water erosion.

The reason for the decline of sage grouse populations is simple. When an animal species is in trouble, biologists look first to their habitat. If the sagebrush landscape were healthy, sage grouse would not be in trouble. They have lost nearly half of their suitable habitat, which provides food, cover, and nesting, and much of what is left has been degraded. The reasons for the loss of that habitat are not so simple. About half of the sagebrush landscape in the West has been taken up for farms, towns, and rural and suburban residential developments. More was intentionally eliminated from federal lands or scourged by fire and replaced by invasive plants. Vast tracts of sagebrush habitat were converted directly to agricultural lands. Many other land uses have chopped additional sage grouse habitat into pieces so small they cannot sustain sage grouse populations. More than 70 percent of sage grouse habitat is on public lands managed by federal or state agencies, and most of it is open to livestock grazing.

The efforts to reap more benefits from western lands led to the decline of the sagebrush ecosystem. The decline began with the removal of beavers by trappers in the 1820s and 1830s, and the subsequent degradation of riparian areas. It continued into the mid-nineteenth century with European settlement, large cattle drives supplying miners in the Rocky Mountains, and the coming of the continental railroad in 1869, which expanded the market for western beef. Livestock ran unregulated until 1897, leading to severe overgrazing in many places. The combined effects of overgrazing and drought in the late 1880s and early 1900s brought changes that still affect sage grouse habitat.

◆

The response of the Bureau of Land Management and the U.S. Forest Service to overgrazing starting in the 1930s exacerbated the problem. In many places, their efforts to increase livestock forage on public lands eliminated large areas of sage grouse habitat. Livestock grazing today is the most widespread land use in the sage grouse range and continues to affect that habitat. Domestic animals still eat and trample vegetation around sagebrush, damaging potential nesting habitat. They trample nests and destroy eggs, and they eat the grasses that sage grouse rely on to hide their nests from predators. Research shows that tall, dense vegetation reduces predation on nesting sage grouse. In the summer livestock also compete for vegetation in riparian areas and wet meadows that are vital to young sage grouse.

Despite changes in policy, the remaining habitat is still being compromised. Federal land managers no longer use large scale treatments to improve livestock forage, but they still build water systems and fences to manage livestock grazing and to increase or maintain the numbers of animals on the range. Sage grouse sometimes collide with fences, which also provide perches for raptors. Water systems allow grazing in more sage grouse habitat, and can be a vector for West Nile virus. Such developments also break up sage grouse habitat.[9] Severe winter weather, cold, and wet weather during the nesting season and predators all take their toll on sage grouse from year to year, but in the long term, habitat loss has played a more important role.

Severe overgrazing along with the invasion of cheatgrass conspired to turn fire into a disaster for sage grouse. Cheatgrass brought back fire with a vengeance as it invaded disturbed soil and previously burned areas. Extremely flammable, it is dry by mid-June or mid-July depending on the elevation, while native grasses still contain much of their moisture.[10] Cheatgrass also grows closer together and carries fire more effectively than bunchgrasses. It recovers quickly after a fire and therefore promotes more frequent fires. Fires in cheatgrass typically return in less than ten years, and as little as every three to five years in some areas. Most native plants, especially big sagebrush, are not adapted to frequent fires. Sagebrush can take cold, heat, and drought, but it is especially vulnerable to fire. It rarely re-sprouts from its roots after a fire but depends instead on seeds left in the soil or spread by animals. In addition, its seedlings do not compete well with grasses, so recovery is usually slow. It can take decades to become reestablished. Fire is an effective way to control big sagebrush, and frequent fires can keep sagebrush from becoming reestablished.[11]

The best natural protection against cheatgrass is the cryptogamic crust, which, when intact, keeps cheatgrass seed from germinating. The hooves of grazing cattle churn up the soil and destroy the integrity of the crust, and cheatgrass moves in faster than the crust can recover. Where cheatgrass has taken over, native grasses and sagebrush decline, degrading wildlife habitat and leaving sage grouse with little food or shelter. It is a rangeland death spiral—cheatgrass promotes fire, and fire favors cheatgrass. Most federal land managers consider cheatgrass a serious threat to the health of the rangeland ecosystems. Some, however, still resort to fire to control cheatgrass, reduce sagebrush density, promote the growth of native grasses and flowering plants, and keep juniper and pinyon pine out of sagebrush lands. Researchers and those familiar with the land say they have found no evidence that such prescribed fires have helped sage grouse.[12] They maintain that prescribed fire in sage grouse nesting, rearing, or winter habitat has been shown to reduce sage grouse numbers.

Fire and its opportunistic accomplice cheatgrass are by no means the only threat. The Oregon Trail brought settlers, and the federal government was in the business of giving western lands away through legislation such as the Homestead Act, Desert Land Entry Act, and the Carey Act. In the hot, dry western states, irrigation made industrial scale agriculture possible, but before the land could be farmed it had to be cleared of sagebrush. Pioneer farmers first cleared it by hand, chopping or grubbing out the stubborn, deep-rooted brush. Later, they used horses. A man and a team of four horses could clear about an acre per day. The most common way was to hitch the horses to an iron rail or heavy-toothed rake to break down the sagebrush. In this way, one man could clear eighty acres in a single summer. The uprooted sagebrush was gathered into piles and burned.[13]

With improved pump technology in the mid-twentieth century, irrigated agriculture gobbled up more acres of sagebrush landscape. In 1946 Julion Clawson, a Salt Lake City businessman, bought several thousand acres of dry farmland at the edge of the Bureau of Reclamation's irrigated Minidoka Project north of the Snake River in southern Idaho. At the time, most farmers irrigated their fields with gravity flows diverted from streams and rivers, some pumped water from canals to reach higher ground, and some pumped water from shallow aquifers. Clawson's land had no surface water, and it was beyond the reach of gravity irrigation canals. Geological reports from 1928 showed large amounts of groundwater more than four hundred feet beneath the arid lava plain, out of reach of older pumps. In 1947 Clawson drilled three deep wells, and found that his modern high-lift pumps could reach enough water to irrigate thirty-eight hundred acres of wheat, potatoes, and beans. Other farmers began to watch with interest. Within four years, he was irrigating twenty-four thousand acres. Others followed. In the early 1950s, nearly one million more acres came into production. People drilled for water as though it were oil.[14] Today about forty million acres are irrigated, much of which was once sage grouse habitat.

Noise and human activity also threatens sage grouse habitat. In a process known as fragmentation, rural residential development, energy production, power lines, and roads all break habitat into patches so small they cannot support viable sage grouse populations. Haul roads, well pads, and pipelines built for oil and gas exploration and extraction bring human disturbance to remote areas and exacerbate the destruction and fragmentation of sage grouse habitat.[15] Biologists say that sage grouse need a four-mile buffer from oil and gas sites for breeding, nesting, and rearing, since they normally stay within four to six miles of their leks during breeding and nesting seasons.

What were once nearly unbroken expanses of sagebrush landscape are today crisscrossed by a spider web of roads. These range from wide multilane interstates and major highways to simple two-track dirt roads, all of which bring an increase in noise and human disturbance. However, they affect more than just the ground they cover. Some researchers estimate that the noise, changes in habitat, and spread of invasive species caused by major highways can extend up to about six miles from the roadway. Most sage grouse habitat is less than two miles from a road.

Vehicles also kill sage grouse outright. Roads increase wildfire potential, block migrations, and can improve access for predators that affect sage grouse. Fragmentation of habitat leads to lower productivity in many areas. In some places the average number of chicks per bird has declined by up to 50 percent since the 1980s, and in some places the number of young is not enough to sustain the population.[16] The cumulative effects of changes in land uses, disturbances, and invasive species combined are more significant than any single cause, researchers say.

———————◆———————

About two hundred years after Lewis and Clark encountered the species, environmental and conservation groups asked the U.S. Fish and Wildlife Service to protect sage grouse under the Endangered Species Act. Between 1999 and 2003, the agency received eight petitions to list sage grouse. The first was for the Columbia Basin populations, in parts of Washington, Oregon, Nevada, and Idaho. In 2001 a petition was filed to list the Mono Basin population, along the border between California and Nevada. Another petition for that population was filed in 2005. In 2002 petitions were filed for the western subspecies, the eastern subspecies, and for the greater sage grouse range-wide. Two more petitions were filed in 2003 for the greater sage grouse throughout its range.

The response to these petitions by Fish and Wildlife officials led to protracted battles in the courts. In 2005 the agency ruled that listing the Columbia Basin population as endangered or threatened was warranted but precluded by other species with a higher priority. Fish and Wildlife combined the three range-wide petitions into one, and ruled that the range-wide listing was not warranted. The rest lacked enough information for any further action, agency officials said. Environmental and conservation groups challenged the decisions in court, and in a settlement, Fish and Wildlife agreed to conduct a new finding for the Mono Basin population. The eastern population legal challenge was dismissed, and the decision on the western population was sent back to Fish and Wildlife. In 2007 the federal court sent the not-warranted decision for the greater sage grouse range-wide petition back to Fish and Wildlife for review.

At this point top level executive branch officials became involved in the fight over sage grouse and their habitat. In a March 5, 2010, news release, Interior Secretary Ken Salazar announced that the greater sage grouse warranted protection under the Endangered Species Act, but listing the species was precluded because the sage grouse species was widely spaced across the West in sufficient numbers, and other species faced more serious and imminent threats.[17] However, since 2005, U.S. Fish and Wildlife had found that new threats had been added to the threats identified earlier, and the scale and intensity of those threats and their combined effects—like the interaction of fire and cheatgrass—had increased. Officials had a better understanding of how those threats affected the continued survival of the species. The primary threats were habitat modification, fragmentation, and destruction. They also found that regulatory mechanisms on federal lands, which made up about two-thirds of the birds' habitat, had not been effective.

Sage grouse, meanwhile, became a candidate for a listing as threatened or endangered under the Endangered Species Act. This left their fate in the hands of the states: Washington, Oregon, California, Nevada, Idaho, Montana, Wyoming, Colorado, Utah, and North and South Dakota. Salazar used as a rationale that biologists expected that some local populations might disappear within thirty to a hundred years if present trends continued. The court then ordered Fish and Wildlife to make a final decision about listing the bird as a threatened species by September 2015. Salazar therefore asked the eleven western states to develop sage grouse conservation plans that could be incorporated into a National Sage-Grouse Planning Strategy to update western federal land-use plans.

Lobbying by grazing, mining, and oil and gas interests that depend on public land resources nearly kept the Fish and Wildlife Service from meeting the court-ordered 2015 deadline. Congress in December 2014 had blocked Fish and Wildlife from spending any federal money to list the sage grouse until October 1, 2015. Furthermore, in the spring of 2015, western Republicans Senator Cory Gardner of Colorado and Representative Rob Bishop of Utah introduced legislation that would have delayed a listing and scaled back federal sage grouse conservation efforts for ten years. They argued that a federal listing would undermine habitat conservation efforts already under way by state officials and landowners. Scientists and researchers argued that some of those conservation efforts did not rely on the best available research.[18] For example, some plans included prescribed fire which, as has been shown, does not benefit sage grouse habitat.

Faced with the hammer of the Endangered Species Act, state officials, ranchers, energy industry officials, and others made a serious effort to conserve sage grouse and its remaining habitat. They worked on ways to stop the decline of sage grouse, not because they cared about the bird so much, but because they feared the consequences an endangered species act listing could have on livestock grazing, mining, oil and gas exploration and extraction, the operations of industrial agriculture, and suburban growth. Forest Service and BLM officials worked to update management plans for about sixty million acres of public land to include conservation measures for sage grouse before the final listing decision in late 2015.

States developed sage grouse conservation plans that focused on protecting the remaining prime sage grouse habitat by limiting some activities in these areas. Unfortunately much of what is considered core habitat is marginal. One example is the desert wilderness of Owyhee County in southwestern Idaho, where stunted sagebrush is interspersed with bare soil and few grasses or other plants. The habitat is better in some places, such as protected river corridors and canyons. Sage grouse experts say that many places considered core habitat areas are in fact not prime sage grouse habitat. Nor did the state plans recognize the role of livestock grazing in the long term decline of sage grouse habitat and how it continues to affect habitat. Mostly they focused on cheatgrass and fire.

Why this eleventh hour effort? Scientists have certainly known for decades about the plight of the sage grouse and about the effects of cheatgrass and fire on sage grouse habitat. There have been plenty of opportunities to address the cheatgrass invasion and to improve rangelands for sage grouse and other species, not just for domestic livestock. In the past, however, ranchers have opposed many of the efforts to improve rangelands that included a reduction in grazing. They resorted to intimidation of federal employees, including death threats and lawsuits, and called upon their powerful political allies in Congress to put financial pressure on the land management agencies, primarily the U.S. Forest Service and Bureau of Land Management. Low-cost grazing—in effect subsidized—on public lands encouraged overgrazing, and unrestrained livestock grazing opened the door to the spread of cheatgrass and the consequent change in fire cycles that eradicated vast tracts of sage grouse habitat. Yet taxpayers continue to subsidize grazing in sage grouse habitat, and land managers appear to accept cheatgrass as inevitable.

Other economic exploitation of public lands has contributed to habitat loss. Crop subsidies spurred the growth of agricultural expansion, and other users have reaped a profit from the vast commons of western public lands, but not without a substantial loss of sagebrush. Without the sagebrush habitat, there would be no sage grouse, and many other wildlife species would disappear. Birds of prey feed on the rodents that thrive in sagebrush grassland. Mule deer hide their fawns under heavy sagebrush cover. Many bird species depend on sagebrush habitat. Countless other plants and insects, most of them invisible to humans, depend on the health of the sagebrush ecosystem.

Nevertheless, on October 2, 2015, the U.S. Fish and Wildlife Service decided that the greater sage grouse no longer warranted protection under the Endangered Species Act. The decision relied on proposed changes in federal land-use plans that would withdraw ten million acres from future mining claims across the West, add restrictions on oil and gas drilling near breeding grounds, and add new reviews of livestock grazing permits. Following legal challenges of its 2005 decision not to list the sage grouse, Fish and Wildlife reviewed its findings and noted that populations had continued to decline, with some local populations wiped out. Officials cited habitat loss, fragmentation, and inadequate regulatory mechanisms as factors leading to a warranted determination.[19]

By 2015, however, conservation efforts in about 90 percent of the breeding habitat by federal, state, and private land owners had eased some of the threats to sage grouse. Across the West about 64 percent of sage grouse habitat is on federal public land, most of it managed by the BLM. Efforts to improve habitat on those lands have placed restrictions on thirty-five million acres of priority bird habitat; marked fences to make them more visible to sage grouse, reducing collisions by more than 80 percent; used conservation easements to limit residential development in core sage grouse areas; reduced the threat of invasive grasses and wildfire risk on 1.8 million acres; and removed invasive conifers on nearly half a million acres of core sage grouse habitat.

In 2010, the U.S. Department of Agriculture launched the Sage Grouse Initiative. By 2014, this voluntary program to encourage sage grouse conservation on private lands in eleven western states had enlisted more than eleven hundred ranchers who were actively involved, mostly in the form of easements that kept private lands from being developed or turned into cropland. Some ranchers also delayed the start of their grazing season and took other measures to reduce the effects of livestock on more than the four million acres of sage grouse habitat included in the program.

In Montana, public and private grants funded efforts to preserve habitat. There, about 70 percent of the remaining sage grouse habitat is on private lands, and conservation efforts included a recent $1.5 million state grant approved in November 2016. The grant would help pay for an eighteen thousand-acre easement on a ranch in central Montana, about 150 miles east of Great Falls. A private donation of $900,000 would bring the amount up to $2.4 million.[20] This easement would allow ranch owners to continue grazing livestock, but ensure that no subdivisions, construction, or other activities would be allowed within six-tenths of a mile of active sage grouse leks. It would also prevent any of the private rangeland from being converted into croplands. An additional $3.4 million in state grants with a $7.85 million match from private and federal sources would be used to protect an additional fifty thousand acres of sage grouse habitat in the state.[21] Critics of the easements contend that such taxpayer money would be better spent getting cattle out of core sage grouse habitat. A better way to protect sage grouse and sage grouse habitat, they say, would be to pay ranchers to retire grazing permits in key sage grouse areas.[22]

Opposition to listing the sage grouse and the conservation efforts it sparked had mixed results. Habitat loss, degradation, and fragmentation—including the spread of invasive plants—did not cease and, in fact, is expected to continue into the future. Fire and cheatgrass continue to be the primary threat to sage grouse. Even though they opposed an endangered species act listing, several state government and industry officials filed or joined lawsuits challenging the land-use restrictions issued in conjunction with the decision not to list the sage grouse. Idaho Governor C. L. Otter in 2015 for instance, complained that without consulting the states, the Fish and Wildlife Service added land-use restrictions on federally managed public lands not included in state sage grouse management plans. Otter's office argued that changes in land-use plans meant to protect sage grouse imposed "unnecessary restriction on Idaho farmers and ranchers, sportsmen, recreationists," and others.[23] Nevada state officials and some mining officials sued Fish and Wildlife over restrictions on grazing, mining, and oil and gas extraction. In nine Nevada counties, ranchers and miners challenged the land use restrictions they said would affect lands they rely on to make their living. These were the same restrictions the Fish and Wildlife Service had relied on to avoid an endangered species listing, which might have brought broader restrictions.

Idaho Fish and Game Director Virgil Moore has argued that such a listing would not bring sage grouse habitat back. His agency favored a recovery solution that would keep management of sage grouse in state hands rather than federal control under an endangered species act listing. He noted that the listing "would not recover the sage grouse population to what it once was because so much of the habitat is gone, and we're not going to get that back." He said further that, "The best chance is to save what's left and that requires the cooperation of land owners and land managers—listing or no listing."[24]

Critics of the Fish and Wildlife Service's decision not to list the sage grouse did not necessarily disagree. In response to the proposed land-use management changes four conservation groups filed their own lawsuit on February 25, 2016, challenging the National Greater Sage-Grouse Planning Strategy, saying it was inadequate because it did not include any comprehensive analysis of sage grouse populations, habitat, or conservation measures. Like much sage grouse habitat, the strategy is fragmented. The Western Watersheds Project, WildEarth Guardians, Center for Biological Diversity, and Prairie Hills Audubon Society of South Dakota together sought instead to require more analysis and changes to include, as the lawsuit puts it, "consistent, science-based conservation measures needed to ensure the survival and recovery of the greater sage grouse across its range into the future."[25] Federal agencies in their proposed land use plan changes failed to include a "range-wide analysis of sage grouse habitats, populations, threats or conservation needs." The agencies had compiled fifteen separate impact statements without a single evaluation of the cumulative effects or the connections between sage grouse habitats and populations. The lawsuit further states that, "Without such comprehensive or range-wide analysis, neither the agencies nor the public have sufficient information to understand how the various measures contained in these different plans may impact sage grouse throughout the species' range."[26] Thus the environmental impact statements violate the National Environmental Policy Act, the Federal Lands Policy and Management Act, the National Forest Management Act, and the Administrative Procedures Act, plaintiffs argued.

The lawsuit also argued that changes in federal requirements to conserve sage grouse are not strict enough and do not follow the best available science or the recommendations of the government's own experts. Specifically, the agencies failed to analyze the effects of livestock grazing, the most wide-spread land use throughout sage grouse habitat, and failed to require changes in grazing management to protect sage grouse habitats. The plans also included exceptions and loopholes for energy development, including in Wyoming, which has the largest sage grouse population with about 37 percent of the remaining birds.

All these plans notwithstanding, fire remains the most immediate threat to sage grouse. Lightning is a major cause of range fires. It strikes where it will, and abetted by cheat grass, drought, and wind, can wreak havoc on remaining sagebrush lands. In a dry year, a lightning storm on a windy day can burn up hundreds of thousands of acres of sagebrush lands, and humans can do little to stop it. In the summer of 2007, a lightning-caused wildfire fueled by cheat grass and pushed by high winds burned more than 650,000 acres of sagebrush grassland on both sides of the Idaho-Nevada border. From 2012 through 2014, more than 2.5 million acres of sage grouse habitat burned on public land.[27] Interior Secretary Sally Jewell, on a visit to Idaho in 2014, clearly expressed her concern about the effects of fire and cheatgrass on sage grouse habitat. She advocated an approach to rangeland fires, including a change in fire-fighting priority, that would put core sage grouse habitat before other resources, except for human lives and property.[28]

It remains to be seen whether the efforts to protect sage grouse will be enough to save it. A study completed in March 2015 estimated that sage grouse numbers had dropped by more than half between 2007 and 2013.[29] Biologists and volunteers conducted nearly ninety thousand counts at more than ten thousand sage grouse leks from 1965 through 2013 in the states where sage grouse are found. The estimated minimum number of breeding males dropped from 109,990 in 2007 to 48,641 in

2013, a decline of about 56 percent.[30] Researchers noted that conservation efforts on private and public lands show little sign of success, and more effort would be required in the face of current trends. Some suggest that the drop in numbers may simply be the bottom of a ten-year population cycle, and in a few years the populations would begin to rise again. Others fear the drop in recent years may be the beginning of a population collapse. Biologists noted that 2013 was a bad year for sage grouse because of ongoing drought and large wildfires. Some have questioned the effectiveness of firefighting efforts and conservation plans and suggest that it is too early to declare any conservation programs successful. On the other hand, it may be too early to write off the results of those efforts.

Though the loss of sage grouse as a species across its range is unlikely in the short term, its survival is by no means assured over the long term.[31] With the lingering damage of a century and a half of overgrazing, cheatgrass firmly established in the West, and the increased potential for drought and more large wildfires with changes in the climate, it may be too late for the sage grouse. Rehabilitation after a fire can take years, decades, and even centuries in some of the driest areas. Sage grouse may not last that long. Officials forecast that in some places, sage grouse will be gone in thirty to a hundred years. Regardless of whether it is listed under the endangered species act, sage grouse are in danger of extinction.

In the face of long odds, we can still leave room for Meriwether Lewis's "cock of the plains." Half of their habitat has been lost to land uses driven by social and cultural issues. We all share responsibility for the loss. We must keep cattle out of nesting areas, close roads through them, avoid drilling for gas and oil or digging for gold there, and keep residential developments out of prime sage grouse habitat. We must deal successfully with raging rangeland wildfires and halt or even reverse the cheatgrass invasion. Then the spike-tailed strut at first light on a frosty morning in early spring will not be the ghost dance of a disappearing species, but the celebration of a brand new day. Hikers in high desert sagebrush might still experience the heart stopping explosion of feathers at their feet when they flush a sage grouse. Then perhaps the West will not lose the numenon of the sagebrush landscape and an important part of its soul.

CHAPTER 7

The Nature of Wildfire

I felt the heat before I saw the pillar of fire. The black and orange fire swirl, like a small tornado, raged outside the plexiglass helicopter window, perhaps fifty yards away. Formed by the hot air from fire rising up a draw, it pulled in oxygen like a giant bellows. Buffeted by turbulent superheated air, the helicopter started shaking as we hovered, making it impossible to hold steady enough to get a picture. We circled for another look, and as we pivoted, I watched a mature lodgepole pine, maybe seventy-five-feet tall, explode and disappear in the inferno.

That hot August day in 1990 I just happened to be in the right place at the right time to get a front row seat to this spectacle. The local newspaper where I worked had sent me out to cover a large wildfire raging near the Idaho-Nevada-Utah border. I had arranged an interview with the fire incident commander, and was to meet him at a remote location where he would board a helicopter that would take him up for a close look at the fire. Armed with notebook, camera, extra film, and sturdy boots, I drove into the hills to the appointed meeting place and waited. Then I heard the clatter and turbine whine of a Bell Jet Ranger. In a whirl of dust and spinning rotor blades, the helicopter set down. The door opened, the U.S. Forest Service fire officer leaned out, and waving me toward the rear door yelled "Come on!" I grabbed my camera bag and notebook and, keeping my head down, ran for the helicopter, pulled open the door, and jumped in. I set my camera bag on the seat beside me and buckled up. The pilot gave me a thumbs up; the whine of the turbines grew in volume and pitch. I yelled an introduction over the roar, but could not hear the response. My stomach sank as we suddenly left the ground in a sweeping, climbing left turn.

I would learn a lot about fire that day: about the role of fire in the western forest ecosystem, why fighting fires can cause more damage to the ecosystem than the fires themselves, and about the future of fuel-choked forests. I also learned an important distinction between forest fires and fires in sagebrush grasslands. Fire once was an important part of sagebrush ecosystems, but the west-wide invasion of non-native cheatgrass has changed the intensity and frequency of fires, threatening sagebrush grasslands and the creatures that depend on them. On the other hand, fire is still an important part of western forest ecosystems.

Not everyone agrees on the role of forest fires on public lands. Some complain that the Forest Service is mismanaging national forests by letting large fires burn, filling the air with smoke and destroying valuable timber. Others, including many fire experts, say the Forest Service is not letting enough fires burn. In the arid West, forest fire is a fact of life, like hurricanes in Florida and the Gulf Coast, blizzards in the Dakotas, and tornadoes in Oklahoma and Kansas. Fire is as much a part of nature as rain, sun, and wind. Letting them burn can be unpopular and at times risky, but some fires burn regardless of human efforts to stop them. Despite evidence to the contrary, many people still resist the idea of a natural role of fire, a role that is vital to the survival of forest ecosystems. Many see fire as catastrophic, unexpected, or unnatural. One thing is for sure: when extended drought, hot weather, and high winds combine, extreme fires will burn until the weather changes or the fire runs out of things to burn. Such fires occur infrequently but are a fact of nature and there is little the Forest Service or anyone else can do about them. The frequency of extreme fires may even be exacerbated by a warming climate.

The fire I witnessed in 1990, named the Indian Spring fire, started on August 7 in the tall grass next to Indian Spring Road where it heads into the hills south of Twin Falls. Five days later it had burned nearly fourteen thousand acres, or about twenty-two square miles. It burned in mixed country, hilly with lodgepole pine and subalpine fir, and small canyons and draws that made perfect little chimneys to fan the flames. More than two hundred firefighters built about thirty miles of fire-lines, and contained the fire on August 11.[1] As we circled the fire, a yellow bulldozer below us cut a fire line across a grass and sagebrush slope. Downhill from the driver, a front of flame moved relentlessly up the draw toward him. His progress was achingly slow as he tried to head off the fast moving fire. We turned a wide circle, and when we came back around, the fire was much closer to the bulldozer, looking like it would overtake him. On our third pass, I could see the raw earth of the dozer cut just ahead of the fire only a few feet from the bulldozer. Flames spread along the fire line behind him, but he had stopped the fire's advance. We made another pass around the perimeter of the fire before heading back to the rendezvous point where my truck was parked. We had been gone an hour and a half, but it did not seem that long. A little wobbly when I stepped down on the ground, I headed back to the office with a lot of questions.

Seen here from the air, the Indian Spring Fire burned about fourteen thousand acres of sagebrush grassland, lodgepole pine, and subalpine fir in hilly country in southern Idaho. *Author photo*

Since that day, though none could match it for excitement, I have seen and reported on several other wildfires. I walked to some, drove to others, watched another from a small airplane, and rode horseback on an overnight expedition with a Hotshot firefighter crew deep into Idaho's Sawtooth Wilderness. The saddest was a fire just outside a community in the central Idaho mountains where I came across the smoking remains of a newly built home. Only a stone chimney and ashes piled among the foundations remained; a burned out hulk sat where the garage would have been. Sadder still, it probably did not have to happen. Often it is not the fires themselves that cause concern but the homes and lives lost to extreme fires, and that can mostly be avoided, experts say. People cannot prevent all wildfires, but they can prepare for them, limit the damages, and reap the benefits.

The broken skeleton is all that remains of this newly built house after a wildland fire near Sun Valley, Idaho. *Author photo*

Fire is impersonal, an immutable force of nature, neither evil nor benign. It is neither for you nor against you, but like the ocean, fire is unforgiving. Its mindless power can be frightening. Obeying only the laws of nature, and responding to the conditions that nature or humans have created, it moves as those conditions dictate. Fire requires fuel, oxygen, and an ignition source, such as a lightning strike, smoldering logging slash, or a discarded cigarette. It will burn until the fuel or oxygen is removed or reduced. The landscape, the amount of fuel and its readiness to burn, temperature, humidity, and especially wind dictate its intensity and movement.

Fire and smoke perform important ecological functions. Fire recycles forest nutrients, stimulating new growth, and regulating forest structure and species composition. In many western forests, where the weather is dry when it is warm, forest litter and dead trees and limbs decay slowly. Without fire to break down dead plant material, productivity declines. Fires burn forest duff, needles, dead limbs, and most seedlings. In addition, the seeds of hundreds of plants need heat to germinate, and surviving seedlings are nourished by the nutrients released by fire. Fire and smoke also help rid the forests of disease, insects, and parasites.[2] The role of smoke is often overlooked as a factor in forest fires. In a 2011 paper, two veteran firefighters, Tom Ribe and Timothy Ingalsbee, explained that scientists studying the ecological functions of fire were discovering beneficial effects of smoke. They learned that some seeds need exposure to smoke to germinate, and that smoke reduces some insect populations and tree diseases.[3]

The role of fire does not end when the flames go out. Burned, still standing dead trees provide habitat for a number of wildlife species. The black-backed woodpecker, in particular, depends on fire killed trees, and local population numbers typically increase after a fire.[4] Woodpecker holes make homes for other birds and mammals, such as bluebirds, nuthatches, and flying squirrels, and perches for flycatchers, swallows, and raptors. The snags also serve as habitat for wood-eating beetles and other insects that provide a food source for woodpeckers and other insect-eaters. When snags fall they provide habitat and cover for insects, fungi, snails, and worms, as well as small animals, such as rabbits, voles, shrews and others that in turn are food for predators. As they rot, snags add humus to the forest soil, increasing fertility and its ability to hold water. When broken trunks and limbs land in streams, they create pools and riffles and habitat for aquatic insects and fish. The fallen snags help stabilize stream banks and reduce the erosive force of water. Because they take a long time to decay in the water—typically fifty to one hundred years—they provide a long-term source of nutrients in the stream.

Sometimes fires create new or improved wildlife habitat. In 1910, 1919, and 1934, large wildfires burned more than a million acres in northern Idaho forests on the west slopes of the Bitterroot Mountains, opening the canopy and creating prime elk habitat. With the subsequent absence of fire, however, new growth choked the once open forests. Elk numbers peaked in the late 1980s, but with deteriorating habitat, the numbers began to drop. Ancient people set fires to create and maintain openings in the forest to attract game animals, and they used it to stimulate the growth of plants used for food, baskets, and medicines.

Natural fires—those not caused by humans—affect different ecosystems in different ways. The common perception that a century of fire exclusion has led to more severe fires is true in some forests, such as low elevation ponderosa pine forest, but it is not true everywhere. Extreme fires burn when conditions are extreme. Even forests where light fires have burned recently or that have been logged or thinned are vulnerable to extreme fires.[5] In high elevation forests dominated by lodgepole pine, subalpine fir, and white pine, fire history shows that large fires have burned with a consistent frequency every few hundred years. In most years such forests are too moist to burn because the snowpack keeps them wet well into the summer. The fire season is short, and conditions favorable to fire come only in late summer.[6] Here too, when conditions are right after decades, or a century or two, without fire, the accumulation of dead wood and young fire-prone trees will carry the fire into the forest canopy of older mature trees. In large, dense stands of lodgepole pine, for example, stand-replacing crown fires, which burn entire stands of trees, are a common natural occurrence. The lodgepole's thin bark offers little protection from fire, but burned areas recover quickly. In fact, some lodgepole cones need the heat of fire to release the seeds onto the bare soil left by the burn. Seeds may also blow in from nearby unburned trees.

The long fire intervals in high elevation forests are similar to those in moist forests on the Pacific Coast. These low elevation forests of western redcedar, hemlock, and Douglas-fir are too wet to burn under normal conditions. Over decades, dead wood and other forest litter accumulates. Even here, when drought is followed by a lightning strike and high winds, rare large fires destroy entire stands, burning several hundred thousand acres. For example, major fires burned in the normally wet Olympic Mountains in Washington in the years 1309, 1442, 1497, and 1668 as a result of extreme climate conditions.[7] On a visit to a forest reserve on the Olympic Peninsula in the late 1890s, forester Gifford Pinchot, who would become the first head of the U.S. Forest Service in 1905, was amazed when he found evidence of past fires in the form of charcoal and ashes in the soil beneath huge Douglas-firs. He found no Douglas-fir seedlings under the cover of the forest, but every opening created by fire had many.[8] As fire historian Stephen Pyne notes, no place is immune to fire, from cypress swamps of the Southeast to the arid lands of the Intermountain West and Southwest, and from the Arctic tundra to the Sonoran desert.[9] Most natural native plant communities and animals in all but the wettest areas are adapted to the frequency and severity of natural fires, and some depend on fire to reproduce.

For thousands of years, fires started by lightning burned unhindered throughout the West. Most such fires burned only small areas and, like similar fires today, went out on their own. A few became large enough to kill entire stands of trees and burned until the weather changed. Fires, natural or set by humans, every few years maintained open, park-like lower elevation ponderosa forests by killing younger and competing trees. When Europeans arrived in the West, however, they saw fire as a threat to the forests. They actively fought fires and punished those who started them.

Excluding fire, however, doomed the open ponderosa forests. Dead plant material accumulated, the species composition changed, and the forests became denser with fewer large, fire-resistant trees. In northern Arizona, for example, lower elevation ponderosa forest density increased from about fifty trees per acre to two hundred or more in the absence of fire. In addition, the composition changed to more fire-prone trees, such as grand fir, Douglas-fir, and subalpine fir.[10] As a result, such forests became more vulnerable to extreme, stand-killing fires.

Wildfire suppression in public forests began in earnest in the late nineteenth century. When the National Forest Reserves were created in 1891, protecting public forests from fire was among its primary responsibilities. "Probably the greatest single benefit derived by the community and the nation from forest reserves is insurance against the destruction of property, timber resources, and water supply by fire," Pinchot wrote, quoting from a forestry handbook, *The Use of the National Forest Reserves*, or more commonly called the *Use Book*.[11]

Some argued that even light, natural fires could turn into raging infernos. The timber industry and its supporters, for example, saw fire as a threat to the resources that fire suppression protected and drove efforts to fight all forest fires. In May of 1908, Edward Gillette, state treasurer of Wyoming, said to the National Governors' Conference in Washington DC, "I believe that our Forest Service, by extinguishing fires in their incipiency, has saved more timber in recent years than has been consumed in a commercial manner. A large forest fire can destroy a million dollars' worth of timber in a day."[12]

Not everyone agreed that excluding fire in general was a good idea. Many argued that light fires kept the forest open and reduced the risk of larger fires. As early as 1890, John Wesley Powell, explorer of the Colorado River and the American West and the second director of the U.S. Geological Survey, warned that, "protecting the forest from small natural fires caused annually by lightning ended up creating larger fires than ever."[13] Aldo Leopold, in a 1924 article in the *Journal of Forestry*, argued that excluding fire had disrupted the ecology of the Southwest and resulted in devastating environmental changes.[14] Leopold had earned a master's degree in forestry from Yale in 1909 and went to work for the U.S. Forest Service in the Southwest. In later years he observed the role of natural, periodic grass fires in keeping open the prairies near his home in Wisconsin. In areas where grass fires were halted, trees quickly invaded the prairies, and in some places formed tall thickets of young trees too dense for a person to walk through.[15] Advocates of light, natural fires claimed that the Forest Service had allowed forests to become overgrown and more vulnerable to disease and extreme fires. They argued that regular natural fires helped maintain forest health.

Nature, however, was about to present the advocates of fire a real challenge. On the same night as the famous Chicago Fire, October 8, 1871, lingering drought, hot weather, and a powerful storm fanned several small fires already burning in northeastern Wisconsin and the upper peninsula of Michigan into the largest forest fire on record in North America. The hardest hit was the town of Peshtigo, Wisconsin, which gave its name to the fire. In the latter half of the 1800s, people moving into the Upper Midwest had cleared millions of acres of forest for farms and pastures. Timber companies, working to meet a growing national demand for lumber, took the largest trees and left small trees, brush, and slash. At the time, the region's vast pine forests dominated the timber industry, and the land around Peshtigo had been extensively logged. Slash from logging was burned or left in tinder-dry piles. Railroad companies left along the tracks the trees and brush cleared from their rights of way. In dry weather, sparks from steam engines ignited grass, brush, and slash. Sawmills held large numbers of logs, lumber, and piles of bark and sawdust. Most buildings in town were wooden, with sawdust on floors, and the streets were lined with boardwalks. This combination set the stage for disaster.

On the night of October 8, high winds fanned a brush fire into an inferno that burned Peshtigo in about an hour.[16] Only two buildings were left standing in the once thriving timber town. When the fire finally stopped, the Peshtigo Fire had burned all or parts of sixteen towns in addition to Peshtigo and nearly four million acres—more than six thousand square miles—killing at least fifteen hundred people in Wisconsin, and as many as twenty-four hundred total.[17] The fire was the first of many large fires over the next five decades that burned millions of acres, destroyed whole towns, and killed thousands of people.[18] Despite the continuing debate over the benefits of letting natural fires burn, other large fires cemented the Forest Service's perceived obligation to protect public forests from fire and eventually led to a strict national policy of fire exclusion.

In March 1910, Henry S. Graves clearly stated the new policy. Graves, who had replaced Pinchot as head of the U.S. Forest Service, issued a bulletin titled, "Protection of Forests from Fire," which declared, "The first measure necessary for the successful practice of forestry is protection from forest fires."[19] Without protection from fire, forest owners would have little incentive to promote natural reproduction, plant trees, or do other work to improve forest production, he wrote. That summer, the Northern Rockies would face catastrophic fires similar to those that began in Peshtigo some thirty years earlier.

In April 1910 drought came to the Northern Rockies, lightning storms without rain followed, and thousands of lightning strikes lit hundreds of small fires.[20] In June dry winds fanned these unusually early fires in the mountains of Idaho, Montana, and Washington. More lightning-caused fires started in July and August. Most of them were in remote backcountry unbroken by development, and areas with few residents, and much of the timber that burned was largely inaccessible. By August 19, firefighters thought they had the fires under control. Then on August 20 and 21 gale force winds whipped the fires into what became known as the Big Blowup. The fires raced through fire lines and natural barriers as though they did not exist, tornados of fire twisted through the forest, fire-generated winds felled mature trees, and smoke blackened the skies.[21] Rain brought a respite on August 23, but it did not last. Despite the best efforts of firefighters, it took the September rain and snow to finally bring the fires to an end. About five million acres of national forests—three million acres of that in Idaho and Montana—had burned. Eighty-five firefighters died. The Forest Service spent about $1.1 million fighting the 1910 fires, about $29 million in 2017 dollars.

In the decades following the 1910 fires, critics of fire exclusion continued to promote the benefits of wildland fire. They also questioned the wisdom of excluding all fire from public forests. They argued that letting fires burn reduced the risk of larger, more intense fires that were more expensive and more dangerous to fight. The official policy, however, remained to exclude wildfire, or to keep fires as small as possible. Fire protection became the foundation of forest conservation, and the Forest Service tied its reputation to suppressing all fires. The agency's firefighting budget increased, and tactics as well as equipment improved and became more effective. In 1913 Graves said: "The necessity of preventing losses from forest fires requires no discussion. It is the fundamental obligation of the Forest Service and takes precedence over all other duties and activities."[22]

A 1930 Forest Service report in support of fire suppression maintained that without fire, trees would benefit from increased competition, and would grow taller, straighter, and cleaner. Despite the agency's assertions, individual ponderosa or lodgepole pines, western larch or Douglas-firs did not become dominant in the absence of fire. The resulting thickets slowed their growth, and eventually fire-prone firs came to dominate. Even with improvements in firefighting tactics and equipment and the resolve of the Forest Service, the increasing number of fire prone trees contributed to an increase in large fires in the West in the following years. Time showed that the lack of fires did not benefit forest ecosystems.[23]

Three years after the Forest Service report, a large fire broke out in western Oregon. On August 14, 1933, two months of drought and windy weather in Oregon's Tillamook County closed logging operations in the Coast Range. At one operation a fire broke out just as workers prepared to shut down. Driven by strong east winds, the fire quickly burned out of control in the logged over area heavy with slash. By the time fog rolled in ten days later, about 40,000 acres had burned. The next day the fog lifted and the wind returned. The fire blew up, growing from 40,000 to 240,000 acres in less than 24 hours. It generated hurricane force winds that knocked down stands of mature Douglas-firs. Flames were reported rising sixteen hundred feet, and a mushroom cloud of smoke rose nearly ten miles into the sky. Heavy rain began falling on September 5, bringing the fire to an end in a cloud of steam. It had burned about 300,000 acres. Parts of the area would burn again into the 1950s.[24]

In 1934 fire returned to the Northern Rockies between Montana and Idaho. The woods dried up early as they had in 1910. Lightning strikes set fires on July 24. A human caused fire started August 8, and 19 lightning fires started on August 11. The fires merged and burned 252,000 acres, and became known as the Selway Fire. Just when firefighters thought they had it under control, high winds breached the fire lines on August 17. A series of blowups followed on August 22, 30, and 31. Not until heavy rains began on September 20 was the fire finally put out.[25]

Ultimately these fires helped shape national fire policy for the next six decades. In 1935 the Forest Service adopted a strict policy of fire exclusion, citing the necessity of protecting the timber supply in public forests from fire. It quickly became known as the 10 a.m. Policy, because it called for control of all fires before 10 a.m. on the day after they were reported. When that was not possible, then 10 a.m. was the aim for each succeeding day.[26]

In the following years the number of acres burned decreased every year, in part as firefighting equipment and tactics improved, especially after World War II. The average annual acreage burned in the lower 48 states dropped to about five million acres by the 1970s, down from forty to fifty million acres in the early 1930s.[27] In the West, wildfires burned an estimated ten to twenty million acres annually before the 1940s. In 1944 the Forest Service launched the Smokey Bear fire prevention campaign, featuring a bear in a hat, spreading the message that forest fires were preventable. In the past few decades, fire suppression has limited wildfires to about four million acres per year. Fire experts consider the difference between the number of acres burned and the number of acres that would have burned without human intervention as a fire deficit. But to many, fewer fires and fewer acres burned seemed like a good thing.

To be sure, while excluding fire has degraded some forest ecosystems, it has not affected all forests. Many fires, despite the buildup of fuels from years of fire exclusion, burned and went out on their own. Not all dense stands of trees are the result of fire exclusion. Some forests, such as the Pacific Coast rain forests and high elevation forests in the Northern Rockies, have not burned since before humans began trying to put out most fires. Under extreme conditions, however, even these forests will burn.

In the last half of 1967 extreme conditions once again prevailed across the West. When the rains stopped in mid-July in the Northern Rockies and the Pacific Northwest, fire danger rose to extreme. More than five thousand fires were reported; thirty were larger than a thousand acres. In the Northern Rockies, 131 fires were reported on July 12, and with little rain, lightning strikes started 118 fires. More were reported in August and September. By the end of the season, 1,400 lightning-caused fires had been reported. Though conditions were similar to the Big Blowup in 1910 when 80 percent of the fires had been controlled, firefighters could do little to stop the 1967 fires, despite improvements in fire suppression that held 95 percent of the fires to less than 10 acres.[28] Several large fires, however, burned out of control. The 56,000-acre Sundance Fire in northern Idaho's Selkirk Mountains combined with other large fires to burn about ninety thousand acres in Montana and Idaho. On one day, winds pushed the fire sixteen miles in nine hours along a four-mile front. Burning debris was thrown as much as twelve miles ahead of the fire.[29] The Sundance Fire burned with an intensity that was stopped only by the weather. Still, only three people died, and only nine of the fires were more than a thousand acres.

The 1967 fires marked the end of Forest Service's dominant role in wildfire suppression. In 1965, inspired by earlier efforts at interagency cooperation elsewhere in the county, the Forest Service, Bureau of Land Management, and the National Weather Service had combined their firefighting efforts to create the Boise Interagency Fire Center to increase cooperation, cut costs, and coordinate firefighting operations. In 1970 Washington and California joined the Interagency Fire Center; the National Park Service and Bureau of Indian Affairs joined in the mid-1970s. The U.S. Fish and Wildlife Service joined in 1979. In 1993, the agency changed its name to the National Interagency Fire Center to reflect its national mission. The U.S. Fire Administration joined in 2003. The center, known casually as NIFC, coordinates wildland firefighting resources for the entire country. It also provides support for other emergencies, such as floods, hurricanes, and earthquakes.[30]

As NIFC was taking shape, attitudes toward fire had begun to change. Fire experts and forest managers recognized that a century of fire exclusion had brought changes that increased the risk of extreme fires in some forests. They also had begun to recognize the ecological values of wildfire and began to allow some fires to burn. A study launched by the Society of American Foresters concluded that fire should not be excluded from forests in the Northern Rockies. The 1971 study found that fire could benefit forest management goals, and it recommended more prescribed fire.[31]

As attitudes toward wildfires changed, so did policies, though not consistently. In the second major policy change, the Forest Service in 1978 abandoned the 10 a.m. policy and allowed more fires to burn, especially in wilderness and remote, inaccessible areas, but only as long as they burned within prescribed boundaries.[32] Moreover that year Congress repealed the Forest Service's blank check legislation. Since then, however, Congress has continued to fund the firefighting efforts of federal agencies, leaving little apparent economic incentive to let more fires burn. Fire suppression has become institutionalized nationally, and it has added an economic interest. In 2015 the average annual salary for a firefighter working for the Forest Service was nearly $50,000.[33] In 2005 about $1.5 billion was spent on fighting forest fires, and by 2017 that had climbed above $2 billion. Still some fire experts suggest the cost of trying to put out forest fires may in some cases exceed the value of the timber lost if the fires were simply allowed to burn. Ironically, the fires that are of most concern are the ones that firefighters cannot control no matter how much they spend.

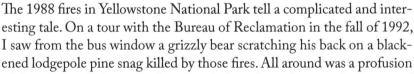

The 1988 fires in Yellowstone National Park tell a complicated and interesting tale. On a tour with the Bureau of Reclamation in the fall of 1992, I saw from the bus window a grizzly bear scratching his back on a blackened lodgepole pine snag killed by those fires. All around was a profusion of fireweed and three- to four-foot lodgepole saplings and a carpet of green undergrowth. As I looked out the window, it struck me that anyone who read the newspaper reports or viewed the television footage of the fires would not believe, four years later, that this could be the same forest. The wildfires that engulfed Yellowstone in the summer of 1988 were the largest in the West since 1910, but this time firefighters managed to protect human lives and park property. However, fighting the fires was expensive, damaging, and all but irrelevant.[34] The fires burned nearly 800,000 acres, or a little more than a third of the 2.2 million acre park; the government spent about $120 million on the immense firefighting effort. Yet hundreds of firefighters, airplanes, helicopters, bulldozers, all applying proven firefighting techniques, could do nothing to stop it.

As usual, weather conditions contributed significantly to the events of 1988. April and May had been wetter than average in the park, but by June drought had set in. That summer turned out to be the driest on record in Yellowstone. No moisture fell in July or August, and the relative humidity stayed below twenty percent (the lowest recorded was six percent), through the summer. By mid-July, grass and litter moisture content was about two to three percent, and fallen dead trees were at about seven percent. Kiln-dried lumber by comparison is about twelve percent.[35] In addition to low humidity, wind also played a key role. Early in the summer, lightning storms started several small fires. Most went out by themselves, but some continued to burn until the fall. Normally the park's fire policy, which had long recognized the natural role of fire in the ecosystem, allowed such lightning-caused fires to burn.[36] From 1972 to 1981, under that policy, only fifteen fires in the park had been larger than one hundred acres, the biggest a little more than 20,000 acres.

In 1988, everything changed. On July 21, when fire activity increased and moisture levels dropped, park managers suspended the fire policy. From then on all fires were fought when reported. Of 248 fires in the Greater Yellowstone Ecosystem that summer, only 31 were allowed to burn. About half of the 800,000 acres burned in just four days of high winds. On August 20, gale force winds pushed the fire and burned more than 150,000 acres in a single day. On September 6 and 7 winds pushed the fire fourteen miles, burning 37,000 acres.[37] Eight large fires accounted for about 95 percent of the total acreage burned and many smaller ones accounted for the rest. On September 11, snow began falling, putting the fires out.

Contrary to some news reports, the fires did not destroy the park. In fact they did little long-term damage. Forest vegetation began to grow back within a few days. Most burned areas came back lush with nutrients released by the fires and because more sunlight reached the forest floor. Thus has fire shaped the Yellowstone ecosystem over thousands of years. It is dominated by lodgepole pine, and large fires that kill most of the mature trees in a stand are common in the park and in subalpine ecosystems like it.[38] Historically large fires have burned in Yellowstone every few hundred years, with major fires previously in 1690 and 1740.[39]

The Yellowstone fires, in dramatic form, reminded us that when lingering drought combines with wind, any spark will set off a Promethean spectacle that mere humans can do little about except get out of the way. Yellowstone had not been subject to extensive fire suppression, but it is subject to extreme fires. Many smaller fires were allowed to burn in Yellowstone over the years, and still when conditions became extreme, fire behavior became extreme. Fighting those smaller fires would not have prevented the 1988 fires.

———————◆———————

Using small, controlled fires to reduce the risk of larger fires does not always work. In May 2000, one such small fire in the Bandelier National Monument north of Albuquerque became the problem. On the evening of May 4, a small flame lit two drip torches that then ignited what was supposed to be a controlled burn in dry forest overloaded with accumulated dead plant materials.[40] Thirty-two people gathered just below the peak of Cerro Grande in New Mexico to help keep the fire within its prescribed boundaries. The 10,207-foot summit on the rim of the Valles Caldera is about fifty miles northwest of Santa Fe and less than ten miles from the town of Los Alamos and the U.S. Department of Energy's Los Alamos National Laboratory. Ponderosa pine, Douglas-fir, white fir, and aspen dominate the forests below the summit. Fire managers set the controlled burn as part of a ten-year fire hazard reduction program. They planned to burn about nine hundred acres, but unusually dry conditions and high winds three days later blew the fire out of control.

Bandelier National Monument posed a dilemma to park officials. They recognized the risk of starting a controlled burn in an area prone to high winds. They also faced what they perceived at the time as a greater risk of an extreme wildfire started by lightning strikes or human activity in an area with tinder dry deadfall and thick underbrush. Fire managers knew, moreover, that no matter how carefully they applied it, using fire always includes a risk. Barry T. Hill wrote in the conclusions to a 2000 GAO report that, "The experience at Cerro Grande illustrates the inherent dangers and risks of introducing fire into the nation's forests, particularly in the western interior of the country, to accomplish forest health or other natural resource objectives. If nothing else, the unpredictability of weather, such as wind, will always be a factor."[41]

The Southwest fire season was just starting, and several other controlled burns had gotten out of control in the area during the previous three weeks. The weather and moisture at eight to nine thousand feet elevation, however, were more favorable. Meanwhile, Forest Service officials at the Santa Fe National Forest bordering the monument had decided to stop all burning in the forest on the same day the prescribed burn at Cerro Grande was started. No one had informed officials at Bandelier of the Forest Service's decision before they started the prescribed burn.

When unpredictable winds pushed the fire outside the prescribed fire line, officials declared it a wildfire at 1 p.m. on May 5. Recognizing the danger, Bandelier officials asked for more help, but help was delayed. Officials then lit a backfire to create a break, and firefighters had the fire contained by late May 6. The next day, however, wind gusts of an estimated twenty to fifty miles per hour blew the backfire in the western portion of the burn out of control. The fire intensified and moved into the Santa Fe National Forest. On May 10, high winds pushed it into the Los Alamos Canyon, threatening the towns of Los Alamos and White Rock, where eighteen thousand residents were evacuated. By the time it was out, it had burned almost 48,000 acres, destroyed or damaged 280 homes and 40 laboratory structures at the Los Alamos National Laboratory, and displaced more than 400 families. No one was killed, but the damage was estimated at about $1 billion.[42]

The Cerro Grande Fire sparked controversy because it had started as a prescribed burn under risky conditions and burned out of control. The resulting investigation of the fire was published under the imposing title: "Managing the Impact of Wildfires on Communities and the Environment: A Report to the President in Response to the Wildfires of 2000."[43] It quickly became known as the National Fire Plan. The plan recognized the long-term effects of a century of fire exclusion, it recognized the value of returning fire to western forests, and it recognized the importance of reducing brush, small trees, and woody debris that accumulate in the absence of fire. The plan also recognized the need to work with local communities and residents about ways to make homes more fire resistant and more easily defended. It focused attention on the growth of residential development in fire-prone areas adjacent to wild lands, increasing the threat to the growing number of homes and communities. Experts quoted in the National Fire Plan 2000 say: "Fires will inevitably occur when we have ignitions in hot, dry, windy conditions...It is one of the great paradoxes of fire suppression that the more effective we are at fire suppression, the more fuels accumulate and the more intense the next fire will be."[44]

Despite that recognition, the Fire Plan recommended fire exclusion as the first priority, and further recommended providing "all necessary resources to ensure that fire suppression efforts are at maximum efficiency in order to protect life and property."[45] The plan's recommended budget requests for fire suppression made up more than ninety percent of the Forest Service and BLM fire budgets.[46] Between 1998 and 2007, an average of about 80,000 fires annually were slated for suppression; only 327 were allowed to burn.[47] In 2008 exclusion still dominated national fire policy. Fire suppression and past fires had done little to prevent the loss of people's homes.

Wildfire expert Jack Cohen noted that intense crown fires did not ignite many buildings. Most of the homes that burned in the Cerro Grande Fire, in fact, were ignited by low ground fires in dead needles, grasses, and brush or by other houses burning nearby. Firefighters were able to save some homes, but so many caught fire at the same time that they were soon overwhelmed. The Cerro Grande Fire was ready to burn. Whether by the hand of land managers or by lightning, fire was inevitable. Cohen and other experts argue that the destruction of homes, however, was not.

A recognized expert on wildfire and home ignitions, Cohen is a fire research scientist with the U.S. Forest Service at the Rocky Mountain Research Station, Fire Sciences Laboratory in Missoula, Montana. At a 2001 workshop for reporters writing about wildfires he tried to dispel the notion of wildfire as catastrophic. A wildfire is a disaster only when it escapes suppression and then only when homes burn. That does not have to happen, Cohen told the small group of writers. All too often, when fire and rural residential development meet, catastrophe follows. Fire officials call it the wildland-urban interface—a handy term for a complex issue graphically demonstrated in California in 2017, where more than nine thousand fires burned about 1.4 million acres, destroying thousands of homes and killing two firefighters and 41 civilians. Wildfires are common in California, but they have become a serious problem in recent years because of the number of people moving into rural, high-risk, fire-prone areas. The issue is not so new, however.

In 1947, the first of two dramatic changes in fire suppression policy occurred. Until then the emphasis had been on protecting timber resources, though fires had burned many homes and towns in the past, as for example the Peshtigo Fire in 1871. In 1947 a series of fires in Maine brought national attention to the wildland-urban issue. That summer and fall, Maine received less than half its average rainfall. Small fires in early October filled many towns with smoke, but on October 21 strong winds fanned them into something more serious. The resulting series of fires burned more than 205,000 acres and took sixteen lives.[48] Entire towns burned, including about eleven thousand homes. The fires showed what can happen when wildfire meets residential development and small, unprepared rural towns.

The response to those Maine fires has been a model for rural fire protection in the rest of the country. Two years later the Northeastern Interstate Forest Fire Protection Compact was formed in the northeastern states to promote integrated and regional fire plans. Those plans called for mutual assistance during fires and for maintaining firefighting services training. In the 1950s the Forest Service began coordinating wildland and rural fire protection, and joined with the Office of Civil Defense to adopt similar compacts throughout the country. In the 1970s, the Pacific Northwest and California adopted the model that eventually led to the formation of the National Interagency Fire Center in Boise.[49]

Fighting fire has its roots in people and communities protecting their homes and families and their economic resources. Most people see fire as a disaster that can be prevented, and those ideas, as they apply to forest fires at least, have been reinforced by the Smokey Bear campaign. Understandably it is difficult to see past the blackened remains of houses. While forest fires are not always preventable, homes at the edge of public forests can be made fire resistant. The key lies in the area within about one hundred feet of a home, known as the home ignition zone, Cohen said.[50] If homes resist ignition, they survive without the help of firefighters, and there is no disaster. Ignition potential depends on building and roofing materials, design of the home, and nearby vegetation. Flames from burning shrubs and tree canopies within a hundred feet can ignite an ordinary wooden house within a few minutes. Most homes that burn, like the homes in the Cerro Grande Fire, are for the most part lit by ground fires in grass, needles, and leaf litter. High winds can carry fire-brands (burning embers) miles ahead of a fire, where they can start new fires on or near a house, often destroying it, even without burning nearby plants. Moreover a burning house can set the nearby forest on fire.[51] Fire safe improvements in the home ignition zone, and fuel reduction within a quarter mile of a community, can provide effective fire protection. Trees and brush near homes can be removed, and vegetation and leaf litter can be cleared. To protect against firebrands, houses can be made with fire resistant materials, such as metal roofs and stone foundations.[52]

Thinning and controlled burns in distant forests do nothing to protect homes and communities from extreme fires. In fact, thinning can increase fire hazard by opening the forest to new growth that may burn hotter and fuel new fires.[53] Ultimately, it might not be necessary to control extreme wildfires if home and community ignition zone conditions prevent or significantly reduce the risk, Cohen told the 2001 workshop participants.

Cohen helped found the Forest Service's Firewise program, which teaches homeowners how to reduce the ignition potential of their homes. He notes with irony that wildland-urban interface disasters result from wildfires that escape control, yet the remedy continues to focus on suppressing fires outside home and community ignition zones. Decades of fire exclusion has left "an organizational mindset that persistently frames the wildland-urban interface fire problem in terms of fire suppression and control, to the exclusion of potentially more effective alternatives," Cohen wrote.[54] There is no evidence that fire suppression can prevent residential fires, he said. It may reduce the number of fires, but it has not prevented the residential disasters that large, extreme fires have caused. Changes in the home ignition zone, such as clearing vegetation around homes, installing metal roofs, and thinning the woods immediately surrounding the community can reduce the risks.[55] That solution, however, is up to the residents and communities, not the Forest Service.

The Forest Service, like other federal agencies, only has authority over public lands. Nonetheless, it spends a substantial portion of its annual firefighting budget on protecting private property, even when no national forest resources are at risk. A 2006 Forest Service audit report noted that up to 95 percent of the cost of fighting fire was spent on private property, and the increasing number of homes built in rural areas near fire-prone forests was driving up that cost.[56]

Local governments have the authority to adopt zoning restrictions and building standards that could reduce the risk of losing homes to wildfire, distasteful as that may be to some local officials.[57] The lack of such restrictions in many rural areas shoves the responsibility for fire protection from developers, builders, home owners, and rural communities onto federal taxpayers. Taxpayers foot the bills for firefighting and disaster relief, essentially subsidizing the decision to build homes in remote fire-prone areas. It is not too different from building homes in a flood plain.[58]

Once homes are built and buyers move in, it is the Forest Service that gets the call when the homes are threatened by wildfire. Some suggest federal agencies should let the fires rage but protect homes and rural communities and focus on creating defensible space around structures. The question then become whether taxpayers, insurance companies, or local fire districts, or a combination thereof, should pay. Fire suppression stops 97 to 99 percent of wildfires. Disasters are the result of the 1 to 3 percent that escape suppression efforts and threaten residential developments, and such fires account for a substantial portion of the cost of fighting forest fires. Lives and property, however, can be protected at a fraction of the cost.

In the years since the Peshtigo Fire of 1871 we have learned some things about fire, though it took some time. Since World War II, firefighting policy has undergone two significant changes that have affected the role of forest fires on public lands. The first recognized the vulnerability of small rural communities and shifted the emphasis to cooperative efforts for protecting property rather than forest resources. The second recognized the role of fire in forest ecosystem health and halted the policy of putting out all fires. Together the two policy changes, if fully embraced, would go a long way to returning fire to its natural role, but only if we recognize that extreme fires will burn regardless of what humans do or do not do. If Cohen's ideas can protect homes, extreme fires are less of a threat. In short, there are better ways to protect property and forest resources than by fighting all forest fires. Granted, the result in the short term could mean more smoke during some fire seasons for a few years, but the eventual result would be healthier forests, which benefit us all.

CHAPTER 8

Bringing Back the Beaver

Shortly after my boss at Idaho Fish and Game retired, I took over his desk and started going through his old files. One day I came across some articles from the 1950s about a most unusual method of transplanting beavers into places where native beavers long ago had been trapped out. In the 1940s, Idaho Fish and Game biologists had been hauling trapped beavers to suitable habitat, some in pickup trucks and others by pack horses or mules. Transporting them was easy in areas with mostly level terrain and lots of back roads. However, in heavily forested and mountainous areas with few good roads, such as the mountain valleys of central Idaho, biologists had to resort to pack animals. Trips took several days and were difficult for the biologists, expensive, and resulted in a lot of dead beavers. They needed to find a better way.

This beaver caught in a steel wire snare was released and rehabilitated before being relocated to the mountains near Boise. *Author photo*

By the middle of the nineteenth century, beavers had been all but wiped out across the country. Unrestrained trapping across North America resulted in the depletion of a public resource. Before it was over the fur trade, especially the trade in beaver pelts, would change our landscape. With beavers gone, the streams and wetland ecosystems that they created and supported began to deteriorate. Dams that went unmaintained collapsed, wetlands drained, water tables dropped, wet meadows dried up, and the wildlife dependent on those ponds and wetlands slowly diminished. The nearly complete disappearance of beavers contributed significantly to the loss of more than half the wetlands that have disappeared since the beginning of the eighteenth century.

In the arid West the beaver's demise set the stage for worse damage from the domestic livestock that followed close behind the trappers. Overgrazing in many places left stream banks denuded and heavily eroded. Once-lush streams turned into dry gulches. The results are still visible in many places today. Some blamed the beavers and others blamed the livestock. Both groups were wrong, mostly. Beavers were not the problem, their absence was. Wildlife biologists, many land managers, and some ranchers have long recognized the importance of beavers to the hydrology of the arid West. Beginning in the early twentieth century, they have been returning beavers, some captured in urban areas, to their former haunts. The return of beavers has been a ray of hope for restoring some ecosystems, recreating islands of native habitat, and bringing back the creatures of those habitats.

In 1948 Idaho Fish and Game biologist Elmo "Scotty" Heter found a better way than pack animals to get beavers into remote areas. The practice of stocking backcountry lakes and streams by airplanes flying low over the water and dropping live fish gave him the idea. He and several other biologists went to work on a way to drop beavers into the backcountry by parachute. They came up with a wooden box big enough to hold two adult beavers. It was made up of two halves, thirty inches long, twelve inches deep, and sixteen inches wide, with air-holes drilled in the wood. The tension of the parachute cord held the two halves together while in the air. The box was designed to pop open when it landed. They used army surplus cargo chutes with a capacity of 140 pounds.[1] A box with two beavers weighed eighty to a hundred pounds, enough to open the chute and still land softly.

Once Heter and his cohorts had figured out the box, they set out to test it. They started with a dummy weight and then used a live subject, a male beaver they named Geronimo. At the first successful drop at an airfield, a biologist was on hand to grab Geronimo when the box opened. Geronimo made several trips as Heter and company refined the drop system. The beaver seemed resigned to his fate, and soon learned the routine. He would even lumber back to the open box when he saw the biologist coming to pick him up. For his reward, Geronimo was the first to be dropped by parachute into the Idaho backcountry along with three females.

The system was fined tuned and successfully carried out that spring and summer. In a typical run, eight crates with two beavers each were loaded onto a single-engine plane with the cabin doors removed. Once in the air over the drop site, the boxes were hooked to a static line and shoved out the door. The best altitude turned out to be five hundred to eight hundred feet, high enough for the chutes to open and low enough for accuracy to avoid landing the boxes in trees. Most drops were made in July and August. Biologists had determined that earlier in the year beavers tended to migrate, and later in the year they would not have time to become established before winter arrived.[2]

By the end of 1948, seventy-six beavers had been dropped by parachute, with only a single casualty. One beaver somehow managed to squeeze out and climb on top of the box on the way down. He jumped or fell off when the box was still about seventy-five feet from the ground. Observations the following year, however, showed all the rest of the beaver transplants had been successful. In the April 1950 issue of the *Journal of Wildlife Management* Heter wrote that beavers, "do much toward improving the habitats of game, fish, and waterfowl and perform important service in watershed conservation."[3] Heter and other Idaho biologists, however, were not the only ones who realized the value of bringing beavers back.

The largest North American rodent, beavers vary in size up to nearly four feet long and weigh twenty-four to sixty-six pounds. Some have reported capturing beavers weighing almost one hundred pounds. Most are reddish-brown but can range from yellow-brown to almost black.

Their bright orange, self-sharpening teeth grow continuously, and the animals must gnaw on something to keep them from growing too long. Awkward on land, beavers are fast swimmers and can remain underwater up to fifteen minutes. A typical beaver colony includes an adult pair, two to four kits from the spring litter, two or three yearlings, and occasionally one or more two-year-olds. The kits weigh about a pound at birth, and can swim the day after they are born. The mother usually drives the two-year-olds from the family den just before her new litter is born. Most beavers apparently mate for life, establishing small, close-knit family units.

The beaver's anatomy is admirably suited to its life and habitat. It uses its distinctive flat, leathery tail as a rudder when swimming, to steady itself while standing on its hind feet, and to slap a warning on the water. With support from its strong tail, it can walk upright while carrying mud or other material held against its chest with chin and forelegs. With its nimble front paws, the beaver can harvest and grasp large leaves as it nibbles, and build its lodges and dams. For its winter larder, it stocks up on the leaves and inner bark of poplar, aspen, alder, cottonwood, and willow branches, secured in the muddy bottom of the pond or stream near the lodge entrance. Beavers also eat grass, sedges, roots and tubers.

Beavers usually live on smaller streams and are expert builders of dams and lodges. They cut trees upstream and use the current to float the wood down to the building site. They start cutting in early summer, but do not start building until August, working mostly at night into October. For their dams they start with logs and larger branches to form the base and then they add smaller branches, twigs, rocks, and mud to seal the dam. They use trunks, branches, twigs, and stones plastered with mud to build lodges. Inside the lodge, the large, main living space above the water line is warm and dry year-round. The animals enter through an underwater tunnel, keeping them and their young safe from most dry-land predators. Whether in dammed pools, lakes, or rivers they build their lodges in water that is deep enough to escape most predators and to remain below the ice in winter. Beavers were once found throughout much of North America, except in the desert Southwest and Arctic tundra, in short, wherever they could find adequate water and plant materials suitable for winter food.[4] They were found living in most rivers from the Rio Grande to the Arctic Ocean in numbers estimated from sixty million to as high as four hundred million.[5]

Wildlife biologists consider the beaver a keystone species. They create and maintain small wetland ecosystems that hold water, recharge groundwater, and recycle nutrients. Areas where beavers cut trees become clearings that attract dozens of other species, including small mammals, deer, moose, muskrats, otters, ducks, fish, and frogs. Some also provide grazing for domestic livestock. Beaver dam ponds provide spawning and rearing habitat for salmon and trout. They are especially important for young fish, and most dams are not high enough to hinder fish migrating upstream. Perhaps the beavers' greatest benefit to humans, however, is in watershed protection, particularly erosion and flood control. Dams and ponds reduce floods from spring snowmelt and summer storms, slowing the water as it spreads across the wide, flat beaver pond or seeps into the ground.

In the arid western states, beavers also helped maintain the verdant lands and wet meadows that border streams, rivers, springs, ponds, and lakes. Though these riparian areas make up only 1 to 2 percent of the land, they are the most productive part of the landscape. In late summer when upland grasses have dried, riparian areas may be the only places wildlife can find green forage that still has the nutrients they need to get through the coming winter. From 75 to 80 percent of western wildlife species depend on riparian areas, which provide bird habitat, including food, cover, and nesting sites. More than half the birds in the Southwest are completely dependent on riparian areas, which also provide key stopovers for many migrating birds.[6] Healthy riparian areas help maintain higher water tables, and build up stream banks and flood plains by trapping water, sediments, and reducing erosion. Woody plants and other vegetation provide shade and block wind, and their roots help hold the soil. Vegetation slows floods, helping to recharge groundwater and to maintain small aquatic species that form the basis of the food chain for a variety of other species.

✦

Beavers' rich, dense fur would ultimately be their demise. The thick underhairs that protect them in cold northern waters are covered with tiny barbs, which made strong, soft, and durable felt, excellent for hats. Demand for the beaver's luxurious pelt resulted in the depletion of European and Russian beaver populations, and largely drove the seventeenth through nineteenth century exploration of North America. Already in the fifteenth century, Basque fishermen may have been the first Europeans to trade for beaver pelts with North American Indians. In July 1534, Frenchman Jacques Cartier encountered Micmac Indians at the mouth of Port-Daniel in Chaleur Bay on Quebec's Gaspé Peninsula ready to trade furs with the French, launching a long relationship. In his account, Cartier noted that the Indians' gestures suggested that other Europeans fishermen had been there before and traded for furs.[7]

Long before the arrival of Europeans, trade in furs already had been well established among North American Indians. On the west coast of British Columbia, for example, native people would gather small fish called olachen, which were rich in oil that was used in food and burned as a source of light. They would trade the fish or its oil for furs from inland tribes.[8] Indians used furbearers for food, clothing, and shelter, and took beavers by means that included netting, shooting, spearing, and trapping with snares and deadfalls. Early European fur traders relied on Indians to gather furs, trading pelts for rifles and gunpowder, metal tools, and cooking utensils.

Sometime in the mid-eighteenth century, Europeans began trapping beavers themselves. Steel traps, used in Europe since the 1600s, made trapping easier. In early eighteenth-century North America a steel trap with a five-foot anchor chain cost twelve to sixteen dollars and weighed about five pounds.[9] Taking care to mask their scent, trappers would wade upstream to set the traps, and wash their hands thoroughly before handling the trap. Traps were placed a few inches under the water near the bank with chains staked securely to the stream bed. Beavers caught in steel leghold traps have been known to gnaw off a paw to escape, but most simply drowned. In his 1831 book, *American Natural History*, John Godman reported that traps were baited with a concoction of castoreum from the scent glands of a male beaver mixed with nutmeg, cloves, and cinnamon and stirred up in whiskey to a consistency of mustard. Kept closely corked the mixture could last several months.[10]

The fur trade ultimately expanded to create a virtual empire. It began in the St. Lawrence River valley where the French dominated beaver trapping. The British were close behind. Then on May 2, 1670, King Charles II of England chartered the Hudson's Bay Company (HBC) to a group of French and English merchants, creating a monopoly that lasted two centuries. One of the largest companies based on beaver trapping, the HBC shaped the face of what became Canada and the northern United States. Its charter granted the company absolute proprietorship and jurisdiction in civil and military affairs, the power to make laws and declare wars against pagans. In other words, the company had the rights and powers of a sovereign, independent government throughout its domain, which covered nearly three million square miles at its peak.[11] The company's trading posts spread from the shores of the Arctic Ocean to San Francisco and as far west as Hawaii. Besides beavers, the fur trade on North American's northern frontiers included fox, mink, and otter.

Trapping was a lucrative business. In the early to mid-1800s, fielding a trapping expedition with twenty trappers, at $400 per year, ten camp keepers and their horses, cost a fur trader up to $2,000. An average beaver pelt would bring four to ten dollars, depending on its size and the prevailing price of furs.[12] Most beavers were skinned near where they were caught, and only the skin, tail, and perineal glands (the source of castoreum) were kept. The trappers would take the skins back to camp where they were cleaned, dried, and packed for the trip out. On average a pack of one hundred pounds contained about eighty skins, and was worth three to five hundred dollars. With average success in a season each hunter would take about 120 beaver skins worth about $1,000 in Boston or New York. The fur trader would earn about $15,000 after accounting for the cost of the return trip.[13] Statistics compiled by an Indian agent for the fifteen years between 1815 and 1830 showed expenses of about $2.1 million, income of about $3.75 million, leaving a profit of $1.65 million. Trappers brought in an average of 25,000 beaver, 26,000 buffalo, 4,000 otter, 12,000 raccoon, 37,500 muskrat, and 150,000 pounds of deer skins per year for those fifteen years. That worked out to about $110,000 a year in profits for the fur trader, the equivalent of about two and a half million in 2018 dollars.[14]

The methodical way trappers took all the beavers from a drainage ensured their demise in much of North America. As beavers were trapped out in the St. Lawrence River valley, trappers and traders followed them west and north.[15] Soon exterminated along the whole Atlantic coast and inland to the middle and upper Missouri River, beaver were dwindling in Hudson's Bay Company territory. By the end of eighteenth century they were gone from the Mississippi and Missouri rivers to the foot of the

Rockies. About the time beavers became extinct east of the Mississippi, beaver hats began to go out of style, slowing but not ending the trade. In 1854, even after the beaver hat had passed its peak in popularity, more than half million beaver pelts were auctioned in London. Hudson's Bay Company officials estimated they sold three million pelts between 1853 and 1877.[16]

West of the Mississippi the fur trade had all but exterminated the beaver in less than half a century. In the upper Missouri River valley and the Rocky Mountains trapping began after the Lewis and Clark expedition showed that the newly purchased territory was rich in furs. After the explorers of the early 1800s, fur trappers were the first white men to visit the great interior wilderness west of the Rocky Mountains. Many of those trappers worked for John Jacob Astor, who had established his Pacific Fur Company in Astoria, the town he established as a fur trading post near the mouth of the Columbia River. The peak of trapping in the Pacific Northwest came in the 1820s and 1830s, and beavers were all but gone before the land became part of the United States. In the process, however, a group of Astor's fur trappers blazed what would become the Oregon Trail.

Soon settlers in numbers were moving West. Seeing the coming migration, Jim Bridger built in 1843 a trading post in the Blacks Fork of the Green River in Wyoming. Fort Bridger, more than a thousand miles from the starting point in Independence, Missouri, became the first trading post for immigrants west of the Mississippi. It marked the start of the era of immigration to the West and the end of the fur trade. With the influx of pioneers on the Oregon Trail, Hudson's Bay Company trappers in the Columbia River Basin made a concerted effort to trap out as many beavers as they could, realizing that the land would soon be part of the United States. In 1846, negotiations between Great Britain and the United States set the border at the forty-ninth parallel, adding what would become the states of Oregon, Washington, Idaho, and parts of Montana and Wyoming.[17]

◆

Beavers in the Northwest, fortunately, were not completely wiped out. In fact, some newcomers to the West recognized the animal's importance to the land. Those old files I had found at work yielded another interesting piece, a story about an eastern Oregon rancher who learned what can happen when beavers are removed, and the potential benefits of bringing them back, with a surprising twist that illustrates a pervasive, though mistaken, attitude toward beavers. The article was written for the Soil Conservation Service by Paul Schaffer in 1941.[18] In 1884 an Oregon rancher bought land in southeastern Oregon's Harney County, not far from today's Malheur National Wildlife Refuge. It was one of the few places in the West where beavers remained. Here the dams and ponds of several beaver families on Crane Creek kept the groundwater level high enough to support meadows green with stirrup-high native grasses. When the owner, Paul Stewart, returned after a year's absence in 1924, he found that poachers had trapped out the beavers. Disaster followed. The untended dams deteriorated, and with the spring flood in 1925, the unchecked stream ran wild. The ponds drained, and the stream flow began to scour a new channel through the sediments accumulated behind the dams. Over the next ten years erosion cut the stream channel fifteen to twenty feet below its original level. The banks collapsed, eating into Stewart's pasture land. As the creek level dropped, water drained from the surrounding land. Sagebrush began to replace the grasses, and a once abundant stock-water well in the pasture often ran dry.

Similar results could be seen in countless places in the West where beavers had been trapped out. With the beaver ponds gone, some streams dried up in the hot summers, others became dry washes for most of the year, flowing only in the spring. Gone also were the willows and the cottonwoods that once lined the ponds and streams, provided cover, and helped cool the water. Former lush and productive riparian areas dried out and eroded away, and the eroded sediments reduced water quality downstream. Fish, bird, and wildlife populations were reduced or eliminated. Some estimates for the United States put the loss of riparian habitat at about 70 percent. Millions of acres have been affected.

It is difficult to estimate how much the eradication of beavers has cost the country. Some have tried. In one example, the loss of more than sixty-four million acres of wetlands in the Mississippi River basin since the 1780s contributed to the damage from the 1993 flood on the upper Mississippi. Nearly 700,000 acres flooded, causing an estimated $16 billion in damages over eighty days.[19] Alice Outwater in her book *Water: A Natural History*, suggests that if the pre-European beaver population was about 200 million and we assumed each beaver created one acre of wetland, that pencils out to about 300,000 square miles of wetlands.[20] Scientists estimate that in 1700 in the lower forty-eight states, wetlands covered more than 221 million acres. Most were fresh water wetlands and about 5 percent marine estuaries. By 1980 more than half of that was gone, in part because of the loss of beavers.[21] Today, wetlands are still being lost, but at a slower rate than in the past. Bringing back beavers in places where they were trapped out is helping to slow the loss and reverse the damage in some places.

Many western landowners continue to shoot and trap the few remaining beavers. They blame beavers for the damage that resulted from improper grazing in riparian areas. It remains a common misconception that beavers "steal" water from downstream users. That misconception has led to countless beaver dams being blown up, adding to the problem with more riparian meadows turned to dry sagebrush flats. During a meeting held in the early 1990s to discuss grazing and beaver issues with U.S. Forest Service officials, an Idaho sheep rancher quipped that beavers did more damage to the land than any livestock. When he was quoted in the local paper the next day, he tried to deny that he had said it, and well he should, because he was wrong. Likewise in the 1990s the Environmental Protection Agency reported that, "The extensive deterioration of western riparian areas began with severe overgrazing in the late nineteenth and early twentieth centuries."[22] That too is incorrect. The deterioration began with the trapping of beavers.

◆

Ranch owner Paul Stewart, whose Harney County, Oregon, land deteriorated after poachers eradicated the resident beavers, ran headlong into those misconceptions when he tried to return beavers to restore his damaged lands (see #2 on map, page 24).

One day in 1936 Stewart looked into a gulch twenty feet deep that had once been a small stream that ran across his eastern Oregon ranch. Just a decade earlier he could drive a team of horses across the same stream. Stewart turned to the beavers that had once kept the stream in check. Later that year, the Oregon State Game Commission gave him sixteen beavers. They went right to work, felling cottonwoods and aspens to start new dams on Crane Creek. The following spring the stream that had flowed wildly was again trapped in the ponds behind new dams, silt settled out and gradually accumulated on the stream bottom, rebuilding the degraded stream. Over the next few years, silt built up the creek to within three feet of the original level in several places. Water flowed over the dams, and the average stream-flow downstream began to increase. Water began to seep back into the soil, and native grasses returned to the meadows, providing hay and grazing for his livestock. Water in the stock well began to rise again.[23]

Stewart's success led to all kinds of trouble. During a dry year, his neighbor's lands dried up while Stewart's beaver ponds were full of water. The neighbor asked him to dynamite the beaver dams so more water would flow through his land. Stewart explained that once the beaver ponds had drained, the flow would be back to where it already was, perhaps less. The neighbor accused Stewart of stealing water. By allowing the dams, Stewart had impounded water that did not belong to him. He accused Stewart of taking more water than he was entitled to under his water right. His downstream neighbor took him to court. In Harney County Circuit Court, Stewart's neighbor argued that Stewart was violating a court decreed water right. Stewart argued that he had a right to use the beavers and their dams to protect his property from erosion. He also argued that more water was available to both Stewart and his neighbor through the year because of the beaver dams.

Stewart lost the first round, but in the end he won the match. In June 1939, the court ruled that Stewart had violated the court's water right decree. The court fined him $300 for contempt and ordered him to pay $500 for damages and gave him five days to have the beavers removed and the dams destroyed, or face three months in the Harney County jail. Stewart did not give up. He appealed to the Oregon State Supreme Court, which upheld his right to protect his land from erosion, so long as he did not interfere with his neighbors' water rights. The court also recognized the importance of preventing erosion to protect valuable lands. When Stewart later sold the place, the beavers were still there, more than 150 of them.[24]

Others have had similar results. Beavers once lived on Copper Creek, where the foothills of the central Idaho mountains meet the Eastern Snake River Plain, not far from the wild and rugged Craters of the Moon National Monument (see #4 on map, page 24). Where the creek runs through the Lava Lake Ranch, it forms a narrow band of green between the gray-brown, sagebrush covered hills. Annual precipitation ranges from less than ten inches on the desert floor to somewhere around twenty inches at the higher elevations where most of it falls as snow. I visited the ranch in the early 1990s to see the results of beavers transplanted on Copper Creek in the mid-1980s.

Beaver dams and ponds on the Lava Lake Ranch have solved flooding problems that the rancher could not. *Author photo*

Like on Stewart's land, the trouble at Lava Lake started when the beavers were trapped out. Later livestock grazing and a string of heavy spring floods in the late 1970s turned the creek into a narrow channel with steep banks and little vegetation. Ranch hands with bulldozers dug earthen dams and felled trees across the stream to stem the floods. The following spring their efforts would wash out. In the spring of 1985 ranch hands built about a hundred small check dams, using old irrigation pipe. Only a few held. "Everything we did made it worse," said Nick Purdy whose family owned the ranch.[25]

Purdy always wondered why the stream had no beavers on it. Then in the fall of 1985, through his work with the U.S. Department of Agriculture's Soil Conservation Service, now known as the Natural Resources Conservation Service, he met Lew Pence, who coordinated a beaver restoration program in central Idaho. Pence convinced Purdy to give the beavers a try. With little to lose, Purdy agreed. They brought in a pair of beavers. Once transplanted to Copper Creek, the animals' first efforts were built on the remains of the former check dams. Soon the water table was rising and thriving, and grasses, willows and brush were returning to the portion of the creek inhabited by the beaver colony. Since the furry reclamation engineers started building dams, the stream came back, wildlife numbers increased, livestock grazing improved, and irrigation wells that used to run dry lasted through the summer, even after a string of dry years.

Wetlands, including beaver ponds, once were considered wastelands. They were seen as the breeding grounds for disease-carrying insects and considered health menaces. Since colonial times settlers and farmers have drained or filled wetlands and put them to other uses. In more recent times, people like Stewart and Purdy have recognized their value and importance as part of the landscape and as a valuable public resource. It is difficult to put a dollar value on an individual beaver pond and its associated wetlands. Though rich in life, most of the benefits of wetlands are often poorly understood. The decision of a landowner to convert a wetland to other uses, such as farming, a shopping center parking lot, or luxury condominiums, or just trap out the beavers for the value of their pelts, is mostly an economic choice for short term gain. The biological and ecologic importance and long-term value of these areas seem to have low priority when compared with the potential economic value of other uses. The benefits to society from wetlands in maintaining the water table, as waterfowl or fish habitat, or as flood or pollution control do not always bring immediate and direct economic benefits to individual landowners.

Wetlands as such may have no immediate market value, but they protect other values. They protect shorelines from erosion, and they are natural buffers, filtering water by removing excess nutrients from urban sewage treatment plants, agricultural fertilizers, manure and leaking septic tanks. They provide aesthetic benefits and educational and recreational opportunities, including hiking, fishing, bird watching, and hunting. About half of North American bird species nest or feed in wetlands. Perhaps most directly valuable, however, wetlands serve as a buffer against floods, in some cases reducing property damage and loss of life. In areas with little rainfall, wetlands keep water on the land and maintain the level of the water table.

Many of those wetlands were created by beavers, which, like other wildlife, are a public resource. Over time they have been exploited for private profit with long-lasting and sometimes costly consequences and stark changes across the landscape. The damage can be reversible. Restoring beavers will not by itself repair all riparian areas or bring back lost wetlands, but in many places where humans have reestablished beavers or where they have returned on their own, the recovery has been rapid and often dramatic.

Beavers today number an estimated seven to twelve million. Most of them are in the Great Lakes region and Mississippi flood plains, but also in many parts of the West. Beavers are no longer dropped from the sky, and land managers and ranchers who once cursed them are recognizing that beavers do far more good than harm. As Scotty Heter wrote in 1950, beavers do a lot for the country's water quality and wildlife habitat. That is still true. The trade in beaver pelts may have made short term profits for a few and built commercial empires, but in the long run they are still worth more for their role in the landscape.

CHAPTER 9

The False Promise of Hatcheries

On a summer morning in 2001, I showed up unshaven at about five thirty on the dock in Newport, Washington. An assignment as outdoor reporter for the *Olympian* newspaper had landed me on an offshore salmon charter fishing boat. I had come to report on the opening of salmon fishing season and rumors of the best salmon return since the Bonneville Dam corseted the Columbia River in 1938. I climbed aboard Phil Anderson's fifty-foot boat, the *Monte Carlo*, along with several officials from the Washington Department of Fish and Wildlife. We were there to find out firsthand about the numbers of salmon returning to the Columbia River system. That year 867,728 Chinook salmon would return to the lower Columbia River, most of them hatchery raised fish, a poor cousin to the wild fish that are still in danger of disappearing. The return was more than three times the ten-year average of 269,416, but just a little more than 5 percent of the number of wild fish that once ran up the big river.[1]

The Columbia River Basin used to be one of the greatest salmon-producing regions in the world. The Columbia River alone once produced as many or more salmon as all the other rivers and streams in Washington, California, and Oregon together. Already by the late 1800s salmon numbers had begun to decline as a result of habitat destruction by trapping, logging, mining, agriculture, commercial fishing, dams, and other means. Rather than enacting and enforcing laws limiting fishing, protecting habitat, or requiring fish passages at dams—all restrictions that would be difficult to enforce—fish managers turned to hatcheries. They based their response on the assumptions that hatcheries could replace natural habitat, and that humans could control the production of salmon much the way they controlled the production of livestock and crops. Some thought hatcheries would make salmon so abundant that limits would not be necessary. Mostly they were wrong. With little

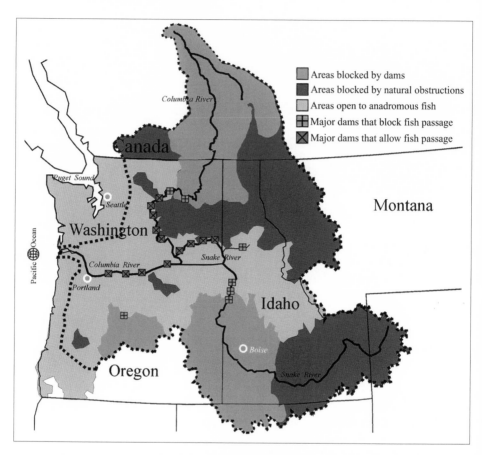

Columbia Basin. *Courtesy of the Northwest Power and Conservation Council*

consideration for the capacity of rivers and the ocean to support salmon or the requirements of the salmon, hatcheries have turned out to be a disaster for wild fish, despite good intentions and billions of dollars spent.

The trip with Anderson turned out to be exciting and enlightening. He navigated his boat out across the Grays Harbor bar into a moderate Pacific Ocean swell. About twelve miles off the coast, he cut the engines when his fish-finding sonar showed schools of herring, anchovies, and sardines, all salmon food. The rumors about salmon numbers were true. The salmon, stocking up for their arduous journey up their natal streams to spawn, started biting almost as soon as the bait went over the side. As the first catch of the day came over the railing only the head remained; a shark had taken the rest. Despite the harassing sharks, everyone soon had their limit. Anderson started the engines, and I shared the bridge with him as we headed back toward Westport, riding a following swell. We talked about salmon and the future of salmon. We were back at the dock before noon, our catch already cleaned and on ice. I had plenty to ponder on the drive back to Olympia.

◆

A biologist friend calls it magic. Young salmon, many of them born in clear mountain waters, migrate to the ocean, navigating barriers such as hydropower dams and road culverts; many of them die along the way. Those that make it spend one or more years in the ocean before returning past those same barriers to their native streams; some as far as two thousand miles from the ocean. The females pick specific stream-bed gravels in which to dig their nests, called redds. Using their tails, they shape the nest to direct the flow of oxygen-rich waters over the eggs. They lay about five thousand eggs, which males then compete to fertilize with their milt. The eggs incubate in the river gravels, where they live until their yolk sacs are depleted and they move into the stream. After hatching, wild salmon learn to grab food quickly and where to hide to avoid predators. They travel along the bottom where the current is slower and rest in eddies behind rocks, logs, and other obstructions. Wild salmon produce thousands of genetically unique offspring; only the few that are best suited for their particular habitat survive.

The salmon that still run up most West Coast rivers from Alaska to the San Francisco Bay are important to the Pacific Northwest for several reasons. They form the foundations of several American Indian cultures, and once made up a substantial portion of the diets of some peoples. They are the basis of both a commercial fishing industry and popular recreational fisheries like Anderson's that support many rural communities and feed people across the country. Moreover, they connect the ocean to the land. Salmon take on 95 percent of their mass in the ocean, bringing back key nutrients to mountain streams and inland watersheds when they return to spawn and die many miles from the ocean. Scientists can track those nutrients through the ecosystem by testing plants, insects, fish, birds, and other animals for a certain form of nitrogen common in the ocean but rare on land. Research suggests than entire forest ecosystems are enriched by the carcasses of ocean-going fish. Microbes feed on the carcasses, insects feed on the microbes, and fish feed on the insects. Some animals, such as bears and other scavengers, feed directly on the carcasses that also nourish the newly hatched young salmon. Thus the salmon nourished the people, the forests, and the river ecosystems of the Columbia Basin in a cycle unbroken for thousands of years.

We have lost much of nature's largesse however. The arrival of Europeans in the Northwest changed the time, places, and methods for harvesting salmon, and that spelled doom for the wild fish. The diseases they brought did the same for the Indians. Beginning in the late eighteenth century, Pacific Northwest Indian populations dropped dramatically, some groups by more than 90 percent.[2] Their harvest dropped accordingly. Before Europeans arrived, an estimated ten to sixteen million salmon returned to the Columbia River Basin. American Indians had harvested up to an estimated 40 million pounds of salmon annually. By 1900 Europeans harvested about the same amount, but their methods were far different. The Indian harvest was dispersed, close to where they lived, and focused on different species of salmon at different times of the year and for different purposes, some for eating fresh, some for smoking, some for drying. European fishermen concentrated on Chinook and sockeye runs more suitable for canning, and therefore fished during a shorter time span and in fewer locations close to canneries. Along with fishing, other activities—such as logging, mining, and hydropower development—damaged, destroyed, or blocked salmon habitat, and some killed the fish outright.[3] By the time the Bonneville Dam was completed in 1938, fewer than half a million fish returned to cross the dam.[4]

No single cause led to the decline of these once teeming salmon runs. It probably began with the fur trappers. As beavers disappeared, so did the dams and ponds that had provided good salmon habitat. The ponds were especially important for rearing young fish. When the pioneers on the Oregon Trail began to arrive in the 1830s, beavers were all but gone in most drainages of the Pacific Northwest. The removal of beavers was only the first of many changes to the ecosystems that once supported wild salmon, contributing to their decline in the Northwest.

Early logging practices and sawmills in the region's forests significantly degraded salmon habitat. In 1852 naturalist James G. Swan, aboard a ship from San Francisco about thirty miles west of the Columbia River mouth, reported that the river current carried "great quantities of drift-logs, boards, chips and sawdust, with which the whole water around us was covered."[5] In those days, loggers used streams to move large old-growth logs to the mill. Some logging operations built low dams to float the logs and move them quickly and cheaply. Downed trees, beaver dams, side channels, and wetlands that provided productive salmon habitat were cleared, sometimes using dynamite, with disastrous results for salmon. Fish biologist Jim Lichatowich wrote in his book *Salmon Without Rivers* that, "Splash dams and log drives became the most effective destroyers of salmon habitat ever devised by humans."[6] The drives and logging operations left streams choked with sawdust and sediments that smothered salmon eggs and clogged the gills of adult salmon. Rotting waste depleted oxygen from the water, and huge logs scoured the stream beds and banks, removing vegetative cover as well as gravel spawning beds. Sediment from logging road failures and landslides also contributed to the death of salmon and the destruction of their habitat.

Gold mining, starting with the Gold Rush in California in 1849 and continuing later in the Columbia Basin, contributed to habitat loss. Some mining methods washed out stream banks and hillsides, filling streams with gravel and sediments. Hydraulic and dredge mining filled rivers with mud, often killing the insects young salmon feed on once they hatch. Huge dredges sucked up the river bed and spit out gravel along the banks. The result was piles of gravel and perhaps a conduit for water, but no longer a living ecosystem. Mining started in the Boise Basin in 1862, and by 1865 salmon were gone from the Boise River system.[7]

Settlers brought agriculture and livestock, which would have their own effects on salmon habitat. Farmers who relied on irrigation built small, low dams that sometime diverted the migrating salmon into irrigation ditches and onto farmland where they died. Some irrigation diversions dried up streams, blocking salmon migration. Fish losses to irrigation diversions were a concern among early game wardens in the West. State laws began to require fish screens of wire mesh on diversions, but the rules were poorly and unevenly enforced. Some diversion dams were large enough to block upstream migration of salmon outright, and only a few were built with fish passage in mind. The Reclamation Act of 1902 allowed the construction of large federal water storage reservoirs that provided stability in irrigation water supplies and expanded the acreage that could be irrigated. The dams were built without consideration of fish passage, and river flows were altered to meet human needs. High spring flows were trapped in the reservoirs behind the dams instead of helping to carry young salmon downstream. Some state water right laws did not account for adequate stream flows to ensure fish survival. Some people considered allowing water to flow to the sea a waste, and some still do.

In addition to the depredation of habitat, mechanized salmon processing contributed directly to the decline of wild salmon runs. Early efforts to cash in on the abundance of salmon in the Columbia River were hampered by the lack of inexpensive and effective ways to preserve the fish to get them to eastern markets. Salting and drying were less than satisfactory. In the latter half of the nineteenth century commercial canning technology became available, and fishing for salmon became serious business. In 1866 George and William Hume, with the help of canning expert Andrew Hapgood, built the region's first cannery at Eagle Cliff in Washington near the mouth of the Columbia River. Canning quickly grew into a major industry, and salmon became an industrial commodity. Unrestricted access to this public resource led to a predictable result. No one owned the fish; they belonged to the people who caught them and hauled them ashore. Fishermen supplying the canneries caught as many fish as they could. The fish they could not sell or that the canneries could not process often simply went to waste.

The most serious long-term threat to salmon has been blocked access to habitat. In the Columbia River Basin, hydropower dams have blocked passage to spawning and rearing streams, and reduced the area of available habitat from about 163,000 square miles to about 73,000 square miles, less than half of what it once was.[8] Along with its largest tributary, the Snake River, the Columbia drains parts of seven states and one Canadian province; that is, nearly all of Idaho, most of Oregon and Washington, parts of British Columbia and western Montana, and slivers of Wyoming, Utah, and Nevada, a total of 259,000 square miles, an area almost the size of Texas. The Columbia links the Continental Divide to the Pacific Ocean, from Yellowstone National Park to Portland. The average flow of 265,000 cubic feet per second is exceeded only by the Mississippi, St. Lawrence, Ohio, and McKenzie Rivers. With all that water, the Columbia also powers the country's largest hydroelectric system. Therein lies the problem. Dam development in the Columbia Basin began in 1888 with the T. M. Sullivan Dam at Willamette Falls in Oregon. Over the next two decades, fourteen hydropower facilities were built on the Snake, Boise, and Spokane Rivers in Idaho; on Rock Creek and the Clackamas and Deschutes Rivers in Oregon; and on the Smilkameen, Noches, Spokane, and Wenatchee Rivers in Washington.[9] Many of them had ineffective or no fish passage.

The Elwha and Glines Canyon dams blocked the Elwha River, which runs into the Strait of Juan de Fuca about ten miles west of Port Angeles, Washington. Though not on the Columbia, the Elwha Dam would play a key role in developing a work-around to state requirements for salmon passage. The river once produced a run of some of the largest Chinook salmon in the Pacific Northwest. Until the 109-foot high Elwha Dam was completed in October 1912, fish weighing a hundred pounds were common. During construction part of the foundation blew out, and builders gave up on the idea of including a fish ladder, even though state law at the time required one. In the late nineteenth century, Oregon and Washington enacted laws requiring structures that blocked salmon passage to include fish ladders or other means of passage to protect the growing fishing industry. Federal laws also required dams to include fish passage, but the laws were poorly enforced. It was difficult to enforce limits on what many thought was an inexhaustible resource, and officials were reluctant to enforce rules that would affect an individual's opportunity to earn a profit, as Bruce Brown wrote in his 1982 book, *Mountain in the Clouds*, "especially when powerful financial interests were involved."[10]

In 1913 a solution to the dam builders' legal dilemma emerged. The Washington fish commissioner suggested that the troubled Elwha Dam owners build a hatchery instead of a fish ladder. If a hatchery was physically connected to it, the dam could be considered a blockage to collect eggs for the hatchery. State law at the time allowed hatcheries to build structures that blocked a river to capture fish. Though technically illegal, the commissioner's suggestion led the Washington legislature two years later to change state law to allow dams to be built without fish passage if a hatchery were built instead. The Elwha hatchery could not live up to its promise, never replacing the salmon run that once spawned above the dam.[11] After a few years, officials gave up on the hatchery. The wild salmon run all but beat itself to death on the base of the dam. The precedent would have a profound effect on Northwest salmon management and cast a shadow that lingers today over wild salmon populations.

Many other dams followed. By 1930 thirty-two dams had been built in the Columbia Basin. In addition hundreds of smaller dams were built for municipal water supplies, livestock water, irrigation, mining, and power generation. Almost all were built without salmon passage, at the same time flooding habitat and altering river flows. In the following decade, decisions about dams and their effect on salmon continued to be based on assumptions that fish ladders would provide adequate passage, that blocked runs could be transplanted to other rivers, and that hatcheries could make up for the runs lost to dams and habitat destruction, despite evidence to the contrary. Many of those decisions left fish managers, to say nothing of Indian or commercial fishermen, with few options and fewer fish.

The major dam building frenzy started in the 1930s with President Franklin D. Roosevelt's public works projects. Columbia Basin projects included large dams on the Columbia River at Bonneville and Grand Coulee, both built without fish passage. A fish ladder was later added to Bonneville, but not Grand Coulee.[12] When completed in 1942, the 550-foot tall dam effectively blocked one of the largest salmon runs on the West Coast, cutting it off from more than a thousand miles of spawning habitat in Washington, Idaho, Montana, and British Columbia. Building a fish ladder was deemed impossible and impractical.

Large dams create lethal barriers for migrating salmon, even with fish passage. Some adults die trying to negotiate fish ladders as exhaustion and delays increase with each dam the fish must pass. The more serious problem is moving the juveniles downstream when they migrate to the ocean. Many young fish are killed in generator turbines and by nitrogen gas saturation when they are washed over spillways, a condition similar to the bends in divers who surface too fast. Each dam reduces the salmon run, and the effects of a series of dams are cumulative.

Damming a river changes it significantly. Salmon like cold, moving water, but most dams turn rivers into warm, slow-moving reservoirs. Young salmon do not swim downstream. They are flushed by the river flow, facing upstream into the current. Without a guiding current, young salmon become disoriented, and it is harder for them to find their way downstream. It once took salmon migrating from Idaho streams ten to fourteen days to reach the ocean. Now it takes fifty or more, disrupting the juvenile salmon's adjustment from fresh water to salt water. Some just lose the drive to migrate, others make easy prey for predators. In addition to hampering salmon migration, dams also change the water chemistry in the reservoirs and trap sediments carried by the river behind the dam. Water released below the dam changes the nature of the river downstream, sometimes removing the gravels that some salmon use for spawning.

As large dams were constructed, concerns began to rise over dwindling salmon runs. In 1938 Congress passed the Mitchell Act, amended in 1946, which called for construction of hatcheries on the lower Columbia River in Oregon and Washington, improved fish passage at dams, irrigation diversion screens, fish refuges without obstructions in several rivers, and transplanting Idaho salmon runs to tributaries downstream of the site of the proposed McNary Dam on the Columbia River, just below the confluence with the Snake River.[13] Most of the $500,000 appropriated to carry out the act was spent on hatcheries, and some characterized it as a hatchery development program. It resulted in forty new or upgraded hatcheries.[14] The Mitchell Act continues to fund a number of hatcheries on the lower Columbia.

Congress passed the act in part as a response to a U.S. Army Corps of Engineers proposal. The Corps wanted to build four navigation and hydropower dams on the lower Snake River in addition to the McNary Dam. Construction of those dams was authorized in the 1945 Rivers and Harbors Act, which also required free passage for salmon to their natural spawning grounds.[15] The requirement of free passage, however, was essentially dropped. The proposed large dams on the Columbia and lower Snake Rivers made fishery managers nervous. They began to fear that the decline of salmon would get worse, and that hatcheries could never make up for the losses to the major dams, even with fish ladders. Fishing interests protested that the dams would be the death warrant for the salmon. Their fears were not unjustified.

In 1947 federal officials decided in favor of hydropower development on the Columbia and Snake. An Interior Department memo dated March 6, 1947, by Assistant Secretary Warner W. Gardner made it clear that some upriver salmon runs would be doomed by design. The memo concluded "that the overall benefits to the Pacific Northwest from a thorough-going development of the Snake and Columbia are such that the present salmon run must be sacrificed. This means that the [Interior] Department's efforts should be directed toward ameliorating the impact of this development upon the injured interests and not toward a vain attempt to hold still the hands of the clock."[16] Meanwhile, during a public meeting in June 1947, officials with the U.S. Army Corps of Engineers had tried to reassure fishing interests that "the dams would not stop salmon from reaching their upriver spawning grounds." U.S. Fish and Wildlife Service biologists asserted that the salmon could be transplanted successfully to the lower tributaries if necessary.[17]

The promises proved hollow. The Interior Department proposed a ten-year moratorium on dam construction to allow biologists to study the needs of salmon and how best to mitigate the anticipated losses. Though federal officials recognized the lethal potential of dams even with fish ladders and other means of fish passage, they rejected the moratorium. It appeared that the four dams on the lower Snake River would be approved. In addition, the mitigating measures did not live up to promises, dams were built in the rivers that were to have been fish refuges, and the transplants did not work, effectively leaving salmon managers with little choice but to switch their focus to hatcheries.

A last ditch effort to block the Snake River dams also failed. In 1959, Assistant Interior Secretary Ross Leffler proposed that the Snake River be protected as a salmon sanctuary.[18] His proposal was blocked. Between 1962 and 1976, the federal government built four dams with navigation locks and fish ladders on the Snake River in southeastern Washington: Lower Granite, Little Goose, Lower Monumental, and Ice Harbor. The dams flooded 140 miles of Chinook habitat in the Snake River, and together reduced access to more than five thousand miles of tributary streams, including the Clearwater River and its tributaries, the Salmon River and its tributaries, the Snake River through Hells Canyon and its tributaries, and hundreds of miles of pristine habitat in central Idaho wilderness. In 1976 Congress required the construction of fish hatcheries to help offset the decline and loss of Idaho's native salmon and trout species as a result of the dams. Under the Lower Snake River Fish and Wildlife Compensation Plan, the U.S. Army Corps of Engineers built twenty hatcheries to raise salmon and trout. That did not help wild salmon in Idaho.

Meanwhile dam and hatchery building continued. In the mid-1950s, Idaho Power Company started to build a complex of three dams farther upstream on the Snake River in Hells Canyon that would block the last wild salmon runs in southern Idaho, southeastern Oregon, and northern Nevada. The Federal Energy Regulatory Commission (FERC), which licenses private power projects on public rivers, required Idaho Power to build hatcheries to compensate for the losses. An estimated one and a half to two million wild salmon once returned to Idaho up the Snake River, the second largest river in the West. Salmon have not returned to the rivers blocked by the Hells Canyon Complex, and wild salmon fishing seasons closed in Idaho in 1978. Salmon hatcheries in Idaho release about ten million Chinook annually. They must navigate eight large dams and their reservoirs. In 2017 the ten-year average return was about 115,000 Chinook salmon, most of them hatchery fish. About 26,000 were wild fish, or about 1 percent of the former run of wild salmon. Despite state, tribal, and federal efforts and millions of dollars spent on hatcheries, the fishing seasons on Idaho's wild salmon are still closed more than thirty-five years later, and wild salmon and steelhead are on the list of threatened and endangered species.

Today about 130 hydro or multipurpose dams in the region, to varying degrees, have flooded or blocked access to salmon spawning and rearing habitat. In the mountains of central Idaho, hundreds of miles of pristine spawning habitat are all but unused because few salmon can get there. Many fishery managers saw hatcheries as their only option to raise more fish in hopes that more would return. It has not worked. In some years, returning runs are not large enough to support any fishing season. Rather than restoring or replacing depleted or wiped out wild salmon runs, hatcheries turned out to be part of the problem. Returning hatchery fish allowed people to ignore overfishing, dam building, and habitat destruction while the degradation continued in a river system that once produced millions of wild salmon annually. Over the long term, hatchery runs are not self-sustaining, but they create the illusion that salmon are doing fine.[19]

Fish culture has a long history that reaches back more than twenty-five hundred years. The ancient Chinese successfully raised carp for food.

In the eighteenth century, fertilizing and hatching salmon eggs artificially started in Europe with experiments on Atlantic salmon. In the mid-nineteenth century, New Englanders began looking into artificial propagation of Atlantic salmon in response to declining numbers.[20] In 1872 the U.S. Commission on Fish and Fisheries decided to try it on Pacific salmon. The commission built a small hatchery on the Sacramento River in California, where salmon eggs were successfully fertilized and hatched artificially. Three years after that limited success, the head of the commission, Spencer Baird, with little evidence of long-term success to back him up, recommended establishing hatcheries on the Columbia River. The stamp of approval from the U.S. fish commissioner cloaked the idea in an aura of legitimacy. Later decisions would build on Baird's recommendation, promoting salmon hatcheries without evidence that they would work over the long term. The prevailing thought held that the shortcomings of nature could be overcome by engineering. It was a small step from there to the conclusion that hatcheries could replace destroyed or blocked habitat as well.

Despite the lack of demonstrable success, hatcheries became the default solution to dwindling salmon runs. In 1878 a group of cannery owners were happy to try Baird's recommendation. They built the first salmon hatchery in the Northwest on the Clackamas River in Oregon to boost salmon runs declining from overfishing and to avoid limits on fishing.[21] Others followed, but growth was slow, hampered by technical problems. In 1909 the Bonneville Hatchery was built to act as a salmon egg clearing house. Eggs fertilized at the Bonneville Hatchery were sent to other hatcheries to be raised and released in other streams in the Columbia Basin with no regard for their origin. Some of these early hatcheries shut down because few adult salmon returned. By about 1940 biologists were learning that salmon runs were unique to the rivers of their origin. Neither the eggs nor the adults could be transferred to other streams with any hope of survival. In later years, with improvements in technology and methods using eggs from local fish, more hatcheries were built, and by 1974, salmon hatcheries were releasing millions of salmon into the rivers of the Columbia Basin.[22]

Today more than one hundred sixty hatcheries operate in Washington, Idaho, and Oregon. The Washington Department of Fish and Wildlife operates sixty-nine hatcheries that produce salmon or steelhead. In

Built in 1909 by the state of Oregon to act as a salmon egg clearing house, the Bonneville Hatchery was the largest of its kind at the time. Eggs fertilized here were sent to other hatcheries to be raised and released in other streams in the Columbia Basin with no regard for their origin. *Courtesy of the Washington Digital Collections, Freshwater and Marine Image Bank*

addition, thirty-five tribal hatcheries and twelve federal hatcheries also produce salmon in the state.[23] Idaho operates fourteen salmon and steelhead hatcheries built as mitigation for losses from hydropower projects in the Snake River drainage. These hatcheries produce about ten million Chinook salmon, five million steelhead, and more than two hundred thousand sockeye salmon for release annually. A new hatchery opened in 2013 with a potential capacity of up to a million sockeye. The Oregon Department of Fish and Wildlife operates thirty-three hatcheries.

Since the late 1980s, hatcheries in the three states have been releasing at least 200 million juvenile fish annually.[24] In spite of that effort, by 1990 salmon returns to the Columbia Basin had declined to just over a million fish, most of them raised in hatcheries. The wild runs were worse off; they had declined to about 3 percent or less of their historic numbers.[25] Despite this apparent failure, most salmon recovery and mitigation efforts continued to rely on hatcheries, even as wild salmon runs continued to decline.

One of the reasons hatcheries have not succeeded well lies in the nature of how hatchery fish are raised. Scientists have questioned whether fish raised in the controlled conditions of uniform concrete raceways and fed automatically could match the rigors of nature that have honed the survival skills and genetic diversity of wild salmon over thousands of years. With eggs stripped from adult females fertilized with milt squeezed from males, hatcheries release millions of salmon into the wild without the natural competition that limits survival and drives evolution. Hatchery fish learn to feed at the surface and swim in schools; they have no need to hide from predators.[26] They do not survive as well as wild fish, since breeding practices can result in genetic defects, and disease spreads in the close quarters of the hatchery raceways.

Wild fish, on the other hand, go through a rigorous selection process. They conserve more of the genetic variation that have allowed the species to survive thousands of years through ice ages, droughts, floods, volcanic eruptions, earthquakes, and ocean conditions that vary with global climate patterns. Genetic diversity spreads the risk. They do not all lay their eggs in the same kinds of places in a river, stream, or lake. The wild fish do not all return at the same time; they tend to be more spread out, and thus some may avoid severe storms or other weather phenomenon that could affect spawning success. "Unlike the salmon raised in a hatchery environment, with its feedlot regime," Lichatowich wrote, "the salmon in a natural population in a healthy river do not all do the same thing in the same place at the same time."[27] Hatchery produced fish tend to be more closely grouped.

Though hatchery fish are less likely to survive, their sheer numbers put pressure on and compete with wild fish.[28] Releases of large numbers of hatchery-raised Chinook salmon have reduced the survival of wild Chinook, especially during years with poor ocean conditions hampering the recovery of wild populations. When hatcheries release millions of juvenile salmon, they can overwhelm the river ecosystem, competing with wild fish for limited food. When food is short, both wild and hatchery fish suffer. In 2002 Washington Trout and the Native Fish Society of Portland sued the Washington Department of Fish and Wildlife to stop the release of hatchery-produced coho salmon and steelhead in Puget Sound. The lawsuit cited an earlier California study that reported 532,000 hatchery salmon ate 7.5 million wild Chinook fingerlings in the Feather River.[29] The lawsuit charged that hatchery operations in Puget Sound helped drive Chinook onto the endangered species list as threatened in 1999. A similar lawsuit in 2014 also made the argument that releases of hatchery raised fish harm wild steelhead, listed as a threatened species in Puget Sound.

After more than 135 years of hatchery operations many wild salmon stocks are on the endangered species list or already extinct. By 1991 researchers found that 214 runs of salmon, steelhead, and sea-run cutthroat trout in the Northwest and California were at high or moderate risk of extinction, and 106 runs already had ceased to exist.[30] Coho salmon became extinct in Idaho in 1986, and are listed as threatened in parts of Oregon, California, and the Lower Columbia River. The Snake River sockeye salmon was listed as endangered in 1991, and has been kept alive only by a captive breeding hatchery program. Sockeye are listed as threatened in parts of Washington. Nine populations of Chinook in Oregon, Washington, California, and Idaho are listed as threatened or endangered. Chum salmon are listed as threatened in parts of Oregon and Washington.

Some have called for a halt to all hatchery operations. Shutting down or limiting the operation of hatcheries might be good for wild salmon, but without changes in dam passage and habitat condition, it would be many years before wild salmon would recover enough to support recreational, tribal, and commercial fishing. Limiting a popular and thriving fishery on hatchery salmon until wild salmon populations recover would be a hard sell. There would be little support for wild salmon restoration if it meant a halt to salmon fishing, even if it were temporary.

Hatcheries have had some benefits though. The ability to mark large numbers of hatchery fish before they are released has allowed anglers to fish for salmon in streams where wild fish also occur. Anglers are allowed to keep only the marked fish. Not all of the unmarked wild fish that are caught and released survive, however, and that incidental mortality limits the fishing on runs that include wild fish. Still, the returning marked hatchery fish support limited tribal, commercial, and recreational fisheries in many streams and rivers, from the Pacific Ocean all the way up to the Sawtooth Valley in the mountains of central Idaho. Hatcheries have become an important part of many state economies. In 2000, fisheries officials estimated that in the Columbia Basin, hatchery fish made up 95 percent of the coho, 70 to 80 percent of the spring and summer Chinook, 50 percent of the fall Chinook, and 70 percent of the steelhead. "Thriving fish populations are good business," then-Washington Fish and Wildlife Director Jeff Koenings said during a public meeting in Olympia, Washington, in 2002.[31]

Hatcheries also have helped to preserve some salmon populations. Perhaps the best example is the captive breeding program launched in 1990 by Idaho Fish and Game. The program has prevented the extinction and preserved the genetic lineage of Snake River sockeye, but the run is far from recovered. Before the turn of the twentieth century, an estimated 25,000 to 35,000 sockeye returned to the mountain lakes of the Sawtooth National Recreation Area in central Idaho, some nine hundred miles from the Pacific. In 1910 the Sunbeam Dam on the Salmon River blocked their passage until it was blown up in 1934 and the sockeye began to return, an estimated average of five thousand per year, by the 1950s. After the four federal dams on the lower Snake River were finished in the 1970s, the numbers dropped again. In most years fewer than a hundred, in others fewer than ten, and in several years none returned. In 1992, when only a single male sockeye returned, Idaho Governor Cecil Andrus dubbed it "Lonesome Larry."

◆

The captive sockeye breeding program has helped. Biologists trap them as they return to Redfish Lake, named for the bright red breeding sockeye, and take them to a nondescript building at a hatchery on Eagle Island west of Boise. A technician kills a female sockeye with a swift, lethal blow to the head and slits open her belly to release a mass of orange eggs. In another part of the building, two biologists hold a male; one of them squeezes its lower abdomen forcing a milky stream of milt into a small container. The milt is mixed with the eggs, and the newly fertilized eggs are placed in trays kept in a controlled environment. Eventually they become new salmon. Each fish's DNA is recorded in a process designed to prevent inbreeding and to conserve the sockeye's unique genetics.

Despite these efforts, Snake River sockeye are still in trouble. In the ten years since 2008, the high return of sockeye was 1,579 in 2014, and the low 91 in the following year.[32] In 2017, 157 returned. The average over the ten years was 690. With the new sockeye hatchery in southeastern Idaho operational, Idaho Fish and Game increased the number released to nearly three-quarters of a million young sockeye in 2017. Managers hope to get up to ten thousand adults to return. Raising more salmon and sending them downriver, however, will not fix the problem. The sockeye, like other salmon, still have to run the same river and the same gantlet of deadly dams and degraded habitat that led to their decline. For many years, fishery managers and government agencies rarely questioned the practice of raising salmon in hatcheries only to release them into degraded and sometimes lethal habitat. The problem is also the failure to see the river basin as a landscape fraught with piecemeal management and often conflicting agendas of state, federal, and tribal agencies, treating salmon runs as individual entities, not as an integral part of the landscape they inhabit.

In 1980 the Northwest Power Act created the Northwest Power Planning Council, now known as the Northwest Power and Conservation Council. The council looked at the Columbia Basin as a cohesive system, and raised important questions about how dams were operated and the role of hatcheries. Critics claim the council is dominated by hydropower interests, but their efforts are at least a start toward restoring once plentiful salmon runs. In the 1940s and '50s when many large hydropower dams were licensed by the Federal Energy Regulatory Commission (FERC), many rivers were managed for energy production, irrigation, and water supplies and known as working rivers. As the licenses of many of those dams expire, FERC may require dam operators to consider the needs of commercial and recreational fisheries as well as the health of fish and streams. Perhaps improved fish passage can become part of license renewal requirements.

Reengineered fish passage is already showing some promise. In 2014, officials counted a little over one million Chinook salmon at Bonneville Dam. Though the most in many decades, that is still less than 10 percent of the historic estimates. The increase is likely the result of improved ocean conditions and increased water flows over hydropower dams and better or more effective fish ladders rather than changes in hatchery operations.[33] Still, such returns hint at the long term potential of salmon runs with improvements in passage and habitat that are even more important in low water years and years when ocean conditions are poorer. Already engineers have been working on ways to get salmon over Grand Coulee Dam, which would return salmon to the extensive habitat in the upper Columbia. Effective catch limits can be set and enforced, damaged salmon habitat can be restored, and most dams—or the way they are operated—can be modified to allow salmon to pass safely. Some cannot. The removal of the Elwha Dam and many others like it across the country have provided promising examples of what the salmon can do if we let them. The dam was removed in 2012, and a hundred years after their passage was blocked wild fish began returning to the upper Elwha River.

Despite their apparent failure, support for salmon hatcheries has become entrenched. Money flowing from regional electricity ratepayers, who buy power generated at federal dams in the Columbia Basin and marketed by the federal Bonneville Power Administration, has gone to operate state, tribal, and federal salmon and steelhead hatcheries. For some fish managers and state fish and wildlife agencies, running hatcheries make up a substantial portion of their budgets. In Idaho, for example, in 2015 about $9 million of the $32 million fishery bureau budget at Idaho Fish and Game came from operating hatcheries.[34] With promises of plentiful hatchery fish, however, hatcheries have all but eliminated the incentive to conserve wild salmon. That is perhaps their worst failing. They have led to the loss of a constituency for wild fish. Wild salmon need people who see landscapes as a system with rivers and mountains, forests, farms, and deserts and who understand their importance from the salmon's perspective.

Salmon recovery is not just about dams and hatcheries. Nor is it about fish passage at dams, barges, gillnetters, trawlers or loggers, farmers or miners. No single cause was responsible for the demise of wild salmon in the Northwest. We all share the blame. We all rely on electricity, we use paper from clear-cut forests, live in houses made of wood, and eat food from sprawling agricultural lands. Our divergent views on the fate of wild salmon have made a political solution to the declining wild runs nearly impossible. But some saw hatcheries as just that, an easy way to solve thorny issues with deep cultural and social roots.[35] So far they have not.

CHAPTER 10

Overcutting Ancient Forests

With a bright sun in a clear blue sky, a gentle east wind, and the temperature in the low seventies, I headed up a former logging road on Long Island, which rises from the shallow waters of Washington's Willapa Bay. I had come with four others to explore a grove of ancient western redcedars hidden deep in the interior and to learn the fate of the ancient forests that once covered most of this region. (See #1 on map, page 24.)

We followed the road north along the spine of the island. Toward noon, we turned onto the Trail of the Ancient Cedars. Soon, huge stumps loomed among the spindly second growth, and then ancient giants rose out of view amid the still-green crowns of lesser trees. Gnarled roots and twisted trunks, some ghostly snags eight to ten feet thick, rose above the forest floor. High up, large sturdy branches still alive reached up to replace long dead, storm killed tops. Western redcedar, *Thuja plicata*, is actually an arborvitae (tree of life) and they are magnificent.

For generations Pacific Northwest Indians and the Chinook tribes depended on the trees for many of their basics needs. From the long, straight-grained trunks of these forest giants, they split long boards to build their distinctive longhouses, carved totem poles, and built sturdy dug-out canoes. Some of these seaworthy craft were up to sixty feet long with an eight foot beam. Native people carved stylized animal spirit faces and profiles in the easily worked wood, artwork that also decorated their homes, ceremonial objects, and tools. The stringy inner bark was twisted into string and thread to make ropes, nets, shoes, and sleeping mats, even padding for cradles. The day we visited the island, however, most of the big trees were long gone.

Like other forests in the Pacific Northwest, Long Island was intensely logged in the early twentieth century. Fortunately the remains of the island's old-growth forest, once nearly all privately owned, are now protected as part of the Willapa National Wildlife Refuge. Here, and in the old-growth forests of Oregon and northern California, years of unrestrained logging landed a medium sized owl on the list of threatened species in 1990.

By then there were few of the big trees left to cut. Nevertheless timber industry officials, their supporters, and many loggers blamed environmentalists, the U.S. Forest Service, and the threatened species listing for the decline of the timber industry in the Pacific Northwest. In fact, automation, overcutting, foreign competition, raw log exports, changes in demand, and a shift of the timber industry to the Southeast United States, all cost the Northwest more jobs than the logging restrictions on the forests set aside as spotted owl habitat in Washington, Oregon, and northern California. The spotted owl listing perhaps became a handy scapegoat for large timber companies that already had begun to tiptoe quietly out of town.

The decline of the timber industry in the Pacific Northwest began long before most people had even heard of the spotted owl. Unfortunately, the uproar over lost jobs and logging restrictions to protect spotted owl habitat all but drowned out any serious discussion of the real issue, particularly, the appropriate use of natural and economic resources. The law that protects the owl also protects clean water, clean air, habitat for other birds, plants, animals, and fish, along with scenic beauty and recreational opportunities. The same logging practices that threatened the owl also contributed to the decline of northwest wild salmon.

On my visit to Long Island I saw examples of many of the issues that have affected forests and the timber industry in the Pacific Northwest. Accessibility is certainly one of those issues. Getting to Long Island is not easy. At a boat ramp across U.S. Highway 101 from the Willapa National Wildlife Refuge headquarters, a couple of hours southwest of Seattle, we put canoes in the water and paddled across the two-hundred-foot channel that separated the island from the mainland. The tide was coming in, and timing here is important. If we lingered too long on the island, the low tide would expose impassable mud flats on both sides of the channel and we would have to wait for the high tide to return. Once across we pulled our canoes up in the marsh grass and set off toward the interior of the island ringed with salt marshes and sand and mud beaches. We took the road that wound from the crossing north to Diamond Point at the other end of the six-mile long, 4,700-acre island, the largest in a Pacific coast estuary. A legacy from the past, several former logging roads crisscross the island, but are now mostly overgrown and closed to vehicles. A thick forest mostly of second-growth Sitka spruce, western hemlock, and western redcedar covers most of the island.

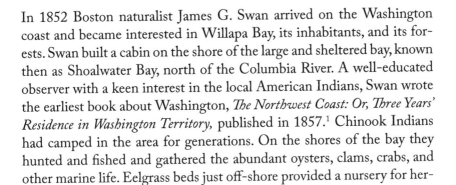

In 1852 Boston naturalist James G. Swan arrived on the Washington coast and became interested in Willapa Bay, its inhabitants, and its forests. Swan built a cabin on the shore of the large and sheltered bay, known then as Shoalwater Bay, north of the Columbia River. A well-educated observer with a keen interest in the local American Indians, Swan wrote the earliest book about Washington, *The Northwest Coast: Or, Three Years' Residence in Washington Territory,* published in 1857.[1] Chinook Indians had camped in the area for generations. On the shores of the bay they hunted and fished and gathered the abundant oysters, clams, crabs, and other marine life. Eelgrass beds just off-shore provided a nursery for herring, sea perch, sole, and salmon.[2]

As more settlers arrived, the bay became popular with commercial oyster gatherers who sold their catch to ships bound for San Francisco. In 1851 the first load of oysters left Shoalwater Bay in wicker baskets. Settlers established a shanty town on the northern tip of Long Island in 1867 and named it Diamond Point for the mounds of oyster shells that sparkled in the sun. A decade later the oyster beds were depleted, and the settlement shriveled.

When Europeans first arrived on the West Coast, Long Island was still covered with thick timber and small, easily cultivated prairie patches with rich soil. Logging on the island began in 1900, decades after the oysters were fished out. Since then the island has been logged twice, in the 1930s and again in the 1960s. In 1939 part of the island was added to the Willapa National Wildlife Refuge, which had been established two years earlier by President Franklin Roosevelt to protect migrating birds. About 1,600 acres, however, which included the 274-acre grove of ancient cedars, had already been acquired by timber giant Weyerhaeuser Company. The grove was left mostly intact because the island was accessible then only at high tide by a ferry across the narrow channel, and because of a hard fought battle to preserve the few remaining old-growth trees.

Logging on the island eventually ended in a complex process, which, while unique in the particulars, was not unlike what was done elsewhere in the Northwest. With the help of some congressional arm-twisting and pressure from environmental groups, Weyerhaeuser in 1983 agreed to trade 1,622 acres on the island for 21 million board feet of standing timber on federal land. In the trade only 119 acres of the 274-acre grove became part of the Willapa National Wildlife Refuge. When cedar prices went up Weyerhaeuser insisted on a re-appraisal. The company wanted $5.5 million for the remaining 155 acres.

Efforts in Congress to raise money were blocked by Idaho Republican Senator Jim McClure, then chairman of the Senate Energy and Natural Resources Committee. Nevertheless, pressure from Senators Slade Gorton and Dan Evans of Washington and Mark Hatfield of Oregon secured $3.38 million in December 1985; Weyerhaeuser continued to hold out for the $5.5 million and threatened to start logging in 1991. Despite objections to paying inflated prices to Weyerhaeuser while cedar prices were dropping, Congress eventually put up the money, and all of Long Island is now protected as part of the Willapa National Wildlife Refuge.[3] Some of the remaining trees in the old grove are more than nine hundred years old and more than ten feet in diameter near the base. It is one of the remnants of the ancient Pacific Coast old-growth rainforest.

◆

Old-growth forest can be difficult to define. In the Pacific Northwest, it is characterized by the number of species and sizes of trees, including many large trees two hundred years old or older, some a thousand years old, that form a multi-layered canopy. It is a complex and diverse forest and typical habitat of the spotted owl, which along with pileated woodpeckers finds nesting cavities in the ancient trees. Red tree voles and flying squirrels, both owl prey, prefer old, mature forests. Bats and frogs find refuge in the bark. Trees continue to play a part in the structure of the forest long after they are dead. Standing snags provide habitat for birds and bats and food for woodpeckers. Woodpecker holes in turn make homes for other birds and mammals, such as bluebirds, nuthatches, and perches for flycatchers, swallows and raptors. The snags also serve as habitat for wood-eating beetles and other insects that are a food source for wood-

Western redcedars like this old giant once covered vast sections of the Pacific Northwest coastal forests. *Author photo*

peckers and other insect-eaters. The forest floor is littered with a tangle of fallen trees and rotting logs that create small openings, hold water, and provide nutrients to the soil and nurseries for young trees. Salamanders hide beneath fallen giants, and ferns and fungi sprout from the rotting logs. They provide habitat and cover for insects, snails, and worms. Most of the species in an old-growth forest, however, live in the soil and are too small to be visible. They evoke little interest from humans, but they are vital to the life of the forest and to life on earth.[4] Fallen snags in streams create pools and riffles and habitat for aquatic insects and fish. They help stabilize stream banks and reduce the erosive force of water. They take a long time to decay, thus providing a long-term source of nutrients in the stream.

The temperate rain forests of the Pacific Northwest included more and larger stands of conifers than almost anywhere else on earth. In 1908 Frank H. Lamb of the Washington State Forest Commission noted that, "Western Washington has the heaviest and most uniform stand of timber in the world."[5] The climate and topography made agriculture difficult in many places, but it was great for growing trees.

As large areas of the forests were lost to overcutting, significant habitat degradation followed. Already in the early 1970s scientists had begun to see a decline in spotted owl numbers. Their research showed past and current forest practices had resulted in wide-spread fragmentation and loss of habitat. In the early 1980s, government biologists designated the spotted owl as an indicator of the health of Pacific Northwest old-growth forest ecosystems.[6] The U.S. Fish and Wildlife Service on June 26, 1990, listed the northern spotted owl as threatened under the Endangered Species Act, citing "loss of habitat across its range and the inadequacy of existing regulatory mechanisms to conserve it."[7] It appeared to the agency to be the only way to protect the remains of the ancient forest ecosystem that supported the owls.

As if to underscore that conclusion, in 1992 the Fish and Wildlife Service added the marbled murrelet, a robin-sized sea bird, to the list of threatened species in Washington, Oregon, and California. The murrelet has been found in many places including the ancient cedars on Long Island. They make their platform nests in the high branches, out of reach of most earth-bound predators. Scientists first described the bird in 1789, but they did not document a nest site until 1974. Murrulets forage at sea within about three miles of the coast, but they nest up to thirty miles from the ocean in large stands of old trees.

The owl listing resulted in logging restrictions on nearly seven million acres of national forest lands designated as critical habitat in Washington, Oregon, and California. Unfortunately but not unexpectedly, residents in timber-dependent communities saw the listing and the harvest restrictions as a threat to their livelihoods.[8] Protecting owl habitat meant the potential loss of about thirty-three thousand jobs, the Fish and Wildlife Service acknowledged, but the effects of the listing and the designation of critical habitat on timber-dependent jobs were not easily isolated from other trends and changes in the timber industry and regional economies.[9]

Critics of the listing complained that environmentalists and Fish and Wildlife were using the Endangered Species Act to bring timber harvest to an end in the Pacific Northwest. The timber industry, many loggers, and timber-dependent communities cast the blame on environmentalists and accused the U.S. Forest Service of mismanagement. Loggers and environmentalists were pitted against each other when they should have been allies. Most of the job losses and harvest restrictions were not the result of the owl listing or designation of critical habitat, though admittedly those did have an effect. Some were mandated by earlier legal actions and changes in Forest Service management plans in response to provisions in the National Forest Management Act and the Federal Lands Policy Management Act, both passed by Congress in 1976. Those acts and resulting plans required old growth forest protection and wildlife conservation.[10] Some harvest reductions had been planned before the owl was listed, and harvest levels had gone down by about 990 million board feet between 1988 and 1989. Many job losses that critics attributed to owl protection were the result of industry changes and trends. It was the decline of old-growth timber in the Pacific Northwest that resulted in the loss of timber jobs, and the listing of the spotted owl was an indicator of efforts to save the last remnants.

Southwestern Washington's Willapa Hills are a case in point. Most of it was private timberland acquired from railroads, through land grants and old homesteads.[11] Most went to large timber corporations, such as Weyerhaeuser, Crown Zellerbach, Longview Fibre, and a few others.

There was no national forest land and little state land here, and federal restrictions on logging old growth to protect the spotted owl did not apply to private forests. No land was set aside for owls, and yet here too, logging declined steeply. It was inevitable. The Willapa Hills, which once held giant Douglas-firs more than ten feet in diameter, were completely logged, unlike Long Island's grove of ancient cedars.

In March 1985 the American Forestry Association predicted the collapse of the timber industry and local economies dependent on what had become a dwindling nonrenewable resource. The association questioned the wisdom of continuing a policy that kept afloat a timber industry and local economy bound to crash as the old growth ran out. The association challenged forest management policy and urged forest managers to wean timber dependent economies from old-growth logging and change to sustainable forestry practices that would make timber a renewable resource. Alas, it was not to be.

Timber companies liquidated the trees as fast as they could in a cutting frenzy that began following World War II. The industry, subsidized by the federal government, cut most of the marketable timber in the northwest, as the demand for lumber increased. Overcutting to meet that demand led to depletion of old-growth timber on private lands, such as in the Willapa Hills, and timber companies began to rely more heavily on national forests. The industry put the Forest Service under intense pressure to increase the timber harvest. Company officials complained to congressional representatives, and Congress set unrealistic harvest levels through the budget process.[12] Some forest supervisors complained that they had come under political pressure to cut more timber than the land could handle, reporter Timothy Eagan wrote in the September 16, 1991, *New York Times.*[13]

Overcutting contributed significantly to the eventual reductions in harvest and the loss of timber jobs. As early as 1969 Forest Service officials realized that harvest rates could not continue as planned and predicted harvest rates and jobs would decline. On private lands harvest increased by 7 percent from 1950 to 1985, while it nearly doubled on national forest lands. Timber companies were cutting trees faster than they could grow back. In 1986, timber harvest exceeded growth by 3.4 billion board feet on private and federal lands in the Pacific Coast region. (A board foot is a piece of wood one inch thick, twelve inches wide and twelve inches long, and twelve board feet equal one cubic foot of wood.)

With the decline in standing trees, experts expected timber harvest in the Northwest woods to drop from about 8 billion board feet in 1986 to 6.7 billion board feet by 2000. Logging reductions for the spotted owl protection made up only a small percentage of the total decline. High harvest rates made the decline in timber harvest inevitable, regardless of the spotted owl listing, the Fish and Wildlife Service said in its economic analysis of the critical habitat designation for the northern spotted owl. Rates on private lands would have forced a 65 percent reduction by 1999.[14] By the 1990s, more than 90 percent of the old-growth forests in the Northwest had been cut, and the industry was clear-cutting 60,000 acres a year.

———————————◆———————————

In the late twentieth century, the most common large-scale logging practice in the Pacific Northwest was clear-cutting. In this process loggers cut down most or all standing trees and snags, often taking only the best trees. The rest were left behind and burned along with the slash, leaving exposed soils vulnerable to erosion and slides.[15] Seen as the most efficient way to turn standing timber into marketable logs, clear-cutting involved heavy machinery, such as large trucks, bulldozers, yarders, loaders, and skidders that compacted forest soils. Typically, when an area was identified for logging, an access road or roads were cut to a site that became the center of operations. Trees were felled and limbed and dragged through the woods by a heavy steel cable to a staging area, where they were loaded onto log trucks and hauled out of the woods. Brush and small trees along with forest soils were torn up in the process.

Other logging methods involve selecting certain trees to be cut, leaving other healthy, mature trees. This practice is used in many parts of the country including the Northwest. The cut trees are often skidded out by tractor or sometimes with teams of horses. The process is less damaging to the forest, but takes more time. The most significant difference is that selective logging does not significantly change the nature of the forest, while clear-cutting removes large sections of forest completely. After a clear cut, it may take several decades or longer before trees can be logged in the same location, if new trees are even planted. In a selective logging program, loggers can return year after year to cut a certain number of trees from the same forest. Selective logging disturbs less soil and is less likely to result in serious erosion. Author and forester Peter Wohlleben argues eloquently and persuasively that selective logging done carefully also produces higher quality timber.[16] One look at second or third growth trees makes it obvious. The trees are skinny and the wood is knotty and open grained. On the other hand, old growth timber in the Northwest is highly valued for its straight, even-grained wood, its strength, and its aesthetic qualities.

While overcutting would lead to a reduction in the available timber by the 1990s, mill automation already had contributed to the loss of timber related jobs. From 1979 to 1988 more than 25,000 timber jobs were eliminated, 195 mills were shut down, while mill production rose by 12 percent and the timber cut increased by 7 percent. Computer monitors and laser-guided saws had replaced about half the employees in many lumber mills. Mechanization and technological changes in the 1980s increased production from 101,000 board feet per worker in 1980 to 146,000 board feet in just seven years. Meanwhile employment dropped by 40,000 workers.[17]

Timber companies were not leaving the Northwest because of the owl listing. In the 1950s, Weyerhaeuser company advertisements promised jobs in southwestern Washington that would last for generations. Thirty years later in 1986 George Weyerhaeuser, speaking in the timber mill town of Longview, Washington, said that excess capacity and depressed prices, along with foreign competition, had forced a reduction in labor. In 1979, a thousand board feet of Douglas-fir two-by-fours sold for $260; by 1986 it was down to $232, he said. He did not mention the spotted owl.[18] Weyerhaeuser was pulling out, closing mills, leaving families, communities, and rural economies to collapse. Other timber giants were doing the same, moving their major operations to the U.S. Southeast.

The move was part of a long industry trend. After harvests peaked and began to decline in one area, the industry moved on to other regions as harvest there became profitable. Since the 1870s, the major lumber producing regions have shifted about every twenty years or so. In 1860 New York and Maine were the biggest timber producers. In 1870 Michigan took the lead through 1890, when Wisconsin moved ahead of New York and Pennsylvania and took the lead. By 1906 the South had taken over. While the timber industry in the Pacific Northwest began soon after the California gold rush, it took off when new markets opened in

Asia in 1880 and when the railroads opened eastern markets to timber from Pacific coast forests. Frank Lamb of the Forest Commission in 1908 predicted that by 1915 the Pacific Northwest would be the chief timber producer, and wondered whether the region would see the same fate as other timber producing regions. He estimated that at the rates being cut in 1908 the supply of trees would last twenty-five to thirty-five years. In his comments to the 1908 governors' conference in Washington, DC, Lamb asked "is it not time to consider if some steps cannot be taken to prevent the inevitable depletion of the nation's last stand of timber?"[19] The trees lasted longer than Lamb had predicted, but the supply ultimately ran out.

By the late 1980s, as private supplies of old growth timber in the Northwest neared exhaustion, costs rose when harvest moved into the rougher terrain of national forests. With steeper slopes and poorer soils, national forest lands were generally less productive than private timber lands, and the Forest Service expected a decline in harvest from federal lands in the 1990s as the supply of standing timber declined. Old growth was being liquidated, and second growth could not make up the difference. As the supply of old-growth declined in the Northwest, however, replanted timber in the Southeast was maturing.[20] In addition, logging on flatter ground in the Southeast cost less. The cost to deliver a thousand board feet in the Pacific Northwest was about twice as much as in the Southeast in 1985. Economic realities like this resulted in many loggers and mill workers losing their jobs.

Raw log exports also led to a loss of Northwest timber industry jobs. On October 12, 1962, the remnants of Typhoon Freda slammed into the Pacific Northwest and British Columbia coast. Known as the Columbus Day Storm, it was the most powerful storm to hit the Northwest in the twentieth century. Gusts as high as 179 mph were recorded as the storm roared across southwestern Washington and Long Island. A radar station near Naselle, Washington, one of the highest points in the Willapa Hills and about seven miles east of Long Island, clocked the winds at 160 mph.[21] The storm leveled more than eleven billion board feet of timber in Washington and Oregon, including many thousand-year-old trees, and many of the standing trees on Long Island. A ferry to the island was installed to harvest the fallen timber, part of the salvage efforts in Washington and Oregon that flooded the market with timber. Much of it was loaded on ships and sent to Asia, most to Japan. Until then log exports had been small. North of Seattle in the late 1970s and early 1980s, large freighters in the port of Everett were piled high with raw logs from Pacific Northwest forests bound for the Far East. At the time automation in the mills, foreign competition, and those raw log exports were—correctly—blamed for lost timber industry jobs. That was before the spotted owl was listed.

The peak of raw log exporting came in 1989, when 3.7 billion board feet of unprocessed logs were shipped to Japan, South Korea, and China. The exports represented about 25 percent of the timber cut that year, and accounted for an estimated 24,000 jobs in the Northwest timber industry. Exporting logs from federal lands had been illegal since the 1970s, but some private timber companies exported logs from their private land and substituted logs from federal public lands for local mills. Legislation in 1990 added restrictions on exports from state lands and on the use of federal logs to replace logs exported from private lands.[22] Officials argued that restrictions on exports would make logs from state and federal lands available and offset reduced harvests that some blamed on spotted owl protection.[23]

Not everybody thought restrictions were a good thing. Timber owners, logging companies, truckers, and those who prepared logs for exports, to say nothing of ship owners, opposed the restrictions. Domestic mill owners, forced to compete with exporters for logs, and the U.S. construction industry supported the restrictions. They argued that exports drove up the cost of logs and reduced the supply for local mills, making them less competitive than other U.S. and Canadian firms.[24]

———————————◆———————————

The issue of lost timber industry jobs resurfaced in January 2013. The Fish and Wildlife Service expanded critical habitat for the spotted owl to nearly ten million acres in California, Oregon, and Washington. Reasons included a steep and unexpected decline in spotted owl population and the effects of increased competition from barred owls moving into spotted owl habitat. Scientists argued that spotted owls needed more high quality habitat and redundancy in suitable habitat, especially in fire-prone areas, so they would have some place else to go if their forest burned. Fish and Wildlife included some state and private lands but only in places where federal lands were not enough to meet the habitat needs of the owl.[25] Critics raised concerns about the inclusion of private land and the loss of timber jobs. Meanwhile, raw logs were still being shipped overseas. In 2010, timber harvest rose by nearly 20 percent in Oregon and Washington, while timber industry jobs dropped by more than four thousand. The increase in harvest largely went to China as raw log exports.[26]

Protecting old-growth forests is not just about owls or marbled murrulets. Timber harvest in the Northwest has been just as hard on wild salmon. The logging practices that brought down the spotted owl population also degraded water quality and destroyed fish habitat and contributed to a dramatic decline and even extinction of several salmon runs. The ancient forests that once were home to some of these fish runs already were beginning to disappear when Swan arrived in Washington in 1852. The Europeans he met here had come seeking riches by cutting timber, harvesting salmon, oysters, clams, and crabs from seemingly limitless sources.

Most destructive logging practices have changed, but modern logging still contributes to salmon population declines.[27] Clear-cuts and logging roads to remote timber stands continue to decrease slope stability, resulting in erosion and landslides that contribute sediments and gravels to streams and eliminate key fish rearing and spawning habitat. Poorly placed culverts can block fish passage. Gravels and sediments make streams wider, shallower, warmer, less stable, with fewer and shallower pools, adding up to poor water quality and degraded fish habitat.

———————————◆———————————

I remember walking in old-growth forest on Washington's Olympic Peninsula after several days of heavy rain. Despite the downpour, the streams ran gin-clear. Clean water is just one of the benefits of restricting timber harvest in large tracts of old-growth forest. An intact forest protects watersheds, fisheries, wildlife habitat, and outdoor recreation opportunities in addition to imperiled owls. These values may not be easily expressed in dollar amounts. They are not marketed and are difficult to compare with commercial uses that have direct and immediate economic benefits. Studies have shown, however, that people generally favor protecting threatened and endangered wildlife and their habitat and are willing to pay for knowing they are protected.[28] That willingness is a recognition of intrinsic value. These so-called "option and existence" values are sometimes referred to as sentimental values. In a July 14, 1989, decision, the Washington, DC Court of Appeals ruled that option and existence values were legitimate components of the total value provided by a natural resource.[29] They represent the value to the public of simply knowing that something exists, such as the Grand Canyon or old-growth forests and spotted owls, and recognition of the importance of the role they play in the environment as well as the value of protecting habitat. It is a willingness to pay for the existence of a resource without actually using it or taking advantage of it. It is quite simply the value of owls and forests for their own sake. Loggers and conservationists both have an interest in the long-term productivity of the forest. For loggers it means steady work, for conservationists, as well as for the wildlife, it means healthy habitats and ecosystems with lots of biological diversity, and that benefits everyone. Timber company officials and their supporters consider old-growth as over-mature forest and argue that it should be liquidated and replaced with more commercially viable plantings. That is faulty logic, wrote naturalist Robert Michael Pyle. Like other living organisms, trees grow old and die. They fall and rot and continue to contribute to the complexity of the forest, and more trees grow.[30] Eventually they too become old-growth trees, with the characteristics that support the complex diversity of life that is a forest, and a lot more than just a stand of commercially viable trees. Forests should not be seen as timber factories, argued Peter Wohlleben. They may serve as habitat for thousands of plant and animal species but only incidentally. Forests have their own intrinsic values apart from anything humans may get from them. Allowed to function on their own, forest ecosystems may include tens of thousands of inextricably linked species and even clean the air we breathe.[31]

It can be difficult to remember, especially in the heat of controversy when people fear their livelihoods are being threatened, that it was not the Endangered Species Act, or environmentalists, or the Forest Service that put timber workers out of work. The real culprits were public lands management and corporate polices, timber industry trends, logging practices, mill automation, raw log exports, economic realities, and the simple fact that the old-growth trees were fast disappearing. The job losses to owl protection were only one part of those changes. Spotted owls are important for their role in the ecosystem, and to humans they are an indicator of the long-term health of Northwest forests.

CHAPTER 11

Saving America's Outback

Lavender shadows stretched across the sagebrush steppe, reaching toward a lava butte that rose more than a hundred feet from its base. The only sounds were the whisper of the wind and the murmur of voices from the two dozen people who had scrambled to the top of the butte and gathered in a loose circle. Ancient inhabitants had carved sacred symbols in the broken lava rock near the rim. In the center of the circle, a Paiute shaman from Salt Lake City prepared a small fire of dry sagebrush twigs for a ceremony to call on the spirits of tribal ancestors. He unwrapped a deer-skin bundle and took out a whistle made from the leg bone of a golden eagle. With the shrill and plaintive tone, he called on the spirits. He knelt before the fire and dropped a pinch of incense made from the leaves of a juniper tree. Fragrant tendrils rose; he waved them reverently with the dried wing of a hawk. He prayed to the Great Spirit, and the setting sun painted his face copper. Two Shoshone-Paiute tribal leaders sang their tribe's creation song. Tribal Chairman Lindsey Manning beat a traditional drum made from animal skin stretched over a round wooden frame. The sun paused on the horizon's rocky rim as if to partake of the solemn moment. From a small pouch, the shaman took a pinch of tobacco and tossed it in the fire for the spirits. He put a pinch on the ground for the ancestors. He packed a pinch into a two-foot-long hand-carved pipe. He continued this ritual until the pipe was full. With the last rays of the sun fading from our faces, Manning lit the pipe with an ordinary butane lighter and passed it to each person in turn around the circle.[1] The tobacco was harsh and burned my lungs. I dared not cough. We all sat in reverent silence in the lingering twilight as the sun slipped beneath the horizon. I imagined the spirits of ancient warriors dancing to Manning's rhythm in the shadows just beyond the sagebrush behind me.

Members of the Shoshone-Paiute tribes of the Duck Valley Indian Reservation and their guests gather for a religious ceremony at a site they hold sacred on Dickshooter Ridge deep in the wild of Idaho's Owyhee County. *Author photo*

Dickshooter Ridge from a distance. *Author photo*

On this September evening in 1993 a battle loomed. A group of Shoshone-Paiutes from the Duck Valley Indian Reservation on the Idaho-Nevada border and a few guests were gathered at the butte the Indians considered sacred in the wild, forbidding, and starkly beautiful heart of the Owyhee River canyon country in the southwest corner of Idaho. They had come to seek help from the spirits of their ancestors— some of whom were buried at the base of the butte—in their continuing struggle against the U.S. Air Force and the state of Idaho. In the 1990s the Air Force tried to turn part of southwestern Idaho into a live-fire bombing range to expand training operations for fighter pilots from the Mountain Home Air Force Base. As part of a three-million acre electronic battlefield, state officials were proposing the Air Force include the butte where I witnessed the ceremony.

I had come to write about how the range expansion plans would affect the Shoshone-Paiutes and the area they considered sacred. The range expansion story was one I had covered through a decade of public controversy. At stake was a vast, wild, windblown landscape, part of the largest area in the lower forty-eight states without a paved road.[2] Mostly public land managed by the federal Bureau of Land Management, it extended about sixty miles into northern Nevada, and well into eastern Oregon. The rugged river canyons stretched from the Bruneau-Jarbidge River of eastern Owyhee County and included the South Fork and East Fork of the Owyhee River, Battle Creek and Deep Creek, the Jacks Creek area, and other smaller tributary streams. The canyons provided some of the best wildlife habitat in southern Idaho, and to those who have seen them, they are some of the most dramatic in the country. Some have called the area the Big Quiet, others have called it America's Outback.

The Shoshone-Paiutes did not just rely on the help of their ancestors, but they joined a coalition of ranchers, conservationists, hunters, recreationists, and naturalists—factions not usually on the same side of most land use issues. Each group had its own reasons for opposing the bombing range expansion, but put their differences aside and agreed to work together to protect the thing they all had in common—the land. The coalition included former military fliers who exposed Pentagon misinformation and interpreted military jargon, and wildlife biologists who explained the importance of the varied habitats in the canyon lands.

The story of this struggle taught an important lesson. People with varied interests learned that protecting areas they valued sometimes required setting aside differences, and it depended on collaboration, compromise, and consideration for those who made their living from the land. It happened in Idaho, but it could have been anywhere. It mattered little whether those places were wilderness or places where three-week river trips were possible in canyons that still looked much like they did before white settlers moved here. Or whether they were places with treasure troves of ancient rock art, herds of elk, deer, pronghorn, and highly prized bighorn sheep, historic artifacts, intact stands of native plants, solitude, and silence; or where the warm summer wind carried the sweet, pungent smell of sagebrush. It mattered only that people who cared for the landscape, for different reasons, agreed to work together to protect those values.

The attention the coalition focused on this remote corner of southwestern Idaho eventually helped resolve some long standing public land-use issues. Their resolution led to protection for significant portions of the Owyhee River canyon lands with historical, cultural, and natural significance, and the designation of half a million acres of wilderness and nearly four hundred miles of stunning scenery protected as Wild and Scenic Rivers. The ancient spirits of the Shoshone-Paiutes may have helped as well. (See #3 on map, page 24.)

America's outback is well worth protecting. From 25,000 feet, lying in the boom pod under the tail of an Air Force KC-135 aerial tanker, Owyhee County looked to me like a topographical map. The canyons showed up clearly, most roads were faint or invisible, and there were no towns to be seen. From that altitude, one gets a perspective of the scale of this wild landscape. There are still only three paved roads in this five-million-acre county. U.S. 95 cuts the northwestern corner, State Highway 78 runs along the northern edge of the county near the Snake River from Bruneau to Homedale, and Highway 51 runs south from the Snake River to the Duck Valley Indian Reservation, roughly bisecting the county. None of them take you into the canyon lands, where the only roads are gravel or dirt, many are rough and rocky, and some are mud.

It requires determination and the right kind of vehicle to get into this outback. The main road into the northern part turns south off Highway 78 outside the town of Grandview on the Snake River. Where the farmlands end, Mud Flat Road turns to gravel and winds up an escarpment

The East Fork of the Owyhee River winds through a scenic canyon that harbors native wildlife. *Author photo*

and out onto a lava-rock-studded plain at about five thousand feet elevation. Up here, vague tracks cross the landscape that stretches to seemingly endless space. No fences, no power lines, just the rugged rolling sagebrush grassland, dotted with occasional juniper trees. Native grasses, shrubs, and wild flowers still grow here. This wild unfettered land, with few signs of human intrusion, a vast wilderness only barely accessible by motor vehicle, has remained an undiscovered national treasure. Most who roam this outback come for the isolation and solitude, and it is isolated for good reason. Rains turn the dirt to gumbo that is as sticky as it is slick on the rough two-track roads that barely qualify as jeep trails, and are impassible after a summer thunder storm or the spring snowmelt.

All is not as flat and empty as it seems. Below the line of sight, in this seemingly endless rolling sea of sagebrush, the East Fork of the Owyhee River cuts a ragged gash hundreds of feet deep across the landscape. At the base of sheer rock walls, the river winds through lush meadows that provide habitat for wildlife, and it all looks much as it did when the Shoshone-Paiute's ancestors were the only human inhabitants here. The country's largest herd of California bighorn sheep introduced in 1963 by Idaho Fish and Game biologists thrive in the canyons, and birds of prey soar on thermal updrafts. On most days, all you hear is the wind and your own heartbeat.

The region's violent geologic past, written in those canyon walls, belies the tranquility found there today. About seventeen million years ago a meteorite slammed into what is now southeastern Oregon. It exploded with such violence that the resulting crater cut into the hot rock of the earth's upper mantle just below the continental crust, creating a hot spot. Lava flowed from the open wound, forming what are now the Columbia and the Owyhee plateaus. Over time the drift of continental rock slowly moved to the southwest, covering the hot spot and creating a string of progressively younger volcanoes in a nearly straight line ending under what is now Yellowstone National Park.[3]

By ten thousand years ago, lava, water, wind, rain, cold, and searing heat had sculpted the features of the Owyhee Plateau. Ancient lava flows dammed up huge Lake Idaho, and when it began to drain, the rushing water cut Hells Canyon of the Snake River. As the lake drained, other streams and rivers, including the Owyhee River, its forks and tributaries, and the Bruneau and Jarbidge Rivers to the east, cut deeper into the

Owyhee Plateau. Erosion excavated canyons to their present depths.[4] The South and East Forks of the Owyhee drain the mountains of northern Nevada, and join and flow into Oregon and north into the Snake River.

Humans have lived on the Owyhee Plateau since the last glaciers receded, perhaps longer. They have left abundant evidence of their presence, including rock shelters, hunting blinds, and stone chips from making arrowheads. Archeologists have dated sites north of the East Fork as much as six thousand years old, but the most active sites are from eight hundred to fourteen hundred years ago.[5] In winter, ancient inhabitants camped in the drainages of the Owyhee River and its tributaries. In spring, summer, and fall they camped in creek bottoms farther north. The harsh, remote landscape offered solitude for vision quests, spiritual outings, and ceremonies, as well as refuge in times of war, and later, from the persecution of invading settlers.

As hunter-gatherers, the people had to keep on the move to gather what the land had to offer in each season. In late winter they found fresh green thistle or squaw cabbage around springs. They gathered seeds of fescue, wheatgrass, Indian rice grass, bluegrass, cattail, rushes, and sunflowers. They winnowed the seeds in broad, flat baskets, ground them into flour, and added water to make a mush. They also stored seeds in pits, baskets, and caves near their winter villages. In the summer, they gathered berries and the bulbs of camas lily as well as arrowroot, wild onions, and wild carrots in moist areas near springs. As winter approached, with freezing winds and deep, driven snow, they moved to protected villages in the canyons. The native plants provided inhabitants with more than just food. They made bows and atlatls from the wood of serviceberry and juniper trees. They carried water in small, tightly woven baskets sealed with pitch. From tough, stringy sagebrush bark, they made bags, blankets, ropes, and sandals, and they mixed various plants for poisons and medicines.

The ancient inhabitants fished and hunted. They caught wild salmon that once ran up the rivers that laced the canyons. Deer, antelope, bighorn sheep, and other animals provided meat year-round. Large complexes of hunting blinds and rock walls were located near major campsites, which in turn were located near major root crops. Some used dogs to herd antelope into corrals. They used traps, nets, and clubs to hunt rabbits, birds, rodents, rock chucks, and other smaller game. Their diet also included caterpillars, larval bees, ants, and other insects.

Many refer to the Owyhee highlands as a desert, but it is really a sagebrush grassland or steppe, and is one of the few areas where native vegetation in good condition still exists. Though precipitation, mostly snow, is limited to five to six inches annually, about seven hundred species of grasses, flowering plants, shrubs, and trees are found here. Wyoming big sagebrush dominates grasslands that include bluebunch grass, Idaho fescue, and Thurber needlegrass. Western juniper is found at the highest elevation. Some ridges and hilltops are dominated by mountain mahogany. The shallow soil of windy ridges supports the low black sagebrush community important to pronghorn, and includes bottlebrush, squirrel tail, Idaho fescue, and bluebunch grasses. Sagebrush, old junipers, and groves of curl-leaf mountain mahogany provide important forage for deer. Aspen communities thrive in areas with more precipitation or near springs, on north-facing slopes, and in canyon bottoms. Between the sagebrush and the aspen grow native shrubs and grasses along with serviceberry, mountain snow berry, wild rose, and chokecherry. On the ground beneath the plants over much of the sagebrush steppe a cryptogamic crust made up of algae and lichens covers the soil, protecting it from wind and water erosion.

The uplands also are rich in puzzling, human-made rock features. Some appear to be ancient hunting blinds, and some may have been used in rituals or in vision quests. Lindsey Manning, the Shoshone-Paiute tribal chairman, demonstrated one of the blinds for me. When he sat down, just his head and shoulders were visible above the wall. The rock walls would have been topped with sagebrush or juniper limbs stuck in the rocks to hide the hunter until the game was driven into easy range.

In addition to the rock structures, the uplands feature rock petroglyphs and pictographs. On rocks near camps, archeologists have found petroglyphs that included circles, human figures, bird tracks, ladders, rain symbols, zigzag lines, and stars. Archeologists, professional as well as amateur, have found stone arrowheads, leaf-shaped knives, milling stones, and large spear points. Descendants of those ancient inhabitants still hunt in the sagebrush steppe.

◆

When European trappers first arrived in the area, Northern Paiute and Western Shoshone inhabited the Owyhee Plateau. In the early 1800s,

British fur trappers were the first to explore southwestern Idaho. American fur trappers soon followed. The word Owyhee is attributed to a mispronunciation of Hawaii. The area was named for three Hawaiians who worked for John Jacob Astor's Pacific Fur Company, and who disappeared in 1819 while trapping beaver on the Owyhee River. One was discovered dead in camp, but the remains of the other two were never found.[6]

In the mid-1800s, southern Owyhee County was still largely unexplored. The area was known only as godforsaken country to the immigrants passing through along the Snake River on the harder but shorter southern alternative of the Oregon Trail. Then in May 1863 prospectors found gold in Jordan Creek in the Owyhee Mountains. On December 31 of that year, Owyhee County was officially established by the Territorial Legislature. Gold and the demand for cattle to feed the miners brought white settlers into Owyhee County. Cattleman Cornelius Shea is credited with bringing the first herd of cattle to Idaho in 1866. More herds trailed up from Texas, and as many as a hundred thousand head roamed Owyhee County before the killing winter of 1888.[7]

The gold mines rivaled the Comstock Lode in Nevada, and a monument to the mining activity that flourished in the Owyhee Mountains still stands. Silver City, "Queen of the Owyhees," established in 1866 by gold miners at the head of Jordan Creek, became the county seat. Perched in a narrow valley at six thousand feet at the end of thirty miles of twisting, hairpin roads, the city depended upon ten- to twelve-horse teams to bring in tons of supplies and to haul the pay dirt back down. In its heyday, the town included six general stores, two hardware stores, a tin shop, two meat markets, two hotels, four restaurants, a brewery and bottling plant, eight saloons, three barbershops, plus a jeweler, a photographer, a tailor, four lawyers, two doctors, and a newspaper.[8] In winter freezing winds heaped drifts of snow deep enough to bury the entire town.

Invading miners, ranchers, and other settlers fought the Indians, who defended their homeland. The residents of Silver City took matters into their own hands, despite a treaty between the United States and the local Indians. A group of residents gathered donations of money, provisions, arms, and horses. Twenty-five men were appointed to hunt Indians, and bounties were set on Indian scalps: $100 for each man, $50 for each woman, and $25 for any Indian under 12 years old.[9] Penniless immigrants were outfitted with horses, rifles, and supplies and sent out in pursuit of Indian scalps. The cost of the equipment was deducted from the bounty on whatever scalps they brought back, but many of the "Owyhee Volunteers" were ill equipped. Stockmen failed to provide the promised horses and supplies, and the Indians were elusive as they sought refuge in the rugged terrain and the canyons along the Owyhee River's East Fork.

At the butte where we gathered in 1993, the ancestors of present-day Shoshone-Paiutes held off and defeated a group of armed volunteers from Silver City in 1866. The place is known to the Indians as *Sihwiyo*, which means "willows growing in a row," and white people know it as Dickshooter Ridge. The Indians were camped in a box canyon at the foot of the butte, repairing equipment and gathering wild roots. A group of volunteers came riding from the west and started shooting. Some of the Indians held them off while the rest of the group took cover in the rocks. They held off the soldiers until nightfall and then set an ambush. They left a trail to water in the canyon and positioned themselves to keep the volunteers from the water. The plan worked. The volunteers, some of them wounded, tried for five days to get to the water and finally gave up and went back to Silver City. The Indians buried their dead, and they too left.[10]

Generations of indigenous people have come to this revered site to pray to the spirits of their ancestors. Benson Gibson, the late tribal chairman of the Duck Valley Shoshone-Paiute Tribe, said of the butte, "I went out into this country with my grandfather for a vision quest in the 1930s. This area is where my people get their medicine."[11] Today Indians still camp here to mend their equipment and gather the plentiful nutritious roots.

The Indians were eventually herded onto what became the Duck Valley Reservation. Established April 16, 1877, it straddles the Nevada-Idaho border.[12] Following their release from captivity at the Yakima Reservation in Washington in the mid-1880s, a group of Northern Paiutes jointed the Western Shoshone already in Duck Valley. Other Shoshone and Paiute tribal members moved to the reservation between 1880 and the early 1900s. In 2010, about thirteen-hundred people lived on the reservation and made their living mostly from ranching and farming.[13] The Owyhee River's East Fork meanders through the reservation, providing water for irrigation. Expansive wetlands provide habitat for many types of waterfowl, especially the ducks that gave the valley its name.

As the twilight faded to black on that September 1993 evening, we clambered down from the butte. The mood was one of reverent awe. Everyone seemed introspective and spoke quietly, if at all. We still faced a ten-mile, bone-jarring ride back to camp in the dark. I bounced along in the back of a stiff-sprung four-wheel-drive pickup, so rough I was unable to speak, much less take notes. We got back to the camp on Battle Creek about midnight, where in the thin, dry air at about six thousand feet elevation and no city lights to compete, the Milky Way sparkled across the sky.

In the 1990s, the Shoshone-Paiutes were fighting for this land again, but this time as part of a coalition. Since 1984, the Air Force had been working quietly on expanding pilot training facilities at the existing 100,000-acre Saylor Creek Bombing Range. The range in the eastern half of Owyhee County, about thirty miles south of Mountain Home, was established in 1943 to train World War II bomber crews. The public first heard about the expansion plans in late 1988 when word leaked out about a proposal for a 1.5 million-acre bombing range and military airspace changes to allow low-level supersonic operations. Pentagon officials said the range was inadequate for training pilots of modern fighter-bombers. Though the expansion was still only a proposal, officials had told Congress that the range had been expanded recently to allow the Air Force to move a wing of fighter jets to Idaho. Later those same officials told the public in Idaho that the proposed expansion was necessary because Congress had approved the transfer of aging Vietnam-era F-4 Phantom fighter jets to Idaho. Military planners at the Pentagon had looked at a map of Idaho and saw nothing in the southwestern corner, and they assumed there would be little public opposition to their proposed bombing range expansion. They were wrong. Public opposition—not just from the Shoshone-Paiute but from others including politically powerful ranchers who ran their livestock on some of the best year-round grazing on the public lands that would be affected by the proposed expansion—beat the Air Force back.

Randall Brewer was one of those ranchers and a member of the National Cattlemen's Public Lands Council. One day I rode with him to his Devil Creek Ranch. The Bruneau-Three Creek Desert Road runs from the town of Bruneau south to ranches in the southeast corner of the county, right through the 1.5 million acres the Air Force wanted for its bombing range expansion. Over forty miles of dusty, kidney-pounding gravel road, we talked as we rattled south toward Brewer's ranch near the Nevada border. He was one of sixty-four ranchers who altogether ran about 14,500 cows and 11,000 sheep on these public grazing lands. Out here in the lower flat lands where the snow melted early, Brewer's cows gave birth and fed on spring grasses. As the higher pastures greened, he moved his cattle up into the ten-thousand foot Jarbidge Mountains of northern Nevada.[14]

Brewer's opposition to the Air Force bombing range expansion started when he met Mountain Home dentist Randy Morris. Morris had been involved for many years in efforts to protect the stunning canyons of Owyhee County, including a proposal to create a national park. When he heard about the Air Force proposal, he arranged a meeting in August 1988 that brought together environmentalists and ranchers, including Brewer, who remarked on the irony of the two factions sitting in the same room on the same side of a public land issue. Brewer and Morris shook hands, effectively launching the coalition that eventually included not just ranchers and environmentalists but also the Shoshone-Paiutes, hunters, hikers, bird watchers, canoeists, and private pilots. The diversity of the coalition gave it political credibility and power—enough to defeat the Air Force proposal.[15]

Victory celebrations, however, were premature. When the Saylor Creek bombing range expansion proposal failed, Idaho's governor, the late Cecil D. Andrus, who said he had the state's economic interest in the Mountain Home Air Force Base in mind, proposed assembling state lands through trades with the BLM to provide the Air Force with another site. That site centered on Dickshooter Ridge, and that got the Shoshone-Paiutes more intimately involved. The new proposal included a 160,000-acre range with two bomb impact areas, but with no live ordnance. It would include the existing Saylor Creek Bombing Range and a three-million-acre electronic battlefield with more than thirty widely scattered sites for mobile electronic enemy air defense simulators in between. Supersonic flights would be allowed above ten thousand feet, generating an average of three hundred sonic booms a month.[16]

In late 1991 opponents of the new proposal included many foes of the earlier range proposal. Their concerns included the effects of the range on 58,700 acres of proposed wilderness, 11,000 acres of critical mule deer winter range, 21,000 acres of prime pronghorn winter range, 22,000 acres of sage-grouse winter habitat, 44 miles of proposed Wild and Scenic Rivers, and 15 river miles of bald eagle winter habitat.[17] In response, state officials proposed moving part of the range operations, including one of the bomb impact areas, south of the East Fork to avoid some of the most sensitive areas.

One summer day, on a ride with a river outfitter scouting for a new take-out spot, I had a first-hand look at the landscape that would be affected. For a number of years Phil Lansing found his livelihood at the base of the canyons' near-vertical basalt cliffs. He had an outfitting permit for eight canoe trips a year on the Owyhee's East Fork. There is enough wild river here to accommodate a twenty-two-day canoe trip. The only other place in the country where that's possible is in the Grand Canyon. "The best way to see these canyons is from a canoe," Lansing told me. "This really is the outback, you know."[18] With a compass and a USGS topographic map balanced in my lap, I navigated as he drove, but the few landmarks in this trackless sagebrush steppe made it difficult to get a compass sighting. One patch of sagebrush looked pretty much like any other, but I could pick out a few high spots that correlated with the map.

After a couple of hours of bouncing through sagebrush, Lansing stopped the Suburban where the tracks faded out at the head of Stove Draw and an old wagon road led down into the canyon. Summer rains had washed out the old track, and the only way down was on foot. We picked our way over talus piles and rock outcrops. About eight hundred feet down, the draw opened into the main canyon. A sheer ocher wall rose on the other side of the river, and its reflection turned the water gold. On the flats along the river we found the stone walls of an old homestead, or perhaps an old line shack, a place of refuge for cowboys far from the home ranch. The tall, thick grass had not seen a bovine for years. Trash littered the burned out cabin and testified to the passers-by—hikers, hunters, or canoeists—who sought occasional refuge here.

We were now at the site where in 1963, Idaho Fish and Game biologists released a group of nineteen California bighorn sheep. Bighorns are commonly depicted in the ancient petroglyhs in the area. Historically abundant in most of the Owyhee River canyons, by the late nineteenth century, they were all but wiped out by unrestricted hunting and disease transmitted from domestic sheep.[19] The bighorns released in 1963 were the first of a group of thirty-eight sheep from the Chilcotin River in British Columbia, a gift from the Canadian government.[20] When biologists left them in a temporary corral overnight to help them acclimate, they kicked it down. Later groups, nine in 1965 and ten in 1966, were simply released from trucks and trailers on the canyon rim and left to make their own way down into the canyon. Since then the herds have flourished in these remote canyons, and now comprise the largest population of California bighorns in the country. Hunters today pay thousands of dollars in an annual auction for a chance to hunt prize bighorn rams in these canyons. The herds became so numerous that in the late 1980s and early 1990s, Idaho Fish and Game trapped forty to sixty sheep annually, some years as many as a hundred, and transplanted them to other places where they once thrived.[21]

As Lansing and I made our way back out of the canyon, I saw signs of sage-grouse. There lay a single egg, olive colored with small brown dots, in a grass-lined depression under a sagebrush. It was cold, and the mother sage-grouse was nowhere to be seen. I wondered if our steps had disturbed her and if she would return to her nest. Much of the area is important sage-grouse habitat.

Back in the Suburban, Lansing and I followed a drift fence, designed to encourage domestic cattle to move in a certain direction to better exploit the scarce forage here. We followed it for what seemed like twenty miles. The area we traversed was accessible only to four-wheel-drive, high-clearance vehicles on rough tracks marked as jeep trails on the USGS map. In the canyons, bighorn sheep found refuge from hard winters and in the spring gave birth to their young. They fed on the early grasses above the canyon rims. Out on the flats mothers could keep a wary eye and spot predators in plenty of time to hustle the young to safety in the rocks below. We also passed high desert water holes vital for migrating shorebirds that stopped on their way to and from breeding grounds in the Arctic.

After another hour or so, we stopped at the edge of the canyon and looked down on a ranch with a few cows grazing in a pasture below us. The 45 Ranch is nestled in a wide spot along the South Fork of the Owyhee River; it is the most remote full-time residence in this rugged empty land where Idaho, Nevada, and Oregon meet. When the road is in good shape, it takes more than two hours to drive the sixty miles to the nearest town, and after a rain storm, the road can be nearly impassable in places. It is about five hours to Boise. Drifting snow and bad roads keep most people from overwintering in this country, but not everyone. Lansing wanted to talk to the ranch manager about permission to cross the ranch for canoe trip take-outs.

This rugged, remote place is stunningly beautiful. From the metal gate on the canyon rim, a set of hairpin turns barely wide enough for the Suburban to navigate dropped about eight hundred feet to the ranch. The house was decorated with Western memorabilia, including old riding gear, rusty leg-hold traps, and an antique rifle. Standing beside the house, a television satellite dish brought the twenty-first century to this remote corner of Idaho that otherwise had not changed much over the past century. The ranch's livestock spent most of the year grazing on the surrounding public lands. Water drawn from the river irrigated several hundred acres of hay. The sigh of wind in the poplars and the gurgle of the nearby South Fork underscored the quiet. Ranch manager Lester Hatch had moved his wife and their seven children here to run the 45 for the absentee owner. He said he liked the isolation.

It was indeed remote and therefore in danger from the modern world. The state's revised proposal would bring training aircraft closer to the ranch and the public grazing lands it relied on. The ranchers, whose operations on the opposite side of the county would have been affected by the Air Force's original Saylor Creek expansion, welcomed Governor Andrus' proposal to move the range to the Dickshooter Ridge. Livestock grazing on Dickshooter was less productive and available only part of the year. Some ranchers here even offered to sell their private holdings. The state's so-called "split-range" proposal drew opposition as more people became aware of the resources that would be at risk. In addition, BLM officials still had lingering concerns about how the range would affect the Shoshone-Paiutes' religious ceremonies. The issue made its way to the White House and the Secretary of the Interior. Members of Congress questioned the need for the range, and things began to unravel. In May 1995 the Air Force dropped the proposal. Everyone thought it was over, and opponents though they had won.

The Air Force, however, still had something up its sleeve. Later in 1995, officials announced yet another proposal, developed behind closed doors, in the same location as the original Saylor Creek range expansion, but smaller in scope and again without live ordnance. It would include a site for practice bombs, simulated target areas, and electronic emitter sites. The proposal included supersonic flights above ten thousand feet and a million-acre electronic combat range in the eastern half of Owyhee County east of Highway 51.[22]

The coalition and the public still had concerns over wildlife and recreation, as well as the Shoshone-Paiute cultural and religious sites. The Air Force had failed to show a need for the expansion that many people feared would put the area's natural values at risk. The Shoshone-Paiutes, however, settled with the Air Force on condition there would be no flights below ten thousand feet over the reservation, and no flights within five miles of the town of Owyhee in Nevada.[23] The BLM and the Air Force agreed to negotiate their differences.

Powers that be, however, were becoming impatient. In 1998 U.S. Senator Dirk Kempthorne of Idaho, who later would become governor, side-stepped the entire public process by introducing a rider to the 1999 Defense Authorization Bill that would create the range. The rider also bought off a prominent rancher, Bert Brackett, now a state senator, whose BLM public land grazing allotment would be used as a target area. Despite public opposition, Congress passed it and President Bill Clinton signed it on October 17, 1998.[24]

The Air Force appeared to have its range, though several legal issues from earlier challenges remained unresolved. Rather than fight it out in court, the two sides agreed to negotiate a settlement. On July 9, 1999, after three days of intense negotiations, they reached an agreement. After fifteen years, the Air Force had its long-sought electronic combat range. Opponents were unable to block the range, which still brought fighter jets into the airspace above Owyhee County. Their cooperative effort did, however, get some meaningful concessions in restrictions that might help protect wildlife, recreation, ranchers, and places sacred to the Shoshone-

Paiutes, who can still gather peacefully at *Sihwiyo* and call on the spirits of their ancestors and find places for their vision quests.

Even as the loose ends were being tied up, other issues came to light. Years of controversy and many public hearings focused attention on the stunning landscape that few but the locals knew about. Increasing recreational use in the area brought new concerns, including reckless off-road vehicle use, looting of archeological sites, spread of cheatgrass, and increased risk of wildfire. It also brought attention to long-standing conflicts over poor grazing practices, proposed wilderness, and other efforts to protect the area.

In the late 1970s, a group known as the Committee for Idaho's High Desert tried to interest the federal government and state officials in creating a national park in the Owyhee River canyon lands.[25] Over the years, BLM officials have recommended many of the creeks and rivers in the area for protection under the federal Wild and Scenic Rivers Act, and the agency has proposed many thousands of acres as wilderness. Officials also have considered designating large portions as national conservation areas to protect the nationally significant recreational, scenic, geological, historic, cultural, and wildlife values. Those ideas mostly went nowhere.

In 2000 conservationists asked the Clinton administration for help. They sought protection for 2.7 million acres of southwest Owyhee County, more than half the county, as a national monument under the Antiquities Act of 1906. The proposal included everything from the Bruneau and Jarbidge Rivers west to the Oregon border, and from the Nevada border north to just south of Highway 78, essentially the mostly uninhabited part of the county. The proposal included more than 700,000 acres already identified as potential wilderness and 288 miles of streams recommended for Wild and Scenic River status.[26]

Lessons learned in the earlier struggles to protect the Owyhee canyon lands were not forgotten. In response to the national monument proposal and the growing interest and recreational use, the Owyhee County Commission in 2001 organized environmentalists, ranchers, Air Force officials, outfitters and others, and most of the earlier coalition members, into a collaborative group known as the Owyhee Initiative. The potential monument designation put pressure on the commissioners and ranchers, who mistakenly feared it would ban grazing, to reach an agreement and to seek federal legislation instead of the monument status. U.S. Senator Mike Crapo agreed to help. Ranchers wanted a plan that protected grazing and conservationists wanted one that protected natural, cultural, and geologic values.[27] Ranchers agreed to support wilderness designations if they could keep their livestock water tanks and fences and continue existing livestock management practices. Conservationists knew that wilderness designations would be unlikely without the support of ranchers. The resulting compromise paved the way to an agreement.

Those involved sorted through the various land-use issues. These included wild and scenic river designations, landscape conservation, livestock grazing, fish and game management, military training, off-road vehicle and recreational uses, and other activities. Field trips and flights over the spectacular canyons took Owyhee Initiative participants and congressional staff members to look at grazing practices and potential wilderness areas. After several years of give and take, compromises were haggled out and a resolution took shape.[28] In early 2009, Senator Crapo, an Idaho Republican, introduced the Owyhee Initiative Implementation Act in Congress to provide the legal basis for the agreement. President Barack Obama signed it in March 2009.

The resulting legislation, part of a larger land management bill, was comprehensive. It designated 517,000 acres as wilderness, including 55,000 acres that would be closed to livestock grazing, protected 384 miles of Wild and Scenic Rivers, closed 200 miles of motorized trails in candidate wilderness areas, and launched a travel planning process to establish a designated system of motorized routes for all public lands in Owyhee County. In addition, the agreement improved regulation and enforcement of illegal off-road vehicle use and increased protection for Shoshone-Paiute cultural sites and resources. Furthermore, roads were opened across private lands to improve public access to the public lands beyond, and the act released about 250,000 acres of wilderness study areas for other uses. The result resolved some long-standing conflicts, but at a cost.

Not all interests were included in the discussion, and that angered some. Critics raised questions about county officials dictating uses of federal lands that belong to everyone, even people who opposed the subsidized grazing on most western public lands and people who live far from

Idaho. Others objected to the wilderness compromise. They argued that livestock do not belong in the fragile sagebrush grasslands and threaten water quality and wildlife habitat. They also objected to provisions in the agreement that allowed ranchers to continue using existing livestock management practices, including using motorized vehicles to herd livestock within designated wilderness areas. They argued that public money subsidized the damage to the land from domestic livestock grazing and to the integrity of wilderness.

Federal land management laws require the BLM to protect values other than grazing. The agency must also protect watersheds and water quality, wildlife habitat and aesthetics, and cultural and historic resources. Sometimes that requires the BLM to place restrictions on destructive or potentially destructive practices on public lands, such as grazing, mining, and logging, to protect the interests of all Americans, the ultimate owners of the land. More important, as a result of years of work, willingness to set aside differences, to collaborate, and to compromise, these canyons now have some protection.

———————◆———————

One day in the spring of 2015, I ventured by truck to one of the areas protected as wilderness by the 2009 Owyhee Initiative. From the 45 Ranch, a dirt track forded the South Fork of the Owyhee River. A steep, rough road the width of a bulldozer blade climbed out of the canyon onto the sagebrush flats above and followed the boundary of the Owyhee River Wilderness. After about two hours of dust and rocks, a vague trailhead appeared where we parked. The 360-degree view showed no sign of human presence to the horizon. From there it was a two-hour hike to the rim and down about seven hundred feet to a wide spot in the canyon and a gravel bank on the west side of the South Fork. A hundred years or so earlier, Basque herders had camped on the east side of the river here and kept a small herd of bulls during the winter, hence the name Bull Camp. The remains of two stone cabins still stood east of the river. In later years, infamous outlaw poacher Claude Dallas made his camp here on the west side of the river. In January 1981, Dallas gunned down two game wardens, Bill Pogue and Conley Elms of Idaho Fish and Game, who had come to confront him over illegally trapping bobcats. It was a long hot and dusty hike back out of the canyon to the vehicle, stopping to admire the expansive views across a stark and empty landscape. Yet on the way back to civilization, I heard two F-15 fighter jets dueling in the sky above the 45 Ranch.

———————◆———————

Thanks to all who cooperated and compromised, the Owyhee River canyon lands still belong to the wildlife, and still deserve reverence. Here anyone can find solitude, humility, and in a good water year, a decent, long canoe trip. It remains profoundly quiet, a place of inspiration, a place that can focus the mind and renew the spirit, a place where ancient warriors still whisper in the wind.

Conclusion

One day in the late 1990s, I came upon a set of big paw prints that crossed deep snow covering a meadow along Big Smoky Creek in the Soldier Mountains of central Idaho. Nearby the remains of an elk calf—hooves, some scraps of hide and tufts of hair, part of a jawbone— lay scattered in the blood-stained snow. The evidence of a life-and-death struggle written in the churned up snow provided mute testimony that the gray wolf once again roamed the Northern Rocky Mountains.

The return of the wolf has brought changes to the Northern Rockies ecosystem. The presence of wolves keeps prey species on the move. Elk and deer no longer concentrate their grazing. The change has allowed more shrubs, willows, and young aspens to grow, increasing age diversity of aspen stands. That in turn has benefitted song birds that depend on the aspen, and they have increased in number and diversity. Beavers, which also depend on aspens in many areas, have expanded their territory and increased in numbers, which in turn has benefitted native fish species that depend on beaver ponds, which in places also raise the local water table. Wolves do not tolerate coyotes much, and their return has brought a decrease in the number of coyotes, allowing many other small animal populations to increase. Those small animals in turn are prey for hawks and owls and small predators, such as weasels, foxes, and lynx.

Wolves have also brought secondary benefits to a variety of other species. Eagles, ravens, and bears, for example, scavenge on wolf kills. By preying on weakened animals, wolves may also stop or slow the spread of chronic wasting disease, a fatal brain disease related to scrapie and mad cow disease, which affects deer, elk, moose, and reindeer but not wolves. Granted, hunters may not find big game animals where they once did, and they may have to look harder to find them or look for new hunting grounds. Even so, over the years elk numbers, for instance, have stabilized, and in spite of the presence of wolves, have increased in some areas where the habitat can support them. Their recovery in the Northern Rockies embodies the concept of thinking like a mountain.

In these eleven chapters I have presented evidence that supports an argument for "thinking like a mountain." The thread that runs through all of them is a set of values and actions that reflect a respect for nature. The issues are not limited to the Northwest, though that is my focus; more importantly, however, they are all connected. As nineteenth-century geographer and naturalist Alexander von Humboldt argued, the threads that make up the web of life all are interconnected, and pulling on one affects them all.[1]

Naturalist E.O. Wilson has pointed out that the main reason species have disappeared and continue to disappear is the loss of habitat.[2] For the long-term benefit to all life on the planet, the choices that preserve habitat, that give us clean air and water, allow salmon to spawn naturally, forests to thrive, and wolves to run free, are preferred. After all, we too depend on the natural world; it's where we live. We all breathe the air, drink the water. Clearly it profits us all if we respect the balance of nature.

To be sure, these issues deal with conflicting values. To resolve such conflicts we might think like the mountain. We can generate some of our electricity by alternative sources, like wind turbines or solar panels, instead of hydroelectric dams or coal-fired power plants in order to nurture landscapes that contain wild salmon runs and support a system of rivers and mountains, forests, farms, deserts, and people that all work together. We can produce commodities responsibly from public and private lands while still protecting the flora and fauna of the western sagebrush steppe, ancient forests, and allowing an endangered top predator in the Northern Rocky Mountains to recover its natural role in the ecosystem. With reasonable zoning restrictions on residential development and fire-safe building codes, we can accommodate human residents in fire-prone forests and still allow fire to play its natural role. Through limited and appropriate uses of public lands, we can raise food for ourselves and still nurture the sagebrush landscape and maintain a stable population of sage grouse and more than three hundred other animal species. We can, if we consider the long-term consequences of our actions, maintain the balance of nature in ways that include us.

These are some of the issues that face us as the owners of those 673 million acres we call public lands. Of course, private lands are also affected by the same conflicts. Individuals are affected differently by these issues, varying with the source of their livelihoods. Still, none of us can escape the limits of the resources available on this little planet, and there are appropriate places for most uses and activities. Some might argue that human needs or values must always take precedence, and they typically value resource uses or extraction at the expense of other values. I would urge them to work with nature, not against it, for nature does not respect our human values.

I am by nature drawn to derelicts, things that have outlived their practical usefulness like old dogs, land that has been allowed to return to its natural state, and the underdogs of nature. I hope to speak for those who cannot speak for themselves. I am cognizant of the needs of people, but also see beyond them to the landscape that supports us all, a landscape that, in the words of Percy Bysshe Shelley, "may be untainted by the misery of man."[3] It is all too obvious when the land is touched by the unseen hand of powers interested only in what can be extracted from it in the pursuit of individual profit. When public resources are put at risk under such circumstances, the public interest and the long-term interests of the landscape must weigh more heavily.

The public interest includes a broad array of users who depend on those same healthy forests, rivers, and grasslands on public lands. They include hunters and anglers, who depend on healthy wildlife habitat and rivers, lakes, and streams; hikers and river runners, who appreciate the beauty and solitude that can still be found on public lands in many places; campers, picnickers, and park visitors, who find respite from their daily stress; the indigenous people of the Northwest who have depended on the salmon in Northwest rivers and streams for ten thousand years; and those who just plain enjoy the outdoors for its own sake, like the magic of star-filled night reflecting in a placid mountain lake while floating in a canoe as if suspended in space. They also include the thousands of people who cater to these users, selling hunting and fishing licenses, equipment, food and fuel, and all those who know it is out there and are willing to pay taxes to support the continued existence of these resources. Thinking like a mountain means recognizing that nature's bounty is far more than a commodity having only a cash value, and using resources wisely and efficiently to meet our needs—not trying to take all we can get, but getting the most out of what we take.

To paraphrase Inupiat elders in northern Alaska, when the oil or the gas is gone, when the trees have all been cut, when only hatchery fish return to the Columbia River system, what is left? The landscape may remain, in most cases, but it is the poorer. The answer, of course, reflects our relationship to nature and how we view the resources on which we all rely. When we think like a mountain, we will have clean air and water, forests will thrive, wild salmon will spawn naturally and make thousand-mile journeys to their natal streams, sage grouse will strut their stuff on their leks in the western sagebrush grasslands, and the wild green fire will burn in the eyes of the wolf—and that benefits us all.

Notes

PREFACE

1. Aldo Leopold, *A Sand County Almanac, and Sketches Here and There,* Special Commemorative ed. (New York: Oxford University Press, 1989), 130.
2. Billy Frank Jr., "The Life and Legacy of Billy Frank Jr.," billyfrankjr.org.
3. Garrett Hardin, "The Tragedy of the Commons," *Science* 162, no. 3859 (December 13, 1968):1243–48.
4. Edward O. Wilson, "The Global Solution to Extinction," Opinion, *New York Times,* March 13, 2016.
5. Wilson, "The Global Solution to Extinction."
6. Wilson, "The Global Solution to Extinction."
7. Fairfield Osborn, *Our Plundered Planet* (Boston: Little, Brown and Company, 1948).
8. Leopold, *A Sand County Almanac,* viii.
9. William O. Douglas, *A Wilderness Bill of Rights* (Boston: Little, Brown and Company, 1965), 136.
10. U.S. Court of Appeals, District of Columbia Circuit. 880 F.2d 432. July 14, 1989.
11. John G. Mitchell, *Losing Ground* (San Francisco: Sierra Club Books, 1975).

CHAPTER 1: SELLING ARCTIC WILDERNESS

1. Faith Gemmill, spokesperson, Gwich'in Nation, writers workshop discussion, Portland State University, Portland, OR, October 2001.
2. N. K. Clough, P. C. Patton, and A. C. Christiansen, eds., *Arctic National Wildlife Refuge, Alaska, Coastal Plain Resource Assessment* (Washington, DC: U.S. Department of Interior, 1987), 46.
3. Jimmy Carter, foreword to *Arctic National Wildlife Refuge: Seasons of Life and Land,* by Subhankar Banerjee (Seattle: Mountaineers Books, 2003), 12.
4. Clough et al., *Arctic National Wildlife Refuge,* 165.
5. Ernest K. Leffingwell, *The Canning River Region Northern Alaska* (Washington, DC: U.S. Government Printing Office, 1919).
6. Ejnar Mikkelsen, *Conquering the Arctic Ice* (London: William Heinemann, 1909; repr. Kessinger Publishing, LLC 2010), 10. Citations refer to the Kessinger edition.
7. Leffingwell, *Canning River Region,* 241.
8. Leffingwell, *Canning River Region,* 54.
9. Leffingwell, *Canning River Region,* 61, 62.
10. Leffingwell, *Canning River Region,* 67.
11. Clough et al., *Arctic National Wildlife Refuge,* 36.
12. Peter Matthiessen, "In the Great Country," in Banerjee, *Arctic National Wildlife Refuge,* 41.
13. Clough et al., 40.
14. Gemmill, October 2001.

15. Clough et al., 30.

16. Erica Goode, "Polar Bears' Path to Decline Runs Through Alaskan Village," *New York Times*, December 19, 2016.

17. U.S. Court of Appeals for The Ninth Circuit. No. 14-35811 D.C. No. 4:13-cv-00018-RRB.

18. Clough, *Arctic National Wildlife Refuge*, 30.

19. Clough, *Arctic National Wildlife Refuge*, 124.

20. Clough, *Arctic National Wildlife Refuge*, 28.

21. Leffingwell, *Canning River Region*, 15.

22. Clough, *Arctic National Wildlife Refuge*, 31.

23. Clough, *Arctic National Wildlife Refuge*, 32.

24. Leffingwell, *Arctic National Wildlife Refuge*, 179.

25. George Marshall, introduction, *Alaska Wilderness: Exploring the Central Brooks Range*, 2nd ed., by Robert Marshall (Berkeley: University of California Press, 1970), xxxiv.

26. Olaus J. Murie, *Journeys to the Far North* (Palo Alto: The Wilderness Society and American West Publishing Co., 1973), 247.

27. Roger Kaye, *The Last Great Wilderness: The Campaign to Establish the Arctic National Wildlife Refuge* (Fairbanks: University of Alaska Press, 2006), 14.

28. John C. Reed, Cdr., USNR, *Exploration of Naval Petroleum Reserve No. 4 and Adjacent Areas, Northern Alaska, 1944–53, Part 1, History of the Exploration* (U.S. Geological Survey, Washington, DC, 1958), 3.

29. BLM Alaska. "What is a Legacy Well?" www.blm.gov/ak/st/en/prog/energy/oil_gas/npra/legacywell/about_legacywells.html.

30. U.S. Geological Survey. *How does the 2017 National Petroleum Reserve–Alaska assessment compare to other assessments USGS has done?* www.usgs.gov/faqs/how-does-2017-national-petroleum-reserve-alaska-assessment-compare-other-assessments-usgs-has?qt-news_science_products=0#qt-news_science_products.

31. Kaye, *The Last Great Wilderness*, 14.

32. George L. Collins and Lowell Sumner, "Northeast Alaska: The Last Great Wilderness," *Sierra Club Bulletin* 38, no.8 (October 1953), 13–26.

33. Collins and Sumner, "Northeast Alaska," 26.

34. William O. Douglas, *My Wilderness: The Pacific West* (Garden City, NY: Doubleday & Company, 1960), 9–31.

35. U.S. Fish and Wildlife Service website, www.fws.gov/refuge/Arctic/about.html.

36. Biographical Directory of the United States Congress. "Stevens, Theodore Fulton." bioguide.congress.gov/scripts/biodisplay.pl?index=s000888.

37. Public Land Order 2214, Department of Interior, December 6, 1960.

38. David Whitney, "Seeking Statehood—Stevens Bent Rules to Bring Alaska Into the Union," *Anchorage Daily News*, August 10, 1994.

39. Whitney, "Seeking Statehood."

40. Ross Coen, *Breaking Ice for Arctic Oil: The Epic Voyage of the SS Manhattan Through the Northwest Passage* (Fairbanks: University of Alaska Press, 2012), 24.

41. William S. Hanable, "Leffingwell: Prudhoe's Pioneer Scientist." *Our Public Lands* 23, no. 3 (Summer 1973), 18–21.

42. U.S. General Accounting Office. *Chandler Lake Land Exchange Not in the Government's Best Interests. GAO/RCED-90-5*, 40, www.gao.gov/products/RCED-90-5.

43. Gemmill, October 2001.

44. Daniel Yergin, *The Prize: The Epic Quest for Oil, Money and Power* (New York: Simon & Schuster, 1991), 573.

45. Ken Boyd, writers workshop discussion, Portland State University, Portland, OR, October 2001.

46. Boyd, October 2001.

47. Cecil D. Andrus, interview with author, Boise, ID, January 2006.

48. Roderick Frazier Nash, *Wilderness and the American Mind*, 5th ed. (New Haven, CT: Yale University Press, 2014), 301.

49. Andrus, interview.

50. Clough, *Arctic National Wildlife Refuge*, 144.

51. Clough, *Arctic National Wildlife Refuge*, v.

52. U.S. General Accounting Office, *Chandler Lake Land Exchange*, 3.

53. U.S. General Accounting Office, *Chandler Lake Land Exchange*, 18.

54. Steve Eder and Henry Fountain, "Arctic Oil Well Hid Its Secrets for 3 Decades," *New York Times*, April 2, 2019, A1.

55. Sen. Frank Murkowski, "It's Not Oil vs. Beauty in the Arctic," Op-Ed, *New York Times*, October 9, 2000.

56. Cecil D. Andrus and Joel Connelly, *Cecil Andrus: Politics Western Style* (Seattle: Sasquatch Books, 1998), 122.

57. Clough, *Arctic National Wildlife Refuge*, 115.

58. Clough, *Arctic National Wildlife Refuge*, 115.

59. Gemmill, October 2001.

60. Gemmill, October 2001.

61. David Warren, "Texas Oil, Gas Discovery Biggest Ever in U.S," Associated Press, *Idaho Statesman* (Boise), November 17, 2016.

62. U.S. Energy Information Administration. "How Much Petroleum Does the United States Import and Export?" www.eia.gov/tools/faqs/faq.php?id=727&t=6.

63. "Expect the Unexpected: The Disruptive Power of Low-carbon Technology," report by the Carbon Tracker Initiative and the Grantham Institute at Imperial College, London. February 2017. www.carbontracker.org/wp-content/uploads/2017/02/Expect-the-Unexpected_CTI_Imperial.pdf.

64. U.S. Energy Information Administration, "Short Term Energy Outlook," *Analysis and Projections*, March 2017), www.eia.gov/outlooks/steo/report/global_oil.cfm.

Chapter 2: Ancient Art in Nine Mile Canyon

1. Climb Utah, "Nine Mile Canyon Guide and Information," www.climb-utah.com/Misc/ninemile.htm.

2. Climb Utah, "Nine Mile Canyon Guide."

3. Troy Scotter, Utah Rock Art Research Foundation, conversation with author, October 2005.

4. N. S. Nokkentved, "Controversy Looms Over Archeologist's 'Conflict of Interest,'" *Daily Herald* (Provo, UT), October 5, 2003.

5. Nokkentved, "Controversy Looms."

6. Michael Smith and Elizabeth S. Merritt, "Re: Disagreement with BLM's 'Finding of No Adverse Effect' Stone Cabin Seismic Exploration Project Utah-70-2003-15," letter to BLM officials in Utah, National Trust for Historic Preservation, September 29, 2003.

7. Nokkentved, "Controversy Looms."

8. National Historic Preservation Act of 1966 (16 U.S.C. 470), Section 106.

9. Mining Law of 1872, 30 U.S.C. §§ 22–42.

10. Mineral Lands Leasing Act of 1920, 30 U.S.C. § 181.

11. Bureau of Land Management, Oil and Gas Lease Information, www.blm.gov/wo/st/en/prog/energy/oil_and_gas/questions_and_answers.print.html.

12. Center for Western Priorities, "A Fair Share: The Case for Updating Oil and Gas Royalties on Our Public Lands," June 18, 2015.

13. U.S. Government Accountability Office, *Energy Policy Act of 2005: Greater Clarity Needed to Address Concerns with Categorical Exclusions for Oil and Gas Development under Section 390 of the Act*, GAO-09-872, September 2009.

14. N. S. Nokkentved, "Ancient Art vs. Natural Gas: A Canyon of Controversy," *Daily Herald* (Provo, UT), October 23, 2005.

15. Bureau of Land Management, Contracted Development Plan, Attachment 1 to *Record of Decision: West Tavaputs Plateau Natural Gas Full Field Development Plan*, July 2010, www.oilandgasbmps.org/docs/UT37-WestTavaputsROD.pdf.

16. Nokkentved, "Ancient Art vs. Natural Gas."

17. Nokkentved, "Ancient Art vs. Natural Gas."

18. U.S. GAO, *Energy Policy Act of 2005*.

19. U.S. GAO, *Energy Policy Act of 2005*.

20. U.S. GAO, *Energy Policy Act of 2005*.

21. Bureau of Land Management, Contracted Development Plan. Attachment 1 to *Record of Decision*.

22. Southern Utah Wilderness Alliance, Nine Mile Canyon Coalition, and The Wilderness Society, "BLM's Approval of 25 Natural Gas Wells in Utah's Nine Mile Canyon Region Sparks Lawsuit," press release, August 7, 2008.

23. Southern Utah Wilderness Alliance et al., "BLM's Approval."

24. Bureau of Land Management, Programmatic Agreement, Attachment 4 to *Record Of Decision: West Tavaputs Plateau Natural Gas Full Field Development Plan*, July 2010.

25. Bureau of Land Management, Contracted Development Plan. Attachment 1 to *Record of Decision*.

26. Bureau of Land Management, "BLM Releases West Tavaputs Plateau Project Final Environmental Impact Statement and Record of Decision Approving Historic Agreement," press release, July 29, 2010.

27. Brian Maffly, "Barrett Walking Away from West Tavaputs Gas Field," *Salt Lake Tribune*, October 30, 2013.

28. David Warren, "Texas Oil, Gas Discovery Biggest Ever in U.S.," Associated Press, *Idaho Statesman* (Boise), November 17, 2016.

29. "Expect the Unexpected," Carbon Tracker Initiative.

Chapter 3: Abandoned Mines, Tainted Water

1. N. S. Nokkentved, "Agreement Resuscitates Mine Cleanup Project," *Daily Herald* (Provo, UT), September 8, 2005.

2. Jim Kuipers, "Putting a Price on Pollution: Financial Assurance for Mine Reclamation and Closure," Mineral Policy Center, Issue Paper No. 4, March 2003. www.earthwork saction.org/files/publications/PuttingAPriceOnPollution.pdf.

3. U.S. Environmental Protection Agency, *Abandoned Mine Site Characterization and Cleanup Handbook*, August 2000, 3.2. www.epa.gov/sites/production/files/2015-09/documents/2000_08_pdfs_amscch.pdf.

4. Donald Worster, *A River Running West: The Life of John Wesley Powell* (Oxford: Oxford University Press, 2002), 472.

5. Worster, *A River Running West*, 390.

6. Biographical Directory of the United States Congress. "Stewart, William Morris." bioguide.congress.gov/scripts/biodisplay.pl?index=s000922.

7. Biographical Directory, "Stewart, William Morris."

8. Ronald James, "General Mining Act of 1872," Nevada Humanities, Online Nevada Encyclopedia, November 3, 2010. www.onlinenevada.org/articles/national-mining-act-1872.

9. James, General Mining Act of 1872.

10. N. S. Nokkentved, "Mining Legacy Lives On: BLM Considers Canyon Claims Active," *Times-News* (Twin Falls, ID), December 3, 2000.

11. Nokkentved, "Mining Legacy Lives On."

12. James, General Mining Act of 1872.

13. Kuipers, "Putting a Price on Pollution."

14. Robert McClure, "Pegasus Gold: from Boom to Bankruptcy," in "The Mining of the West: Profit and Pollution on Public Lands," *Seattle Post-Intelligencer*, reprint, June 11–14, 2001, 13.

15. Phillip Argall, "History of Cyanidation," *Mining and Scientific Press* 95, November 23, 1907, 655.

16. N. S. Nokkentved, "Gold in Them Hills: Pegasus Launches Black Pine Mine Project," *Times-News* (Twin Falls, ID), September 4, 1992.

17. Nokkentved, "Gold in Them Hills."

18. Clark Fork Coalition, "Beal Mountain: A Mining Mess We Could Do Without" in *Mine Waste Cleanups: A Legacy of Mining Pollution in the Clark Fork.* clarkfork.org/why-were-here/watershed-history-challenges-need/mine-waste-cleanups.

19. Montana Bureau of Mines and Geology, Environmental Studies Berkeley Pit and BMF Operable, April 11, 2015. www.mbmg.mtech.edu/env/env-berkeley.html.

20. Montana Bureau of Mines and Geology, Environmental Studies Berkeley Pit.

21. Matt Volz, "Thousands of Geese Deaths Put Focus on Toxic Pit That Concerns Montana City, EPA" Associated Press, *Idaho Statesman* (Boise), January 29, 2017.

22. U.S. Environmental Protection Agency, "Superfund Policy, Guidance and Laws," www.epa.gov/superfund/superfund-policy-guidance-and-laws.

23. Richard Pérez-Peña, "Study Faults E.P.A. for Toxic Wastewater Spill in Colorado Rockies," *New York Times*, October 22, 2015.

24. Julie Turkewitz, "Colorado Spill Heightens Debate Over Future of Old Mines," *New York Times*, August 16, 2015.

25. Brian Handwerk, "Why Tens of Thousands of Toxic Mines Litter the U.S. West." *Smithsonian.com*, August 13, 2015. www.smithsonianmag.com/science-nature/why-tens-thousands-toxic-mines-litter-us-west-180956265.

26. N. S. Nokkentved, "Funds Approved for American Fork Canyon Mine Cleanup," *Daily Herald* (Provo, UT), November 9, 2005.

27. N. S. Nokkentved, "Agreement Resuscitates Mine Cleanup Project," *Daily Herald* (Provo, UT), September 8, 2005.

28. Nokkentved, "Agreement Resuscitates Mine Cleanup Project."

29. Nokkentved, "Agreement Resuscitates Mine Cleanup Project."

30. Nokkentved, "Agreement Resuscitates Mine Cleanup Project."

31. Nokkentved, "Funds Approved for American Fork Canyon Mine Cleanup."

32. Anu K. Mittal, in "Abandoned Mines: Information on the Number of Hardrock Mines, Cost of Cleanup, and Value of Financial Assurances," U.S. Government Accountability Office, GAO-11-834T, Abandoned Mines, Washington, DC, July 14, 2011.

33. Pew Campaign for Responsible Mining, "Reforming the U.S. Hardrock Mining Law of 1872: The Price of Inaction," January 27, 2009. www.pewtrusts.org/en/research-and-analysis/reports/2009/01/27/reforming-the-us-hardrock-mining-law-of-1872-the-price-of-inaction.

34. Mittal, in "Abandoned Mines."

35. Robin M. Nazzaro, statement in "Hardrock Mining: Information on State Royalties and the Number of Abandoned Mine Sites and Hazards," U.S. Government Accountability Office, GAO-09-854T, Hardrock mining, Washington, DC, July 14, 2009.

36. Mittal, in "Abandoned Mines."

37. President Richard M. Nixon, State of the Union Message to Congress, February 2, 1973. www.infoplease.com/t/hist/state-of-the-union/186.html.

38. Anne-Marie Fennell, statement in "Mineral Resources: Mineral Volume, Value, and Revenue," U.S. Government Accountability Office, GAO-13-45R Mineral Resources, November 15, 2012.

39. "137 Years Later," *New York Times*, editorial, July 20, 2009.

Chapter 4: Lurching Toward Wolf Recovery

1. Leopold, *A Sand County Almanac*, 129.

2. Adolph Murie, *A Naturalist in Alaska* (New York: The Devlin-Adair Company, 1961), 11.

3. Peter Matthiessen, *Wildlife in America* (New York: Viking Penguin Inc., revised edition, 1987), 57.

4. Barry Lopez, *Of Wolves and Men* (New York: Charles Scribner's Sons, 1978), 171.

5. Henry W. Henshaw, "Report of Chief of Bureau of Biological Survey," U.S. Department of Agriculture, Washington, DC, August 31, 1916.

6. Wildlife Services, Data Reports, 2014, USDA Animal and Plant Health Inspection Service, www.aphis.usda.gov/aphis/home.

7. National Park Service, "Natural Resources Report Number 11," U.S. Department of the Interior, 1978.

8. N. S. Nokkentved, "Wolves Face Long History of Persecution," *Times-News* (Twin Falls, ID), March 18, 2001.

9. U.S. Fish and Wildlife Service, "Reclassification of the Gray Wolf in the United States and Mexico, with Determination of Critical Habitat in Michigan and Minnesota," *Federal Register* 43, no. 47, 9608, March 9, 1978.

10. N. S. Nokkentved, "Relating to Beast and People," *Times-News* (Twin Falls, ID) September 3, 2000.

11. Boulder-White Clouds Council, news release, August 7, 2000.

12. Boulder-White Clouds Council.

13. N. S. Nokkentved, "Feds OK the Killing of Wolves," *Times-News* (Twin Falls, ID), September 7, 2000.

14. N. S. Nokkentved, "Wolf Trapping Ends; Road Reopens," *Times-News* (Twin Falls, ID), August 11, 2000.

15. William Brailsford, interview with author, March 18, 2001.

16. U.S. Fish and Wildlife Service, "Rocky Mountain Wolf Recovery 2012 Interagency Annual Report," Table 5b: Northern Rocky Mountain Confirmed Wolf Depredations by State, 1987–2012.

17. The total numbers of cattle and sheep include animals that have not grazed on public land. The numbers are compiled from the National Agricultural Statistics Service, Statistics by State, www.nass.usda.gov.

18. National Agricultural Statistics Service, www.nass.usda.gov.

19. Nokkentved, "Relating to Beast and People."

20. Nokkentved, "Relating to Beast and People."

21. Peter Zager and Michael W. Gratson, "Elk Ecology Study IV: Factors Influencing Elk Calf Recruitment July 1, 2000, to June 30, 2001," Idaho Department of Fish and Game, Boise, April 2002.

22. Peter Zager, Craig White, and George Pauley, "Elk Ecology Study IV: Factors Influencing Elk Calf Recruitment July 1, 2005 to June 30, 2006," Idaho Department of Fish and Game, Boise, September 2007.

23. Mark Hurley and Pete Zager, "Influence of Predators on Mule Deer Populations Study," Idaho Department of Fish and Game, Boise, September 2007.

24. Natural Resources Defense Council and Defenders of Wildlife, "Petition to Prepare a Recovery Plan for the Gray Wolf," February 20, 2008. www.nrdc.org.

25. Defenders v. Salazar, September 8, 2009, U.S. District Court for the District of Montana, Missoula Division.

26. Defenders v. Salazar, September 8, 2009.

27. Defenders v. Salazar, August 5, 2010, U.S. District Court for the District of Montana, Missoula Division.

28. Center for Biological Diversity, "Lawsuit Challenges Constitutionality of Anti-Wolf Rider," May 5, 2011.

29. U.S. Fish and Wildlife Service, "Memorandum Regarding a Viable Wolf Population in the Northern Rocky Mountains," Appendix 9 in *The Reintroduction of Gray Wolves to Yellowstone National Park and Central Idaho*, Final Environmental Impact Statement, April 14, 1994.

30. Nokkentved, "Wolves Face Long History of Persecution."

31. William J. Ripple and Robert L. Beschta, "Trophic Cascades in Yellowstone: The First 15 Years after Wolf Reintroduction," *Biological Conservation* 145, no. 1 (January 2012), 205–13, www.sciencedirect.com/science/article/pii/S0006320711004046.

32. Michael Jamison, "Tracking Science: Biologist's Findings Show Forest Diversity, Health Influenced by Wolves," *Missoulian* (Missoula, MT), October 25, 2009.

33. Jamison, "Tracking Science."

34. Ripple and Beschta, "Trophic Cascades in Yellowstone."

35. Douglas Smith et al., "Yellowstone after Wolves," *BioScience* 53, no.4, April 2003.

36. Ripple and Beschta, "Trophic Cascades in Yellowstone."

37. Smith et al. "Yellowstone after Wolves."

CHAPTER 5: PRIVATE LIVESTOCK, PUBLIC LANDS

1. N. S. Nokkentved, "A Walk on the Range: Critic, Rancher Meet to Talk Grazing," *Times News* (Twin Falls, ID), September 30, 2000.

2. U.S. Department of Interior, Bureau of Land Management and USDA Forest Service. "Rangeland Reform '94; A Proposal to Improve Management of Rangeland Ecosystems and the Administration of Livestock Grazing on Public Lands," August 1993.

3. N. S. Nokkentved, "Cattle Foul Mountain Lakes: Trout Listing May Help Resolve Issue," *Times-News* (Twin Falls, ID), September 19, 1999.

4. George Wuerthner, "Sage Grouse, Livestock Grazing, and the Bovine Curtain," *The Wildlife News*, www.thewildlifenews.com/2013/08/03.

5. Nokkentved, "A Walk on the Range."

6. Nokkentved, "Cattle Foul Mountain Lakes."

7. N. S. Nokkentved, "Cattle Keep Ranchers in Trouble over Sensitive Frog Lake Area," *Times-News* (Twin Falls, ID), July 12, 2000.

8. Nokkentved, "Cattle Foul Mountain Lakes."

9. Bruce D. Smith, *The Emergence of Agriculture* (New York: Scientific American Library, 1998), 53–67.

10. Bernard Shanks, *This Land is Your Land: The Struggle to Save America's Public Lands* (San Francisco: Sierra Club Books, 1984), 174.

11. W. C. Lowdermilk, *Conquest of the Land Through 7,000 Years*, Agriculture Information Bulletin No. 99, U.S. Department of Agriculture, Soil Conservation Service, August 1953; reprinted 1989, 12.

12. Richard Manning, *Grassland: The History, Biology, Politics, and Promise of the American Prairie* (New York: Penguin Books USA Inc., 1995), 111.

13. George Wuerthner and Mollie Matteson, eds., *Welfare Ranching: The Subsidized Destruction of the American West* (Washington, DC: Island Press, 2002), 5.

14. Wuerthner and Matteson, *Welfare Ranching*, 5.

15. Shanks, *This Land is Your Land*, 178.

16. Dutton, W. L. "History of Forest Service Grazing Fees," *Journal of Range Management* 6, no. 6 (November 1953), 393–98. journals.uair.arizona.edu.

17. Gifford Pinchot, *Breaking New Ground* (New York, NY: Harcourt, Brace and Company, 1947), 273.

18. The Taylor Grazing Act of 1934 (43 USC 315) (Pub.L. 73–482).

19. Shanks, *This Land is Your Land*, 80–81.

20. Taylor Grazing Act of 1934.

21. U.S. Department of Interior, *Study of Fees for Grazing Livestock on Federal Lands: A Report from the Secretary of the Interior and the Secretary of Agriculture* (Washington, DC: U.S. Government Printing Office, 1977), 3–21.

22. Shanks, *This Land is Your Land*, 188.

23. U.S. Department of Interior, Bureau of Land Management and USDA Forest Service. "Rangeland Reform '94," August 1993.

24. Shanks, *This Land is Your Land*, 190.

25. U.S. Government Accountability Office, *Livestock Grazing: Federal Expenditures and Receipts Vary, Depending on the Agency and the Purpose of the Fee Charged*, GAO-05-869, September 2005.

26. U.S. Government Accountability Office, *Livestock Grazing*.

27. Mark Salvo, "Western Wildlife Under Hoof: Public Lands Livestock Grazing Threatens Iconic Species," WildEarth Guardians, Chandler, Arizona, April 2009.

28. U.S. Department of Interior, *Study of Fees for Grazing Livestock on Federal Lands*, 3-3.

29. U.S. Fish and Wildlife Service, "2011 National Survey of Fishing, Hunting, and Wildlife - Related Recreation," digitalmedia.fws.gov/digital/collection/document/id/859.

30. J. W. Connelly, S. T. Knick, M. A. Schroeder, and S. J. Stiver, "Conservation Assessment of Greater Sage-grouse and Sagebrush Habitats," Western Association of Fish and Wildlife Agencies, Cheyenne, WY, 2004, 7-28. sagemap.wr.usgs.gov/docs/Greater_Sage-grouse_Conservation_Assessment_060404.pdf.

31. Stephen Trimble, *The Sagebrush Ocean: A Natural History of the Great Basin*, 10th Anniversary ed. (Reno: University of Nevada Press, 1989), 107.

32. Connelly, et al. *Conservation Assessment of Greater Sage-grouse*, 7-25.

33. Trimble, *The Sagebrush Ocean*, 107.

34. Mike Pellant, "Cheatgrass: The Invader That Won the West," report prepared for the Interior Columbia Basin Ecosystem Management Project, 1996.

35. Pellant, "Cheatgrass."

36. Pellant, "Cheatgrass."

37. Ed Chaney, Wayne Elmore, and William S. Platts, *Managing Change: Livestock Grazing on Western Riparian Areas*, report prepared for the Environmental Protection Agency by the Northwest Resource Information Center Inc., July 1993.

38. John Burroughs, *The Writings of John Burroughs* (Boston: Houghton, Mifflin, 1905), 11.

39. Salvo, "Western Wildlife Under Hoof."

40. Vickery Eckhoff, "Exposing America's Billionaire Welfare Ranchers." AlterNet, March 24, 2015, www.alternet.org/economy/exposing-americas-billionaire-welfare-ranchers.

41. Eckhoff, "Exposing America's Billionaire Welfare Ranchers."

42. Shanks, *This Land is Your Land*, 180.

43. N. S. Nokkentved, "Bankable Resource: Value of Grazing Permits Raises Many Questions." *Times-News* (Twin Falls, ID), September 22, 1997.

44. Nokkentved, "Bankable Resource."

45. Salvo, "Western Wildlife Under Hoof."

46. Carl Nellis, conversation with author, January 2010.

47. Wuerthner and Matteson, *Welfare Ranching*, 5.

48. U.S. Environmental Protection Agency, *Polluted Runoff: Nonpoint Source* (NPS) Pollution, www.epa.gov/nps.

CHAPTER 6: VANISHING SAGE GROUSE

1. N. S. Nokkentved, "Night Moves on the Lek," *Times News* (Twin Falls, ID), April 22, 1991.

2. Nokkentved, "Night Moves on the Lek."

3. Kent L. Christopher and Tom J. Cade, "How to Conserve and Restore the High Desert Environment and Rebuild Sage Grouse Populations: A Challenge for the Western Governors' Association and Western Association of Fish and Wildlife Agencies," unpublished report, n/d.

4. Meriwether Lewis and William Clark, et al., *The Journals of the Lewis and Clark Expedition*, June 5, 1805, and March 2, 1806 (Lincoln: University of Nebraska Press), online edition, lewisandclarkjournals.unl.edu.

5. N. S. Nokkentved, "Mating Rituals among Grouse Similar to Those in other Species." *Times News* (Twin Falls, ID), April 22, 1991.

6. Nokkentved, "Mating Rituals."

7. Hugh N. Mozingo, *Shrubs of the Great Basin: A Natural History* (Reno: University of Nevada Press, 1987), 271–72.

8. Niels S. Nokkentved, *A Forest of Wormwood: Sagebrush, Water and Idaho's Twin Falls Canal Company* (Twin Falls, ID: The Twin Falls Canal Company, 2008), 37.

9. J. W. Connelly, S. T. Knick, M. A. Schroeder, and S. J. Stiver. *Conservation Assessment of Greater Sage-grouse and Sagebrush Habitats*. Western Association of Fish and Wildlife Agencies, unpublished report (Cheyenne, WY, 2004), 7-35.

10. Pellant, "Cheatgrass."

11. Mozingo, *Shrubs of the Great Basin*, 280.

12. Connelly, et al., *Conservation Assessment*, 7-36.

13. Nokkentved, *A Forest of Wormwood*, 104.

14. Nokkentved, *A Forest of Wormwood*, 154–56.

15. Connelly, et al., *Conservation Assessment*, 7-1.

16. Don Smurthwaite, *Sage Grouse: A Part of Idaho's High Desert Heritage*, brochure, Idaho Department of Fish and Game, May 1998.

17. U.S. Fish and Wildlife Service and Bureau of Land Management, "Interior Expands Common-Sense Efforts to Conserve Sage-Grouse Habitat in the West," news release, March 5, 2010, www.fws.gov/mountain-prairie/pressrel/dc02.html.

18. William Baker, et al., letter to Secretary of the Interior Sally Jewell and Secretary of Agriculture Tom Vilsack, March 12, 2015, www.eenews.net/assets/2015/03/12/document_gw_06.pdf.

19. U.S. Fish and Wildlife Service, Department of the Interior, *Federal Register* 80, no. 191, October 2, 2015, 59858, www.govinfo.gov/content/pkg/FR-2015-10-02/html/2015-24292.htm.

20. David Murray, "State Conservation Team Approves $1.5 million for Sage Grouse," *Great Falls (MT) Tribune*, November 21, 2016.

21. Murray, "State Conservation Team."

22. George Wuerthner, "Sage Grouse Funding Priorities are Misplaced." *The Wildlife News.* November 22, 2016, *www.thewildlifenews.com/?s=sage+grouse.*

23. C. L. Otter, "Governor Otter, Legislature Sue Feds Over Flawed Process Behind Sage-Grouse Decision," news release, September 25, 2015.

24. Virgil Moore, personal communication, January 2014.

25. Western Watersheds v. Schneider, Complaint, Case 1:16-cv-83, February 25, 2016, U.S. District Court for the District of Idaho, www.advocateswest.org/wp-content/uploads/2009/06/SG-RMP-Complaint-FILED.pdf.

26. Western Watersheds v. Schneider.

27. Keith Ridler, "Jewell Orders Firefighting Strategy That Protects Habitat," Associated Press, *Missoulian* (Missoula, MT), January 6, 2015.

28. Ridler, "Jewell Orders Firefighting Strategy."

29. Edward O. Garton et al., "Greater Sage-Grouse Population Dynamics and Probability of Persistence," Final Report to Pew Charitable Trusts, March 18, 2015, www.pewtrusts.org/~/media/assets/2015/04/garton-et-al-2015-greater-sagegrouse-population-dynamics-and-persistence-31815.pdf.

30. Garton et al., "Greater Sage-Grouse Population Dynamics."

31. Garton et al., "Greater Sage-Grouse Population Dynamics."

Chapter 7: The Nature of Wildfire

1. N. S. Nokkentved, "Thorn Creek, Indian Spring Fires Contained," *Times-News* (Twin Falls, ID), August 12, 1990.

2. George Wuerthner, "Logging and Wildfire: Ecological Differences and the Need to Preserve Large Fires," in *The Wildfire Reader: A Century of Failed Forest Policy*, edited by George Wuerthner (Washington, DC: Island Press, 2006), 186.

3. Tom Ribe and Timothy Ingalsbee, "Smoke Signals: The Need for Public Tolerance and Regulatory Relief for Wildland Smoke Emissions," Firefighters United for Safety, Ethics, and Ecology (FUSEE), August 2011. www.fusee.org/documents/FUSEE_SmokeSignals5_print.pdf.

4. Wuerthner, "Logging and Wildfire," 189.

5. George Wuerthner, "Burning Questions," Counter Punch, www.counterpunch.org, June 12, 2009.

6. Wuerthner, "Logging and Wildfire," 184.

7. Wuerthner, "Logging and Wildfire," 183.

8. Gifford Pinchot, *Breaking New Ground* (New York: Harcourt, Brace and Company, 1947), 127.

9. Stephen J. Pyne, *Fire in America: A Cultural History of Wildland and Rural Fire* (Seattle: University of Washington Press, 1997), 38.

10. National Fire Plan, "Managing the Impact of Wildfires on Communities and the Environment: A Report to the President in Response to the Wildfires of 2000," U.S. Departments of Agriculture and Interior, September 2000, 8. www.forestsandrangelands.gov/documents/resources/reports/2001/8-20-en.pdf.

11. Pinchot, *Breaking New Ground*, 276.

12. Edward Gillette, "Suggestions on the Conservation of Some of Our Resources," in *Proceedings of a Conference of Governors*, ed. W. J. McGee (Washington, DC: Government Printing Office, 1909), 395.

13. Worster, *A River Running West*, 487.

14. Aldo Leopold, "Grass, Brush, Timber, and Fire in Southern Arizona," *Journal of Forestry* 22, no.6 (October 1, 1924), 1–10.

15. Leopold, *A Sand County Almanac*, 29.

16. National Fire Plan, 6.

17. National Interagency Fire Center, www.nifc.gov/fireInfo/fireInfo_stats_histSigFires.htm.

18. Jack D. Cohen, "The Wildland-Urban Interface Fire Problem: A Consequence of the Fire Exclusion Paradigm," *Forest History Today* (Fall 2008), 20–26.

19. Henry S. Graves, *Protection of Forests from Fire*, Bulletin 82, U.S. Department of Agriculture, Forest Service (Washington, DC: Government Printing Office, 1910; repr. Delhi, India: Facsimile Publisher, 2015), 7.

20. National Fire Plan, 6.

21. Pyne, *Fire in America*, 246.

22. Henry S. Graves, "Report of the Forester for 1913," in *Annual Reports of the Department of Agriculture for the year ended June 30, 1913* (Washington, DC: Government Printing Office, 1914; repr. GoogleBooks.com), 150.

23. Ribe and Ingalsbee, "Smoke Signals."

24. Pyne, *Fire in America*, 331.

25. Pyne, *Fire in America*, 256.

26. Pyne, *Fire in America*, 260.

27. National Fire Plan, 7.

28. Pyne, *Fire in America*, 257.

29. Pyne, *Fire in America*, 25.

30. National Interagency Fire Center, www.nifc.gov/fireInfo/fireInfo_stats_histSigFires.htm.

31. Pyne, *Fire in America*, 259.

32. Pyne, *Fire in America*, 259.

33. Forest Firefighter: Salary Info, Job Duties and Requirements, study.com/articles/Forest_Firefighter_Salary_Info_Job_Duties_and_Requirements.html.

34. George Wuerthner, "The Yellowstone Fires of 1988: A Living Wilderness," in *The Wildfire Reader*, 91.

35. Wuerthner, "The Yellowstone Fires of 1988," 97.

36. Conrad Smith, "Hot News: Media Coverage of Wildfire," in *The Wildfire Reader*, 56.

37. Wuerthner, "The Yellowstone Fires of 1988," 97, 98.

38. Wuerthner, ed., *The Wildfire Reader*, 89.

39. Wuerthner, "The Yellowstone Fires of 1988," 94.

40. Tom Ribe, *Inferno by Committee: A History of the Cerro Grande (Los Alamos) Fire* (Victoria, BC: Trafford Publishing, 2010), 110.

41. Barry T. Hill, in "Fire Management: Lessons Learned From the Cerro Grande (Los Alamos) Fire," U.S. General Accounting Office, GAO/T-RCED-00-257 (July 20, 2000), 13.

42. Hill, "Fire Management," 1.

43. National Fire Plan.

44. National Fire Plan, 9.

45. National Fire Plan, 21.

46. National Fire Plan, 30.

47. Cohen, "The Wildland-Urban Interface Fire Problem," 20–26.

48. National Interagency Fire Center website, www.nifc.gov/fireInfo/fireInfo_stats_histSigFires.htm.

49. Pyne, *Fire in America*, 7, 357, 358.

50. Jack Cohen, writers' workshop discussion, Portland State University, October 2001.

51. John Krist, "Burning Down the House: The Role of Disaster Aid in Subsidizing Catastrophe," in *The Wildfire Reader*, 319.

52. Brian Nowicki and Todd Schulke, "The Community Protection Zone: Defending Homes and Communities from the Threat of Forest Fire," in *The Wildfire Reader*, 318.

53. Nowicki and Schulke, "The Community Protection Zone," 322.

54. Cohen, "The Wildland-Urban Interface Fire Problem," 20–26.

55. Mollie Matteson, "A Spiral Dance: The Necessity of Fire to Wildness," in *The Wildfire Reader*, 29.

56. U.S. Department of Agriculture. "Forest Service Large Fire Suppression Costs." *Audit Report*, Office of Inspector General, Western Region. Report No. 08601-44-SF (November 2006), www.usda.gov/oig/webdocs/08601-44-SF.pdf.

57. Michael Jamison, "Timber in Transition: Subdivisions in Remote Areas Increase Cost County Services," *Missoulian* (Missoula, MT), February 6, 2007.

58. John Krist, "Burning Down the House," 314.

CHAPTER 8: BRINGING BACK THE BEAVER

1. Elmo W. Heter, "Transplanting Beavers by Airplane and Parachute," *Journal of Wildlife Management* 14, no. 2 (April 1950), 143–47.

2. Heter, "Transplanting Beavers."

3. Heter, "Transplanting Beavers."

4. Matthiessen, *Wildlife in America*, 79.

5. Peter C. Newman, *Company of Adventurers: The Story of the Hudson's Bay Company*, vol. 1 (New York: Viking Penguin, 1985), 50.

6. Ed Chaney et al., "Livestock Grazing on Western Riparian Areas," Northwest Resource Information Center, Eagle, ID, for the U.S. Environmental Protection Agency, July 1990 and August 1993.

7. Samuel Eliot Morison, *The European Discovery of America: The Northern Voyages A.D. 500–1600* (New York: Oxford University Press, 1971), 369, 370.

8. Eric R. Wolf, *Europe and the People Without History* (Berkeley: University of California Press, 1997), 185.

9. John Davidson Godman, *American Natural History*, vol. 2, 2nd ed. (Philadelphia: Stoddart and Atherton, 1831), 35.

10. Godman, *American Natural History*, 36.

11. Hiram M. Chittenden, *The American Fur Trade of the Far West*, repr. ed. vol. 1 (Lincoln: Bison Books, University of Nebraska Press, 1986), 90.

12. Hiram M. Chittenden, *The American Fur Trade of the Far West*, repr. ed. vol. 2 (Lincoln: Bison Books, University of Nebraska Press, 1986), 807.

13. Chittenden, *The American Fur Trade*, vol. 1, 7.

14. Chittenden, *The American Fur Trade*, vol. 1, 8.

15. Newman, *Company of Adventurers*, 1:42.

16. Newman, *Company of Adventurers*, 1:50.

17. Richard W. Behan, *Plundered Promise: Capitalism, Politics and the Fate of the Federal Lands* (Covelo, CA: Island Press, 2001), 66.

18. Paul Schaffer, "Beaver on Trial," *Oregon Fish and Wildlife Magazine*, December 22, 1941.

19. Donald L. Hey, et al. *Flood Damage Reduction in the Upper Mississippi River Basin: An Ecological Alternative*, The Wetlands Initiative (Chicago, IL, 2004), 16.

20. Alice Outwater, *Water: A Natural History* (New York: Basic Books, 1996), 33.

21. Thomas E. Dahl, *Wetlands Losses in the United States 1780s to 1980s*. U.S. Department of the Interior, Fish and Wildlife Service, Washington, DC, 1990. www.fws.gov/wetlands/documents/Wetlands-Losses-in-the-United-States-1780s-to-1980s.pdf.

22. Chaney, "Livestock Grazing on Western Riparian Areas."

23. Schaffer, "Beaver on Trial."

24. Schaffer, "Beaver on Trial."

25. N. S. Nokkentved, "Ranchers Bank on Furry Engineers to Save Streams," *Times-News* (Twin Falls, ID), September 28, 1992.

CHAPTER 9: FALSE PROMISE OF SALMON HATCHERIES

1. Columbia Basin Research, Columbia River DART (Data Access in Real Time), Adult Passage Daily Counts for All Species, www.cbr.washington.edu/dart/query/adult_daily.

2. Joseph E. Taylor III, *Making Salmon: An Environmental History of the Northwest Fisheries Crisis* (Seattle: University of Washington Press, 1999), 41.

3. Taylor, *Making Salmon*, 63.

4. Bill M. Bakke, *Chronology of Salmon Decline in the Columbia River 1779 to the Present*, www.nativefishsociety.org, 2009.

5. James G. Swan, *The Northwest Coast, Or Three Years' Residence in Washington Territory*, 5th ed. (Seattle: University of Washington Press, 1992), 19.

6. Jim Lichatowich, *Salmon Without Rivers: A History of the Pacific Salmon Crisis* (Covelo, CA: Island Press, 1999), 131.

7. Taylor, *Making Salmon*, 51.

8. Dale D. Goble, "Salmon in the Columbia Basin: From Abundance to Extinction," in *Northwest Lands, Northwest Peoples: Readings in Environmental History*, eds. Dale D. Goble and Paul W. Hirt (Seattle: University of Washington Press, 1999), 245.

9. Goble, "Salmon in the Columbia Basin," 244.

10. Bruce Brown, *Mountain in the Clouds: A Search for the Wild Salmon* (New York: Simon & Schuster, 1982), 66.

11. Brown, *Mountain in the Clouds*, 71.

12. Keith Petersen, *River of Life Channel of Death: Fish and Dams on the Lower Snake* (Lewiston, ID: Confluence Press, 1995), 113.

13. Douglas W. Dompier, "What the Mitchell Act Promised the Salmon," in *The Northwest Salmon Crisis: A Documentary History*, Joseph Cone and Sandy Ridlington, eds. (Corvallis: Oregon State University Press, 2000), 114–15.

14. Joseph Cone, *A Common Fate: Endangered Salmon and the People of the Pacific Northwest* (New York: Henry Holt and Company, 1995), 53.

15. Rivers and Harbors Act, 1945, Public Law 79-14, Ch. 19, S.35.

16. Warner W. Gardner, Memorandum to Secretary of Interior: Columbia River Dams or Salmon, Department of the Interior, March 6, 1947, Washington, DC: National Archives, RG48.

17. "Future of Area's Salmon at Stake: Whether to Sacrifice Industry for Dams up for Decision." *Spokesman-Review* (Spokane, WA), June 25, 1947.

18. Lichatowich, *Salmon Without Rivers*, 138.

19. Goble, "Salmon in the Columbia Basin," 249.

20. Lichatowich, *Salmon Without Rivers*, 115–19.

21. Bakke, *Chronology of Salmon Decline in the Columbia River*.

22. Goble, "Salmon in the Columbia Basin," 249.

23. "Conservation: Hatcheries," Washington Department of Fish and Wildlife, wdfw. wa.gov/hatcheries/overview.html.

24. James A. Lichatowich et al., "Artificial Production and the Effects of Fish Culture on Native Salmonids," in *Return to the River: Restoring Salmon to the Columbia River*, ed. Richard N. Williams (San Diego: Elsevier Academic Press, 2006), 440.

25. Joseph Cone, *A Common Fate*, 56.

26. Alice Outwater, *Water: A Natural History* (New York: Basic Books, 1996), 111.

27. Lichatowich, *Salmon Without Rivers*, 79.

28. Outwater, *Water*, 114.

29. Sam Wright, Declaration in support of plaintiff's motion for preliminary injunction, Case No. CV03-0687Z in U.S. District Court Western Washington, Seattle, Hon. Thomas S. Zilly, March 2003.

30. Lichatowich, *Salmon Without Rivers*, 204.

31. N. S. Nokkentved, "Salmon Hatchery Changes Recommended," *Olympian* (Olympia, WA), February 20, 2002.

32. NOAA Fisheries Proposed ESA Recovery Plan for Snake River Sockeye Salmon (*Oncorhynchus nerka*), June 30, 2014, 15.

33. John Harrison, "Dams: Impacts on Salmon and Steelhead," Northwest Power and Conservation Council, October 31, 2008, www.nwcouncil.org/history/DamsImpacts.

34. Idaho Department of Fish and Game, "Director's Annual Report to the Commission, FY2015," idfg.idaho.gov/sites/default/files/directors-annual-report-2015.pdf.

35. Taylor, *Making Salmon*, 236.

CHAPTER 10: OVERCUTTING ANCIENT FORESTS

1. Swan, *The Northwest Coast*.

2. Swan, *The Northwest Coast*, 27, 28.

3. Robert M. Pyle, *Wintergreen: Rambles in a Ravaged Land* (Seattle: Sasquatch Books, 2001), 179–82.

4. Peter Wohlleben, *The Hidden Life of Trees: What They Feel, How They Communicate* (Vancouver, BC: Greystone Books, 2016), 86.

5. Frank H. Lamb, "What Washington as a State Has Done and Can Do for Forest Conservation," in *Proceedings of a Conference of Governors*, ed. W. J. McGee (Washington, DC: Government Printing Office, 1909; Google Books repr. nd.), 385.

6. M. L. Schamberger, M. J. Hay, and R. L. Johnson. "Economic Analysis of Critical Habitat Designation Effects for the Northern Spotted Owl," U.S. Fish and Wildlife Service, Washington, DC, 1992, pubs.er.usgs.gov/publication/70127880, 2.

7. Schamberger et al., "Economic Analysis," ii.

8. Schamberger et al., "Economic Analysis," 62.

9. Schamberger et al., "Economic Analysis," v.

10. Schamberger et al., "Economic Analysis," 16.

11. Pyle, *Wintergreen*, 139.

12. Paul W. Hirt, "Getting out the Cut: A History of National Forest Management in the Northern Rockies," in *Northwest Lands, Northwest Peoples: Readings in Environmental History*, Dale D. Goble and Paul W. Hirt, eds. (Seattle: University of Washington Press, 1999), 440.

13. Timothy Egan, "Forest Supervisors Say Politicians Are Asking Them to Cut Too Much," *New York Times*, September 16, 1991.

14. Schamberger et al., "Economic Analysis," 25, 26.

15. Schamberger et al., "Economic Analysis," 74.

16. Sally McGrane, "German Forest Ranger Finds that Trees Have Social Networks, Too," *New York Times*, January 29, 2016.

17. Schamberger et al., "Economic Analysis," 21.

18. Jim Pissot, "Timber Troubles: The Spotted Owl is Not the Cause of the Northwest Forest Crisis," *Washington Post*, Op-Ed, April 2, 1993.

19. Lamb, "What Washington as a State Has Done," 385, 386.

20. Schamberger, "Economic Analysis," 21.

21. Wolf Read, "The 1962 Columbus Day Storm," www.climate.washington.edu/stormking/October1962.html.

22. Schamberger et al., "Economic Analysis," 23.

23. Schamberger et al., "Economic Analysis," 66.

24. Jean M. Daniels, "The Rise and Fall of the Pacific Northwest Log Export Market," U.S. Department of Agriculture, Forest Service, Pacific Northwest Research Station, General Technical Report PNW-GTR-624, February 2005.

25. U.S. Fish and Wildlife Service, "Designation of Revised Critical Habitat for Northern Spotted Owl," Final Rule, effective January 3, 2013.

26. Jerry Crane, "Oregon and Washington Log Exports Cost Thousands of Jobs," 2015 OregonLive.com, August 11, 2011.

27. Schamberger et al., "Economic Analysis," 77.

28. Schamberger et al., "Economic Analysis," 79.

29. U.S. Court of Appeals, District of Columbia Circuit. 880 F.2d 432. July 14, 1989.

30. Pyle, *Wintergreen*, 177.

31. Wohlleben, *The Hidden Life of Trees*, 244.

CHAPTER 11: SAVING AMERICA'S OUTBACK

1. Niels S. Nokkentved, *Desert Wings: Controversy in the Idaho Desert* (Pullman: Washington State University Press, 2001), 93.

2. Nokkentved, "More Protection? Owyhee Dispute Simmers," *Times-News* (Twin Falls, ID), April 22, 2001.

3. Nokkentved, "Birth of a Hotspot: Canyonlands Have a Violent Past," *Times-News* (Twin Falls, ID), April 22, 2001.

4. Nokkentved, "Birth of a Hotspot."

5. Nokkentved, *Desert Wings*, 6.

6. Jack Trueblood, "Driving Guide to the Mud Flat Road," *Idaho Wildlife* 16, no. 2, Idaho Department of Fish and Game, Boise, ID.

7. Trueblood, "Driving Guide to the Mud Flat Road."

8. Julia Conway Welch, *Gold Town to Ghost Town: The Story of Silver City, Idaho* (Moscow: University of Idaho Press, 1982), 77.

9. Nokkentved, *Desert Wings*, 92.

10. Nokkentved, *Desert Wings*, 92.

11. Benson Gibson, interview with the author, September 1993.

12. Nokkentved, "Indians, Trappers and More Mark Owyhee History," *Times-News* (Twin Falls, ID), April 22, 2001.

13. Nokkentved, *Desert Wings*, 93.

14. Nokkentved, *Desert Wings*, 24.

15. Nokkentved, *Desert Wings*, 17.

16. Nokkentved, *Desert Wings*, xii, 47.

17. Nokkentved, *Desert Wings*, 51.

18. Nokkentved, *Desert Wings*, 68.

19. Nokkentved, *Desert Wings*, 69.

20. Idaho Department of Fish and Game, Bighorn Sheep Management Plan, Appendix B: Translocation, Table 1, July 30, 2010. idfg.idaho.gov/old-web/docs/wildlife/planBighorn.pdf.

21. Nokkentved, *Desert Wings*, 69.

22. Nokkentved, *Desert Wings*, 114.

23. Nokkentved, *Desert Wings*, 115.

24. Nokkentved, *Desert Wings*, 122.

25. Nokkentved, "Saving Idaho's Outback: Conservationists Push Monument Proposal," *Times-News* (Twin Falls, ID), November 12, 2000.

26. Nokkentved, "Saving Idaho's Outback."

27. Rocky Barker, "The Owyhee Canyonlands: The Heart of Nowhere," *Idaho Statesman* (Boise), December 1, 2002.

28. Barker, "The Owyhee Canyonlands."

CONCLUSION

1. Andrea Wulf, *The Invention of Nature: Alexander von Humboldt's New World* (New York: Alfred A. Knopf, 2015), 87.

2. Wilson, "The Global Solution to Extinction."

3. Percy Bysshe Shelley, "Song: Rarely, rarely comest thou."

Bibliography

Andrus, Cecil D. and Joel Connelly. *Cecil Andrus: Politics Western Style*. Seattle: Sasquatch Books, 1998.

Argall, Philip. "History of Cyanidation." *Mining and Scientific Press* 95 (November 23, 1907): 655–657.

Baker, William, et al. Letter to Secretary of the Interior Sally Jewell and Secretary of Agriculture Tom Vilsack. March 12, 2015. www.eenews.net/assets/2015/03/12/document_gw_06.pdf.

Bakke, Bill M. *Chronology of Salmon Decline in the Columbia River 1779 to the Present*, 2009. Native Fish Society. nativefishsociety.org.

Banerjee, Subhankar. *Arctic National Wildlife Refuge: Seasons of Life and Land*. Seattle: Mountaineers Books, 2003.

Barker, Rocky. "The Owyhee Canyonlands: The Heart of Nowhere." *Idaho Statesman* (Boise, ID), December 1, 2002.

Behan, Richard W. *Plundered Promise: Capitalism, Politics and the Fate of the Federal Lands*. Covelo, CA: Island Press, 2001.

Biographical Directory of the United States Congress. "Stevens, Theodore Fulton." bioguide.congress.gov/scripts/biodisplay.pl?index=s000888

―――. "Stewart, William Morris." bioguide.congress.gov/scripts/biodisplay.pl?index=s000922

BLM Alaska. "What is a Legacy Well?" www.blm.gov/ak/st/en/prog/energy/oil_gas/npra/legacywell/about_legacywells.html.

Bureau of Land Management. "BLM Releases West Tavaputs Plateau Project Final Environmental Impact Statement and Record of Decision Approving Historic Agreement." News release, July 29, 2010. (In author's possession.)

―――. Contracted Development Plan. Attachment 1 to *Record of Decision: West Tavaputs Plateau Natural Gas Full Field Development Plan*. July 2010. www.oilandgasbmps.org/docs/UT37-WestTavaputsROD.pdf.

―――. "Programmatic Agreement." Attachment 4 to *Record of Decision: West Tavaputs Plateau Natural Gas Full Field Development Plan*. July 2010. www.oilandgasbmps.org/docs/UT37-WestTavaputsROD.pdf.

―――. Oil and Gas Lease Information, retrieved from www.blm.gov/wo/st/en/prog/energy/oil_and_gas/questions_and_answers.print.html.

Boulder-White Clouds Council. "Stanley Wolf Pack Peril Continues." News release, August 7, 2000. (In author's possession.)

Brown, Bruce. *Mountain in the Clouds: A Search for the Wild Salmon*. New York: Simon & Schuster, 1982.

Burroughs, John. *The Writings of John Burroughs*. Boston: Houghton, Mifflin, 1905.

Center for Biological Diversity. "Lawsuit Challenges Constitutionality of Anti-Wolf Rider." News release, May 5, 2011. www.biologicaldiversity.org/news/press_releases/2011/wolves-05-05-2011.html.

Center for Western Priorities. "A Fair Share: The Case for Updating Oil and Gas Royal-ties on Our Public Lands," June 18, 2015. westernpriorities.org/2015/07/08/a-fair-share-the-case-for-updating-oil-and-gas-royalty-rates-on-our-public-lands.

Chaney, Ed, Wayne Elmore, and William S. Platts. *Managing Change: Livestock Grazing on Western Riparian Areas.* Report produced by the Northwest Resource Information Center of Eagle, Idaho, for the U.S. Environmental Protection Agency, August 1993.

Chittenden, Hiram M. *The American Fur Trade of the Far West.* Lincoln: University of Nebraska Press, 1986.

Christopher, Kent L. and Tom J. Cade. "How to Conserve and Restore the High Desert Environment and Rebuild Sage Grouse Populations: A Challenge for the Western Governors' Association and Western Association of Fish and Wildlife Agencies." Unpublished, n.d. (In author's possession.)

Clark Fork Coalition. "Beal Mountain: A Mining Mess We Could Do Without." In *Mine Waste Cleanups: A Legacy of Mining Pollution in the Clark Fork.* clarkfork.org/why-were-here/watershed-history-challenges-need/mine-waste-cleanups.

Climb Utah. "Nine Mile Canyon Guide and Information." www.climb-utah.com/Misc/ninemile.htm.

Clough, N. K., P. C. Patton, and A. C. Christiansen, eds. *Arctic National Wildlife Refuge, Alaska, Coastal Plain Resource Assessment.* U.S. Department of Interior. Washington, DC: U.S. Government Printing Office, 1987. Reprint.

Cohen, Jack D. "The Wildland-Urban Interface Fire Problem: A Consequence of the Fire Exclusion Paradigm." *Forest History Today,* Fall 2008: 20–26. foresthistory.org/Publications/FHT/fhtfall2008.html.

Coen, Ross. *Breaking Ice for Arctic Oil: the Epic Voyage of the SS Manhattan Through the Northwest Passage.* Fairbanks: University of Alaska Press, 2012.

Collins, George L. and Lowell Sumner. "Northeast Alaska: The Last Great Wilderness." *Sierra Club Bulletin* 38, no. 8 (1953): 13–26.

Columbia Basin Research. Columbia River DART, Adult Passage Daily Counts for All Species, www.cbr.washington.edu/dart/query/adult_daily.

Cone, Joseph. *A Common Fate: Endangered Salmon and the People of the Pacific Northwest.* New York: Henry Holt and Company, 1995.

Cone, Joseph and Sandy Ridlington, eds. *The Northwest Salmon Crisis: A Documentary History.* Corvallis: Oregon State University Press, 2000.

Connelly, J. W., S. T. Knick, M. A. Schroeder, and S. J. Stiver. "Conservation Assessment of Greater Sage-grouse and Sagebrush Habitats." Western Association of Fish and Wildlife Agencies. Cheyenne, WY, 2004. sagemap.wr.usgs.gov/docs/Greater_Sage-grouse_Conservation_Assessment_060404.pdf.

Crane, Jerry. "Oregon and Washington Log Exports Cost Thousands of Jobs." Oregon-Live.com. August 11, 2011. www.oregonlive.com/opinion/index.ssf/2011/08/oregon_and_washington_log_expo.html.

Dahl, Thomas E. "Wetlands Losses in the United States 1780s to 1980s." U.S. Department of the Interior, Fish and Wildlife Service. Washington, DC, 1990. www.fws.gov/wetlands/documents/Wetlands-Losses-in-the-United-States-1780s-to-1980s.pdf.

Daniels, Jean M. "The Rise and Fall of the Pacific Northwest Log Export Market," U.S. Department of Agriculture, Forest Service, Pacific Northwest Research Station,

General Technical Report PNW-GTR-624, February 2005. www.fs.fed.us/pnw/pubs/pnw_gtr624.pdf.

Defenders v. Salazar. U.S. District Court for the District of Montana, Missoula Division. 729 F.Supp.2d 1207 (2010)

Defenders v. Salazar. U.S. District Court for the District of Montana, Missoula Division. 812 F.Supp.2d 1205 (2009).

Dompier, Douglas W. "What the Mitchell Act Promised the Salmon." In *The Northwest Salmon Crisis: A Documentary History*, edited by Joseph Cone and Sandy Ridlington. Corvallis: Oregon State University Press, 2000.

Douglas, William O. *A Wilderness Bill of Rights*. Boston: Little, Brown and Company, 1965.

———. *My Wilderness: The Pacific West*. Garden City, NY: Doubleday & Company, 1960.

Dutton, W. L. "History of Forest Service Grazing Fees." *Journal of Range Management* 6, no. 6 (1953): 393–98. journals.uair.arizona.edu.

Eckhoff, Vickery. "Exposing America's Billionaire Welfare Ranchers." AlterNet, March 24, 2015. www.alternet.org/economy/exposing-americas-billionaire-welfare-ranchers.

Eder, Steve and Henry Fountain. "Arctic Oil Well Hid Its Secrets for 3 Decades." *New York Times*, April 2, 2019.

Egan, Timothy. "Forest Supervisors Say Politicians Are Asking Them to Cut Too Much" *New York Times,* September 16, 1991.

"Expect the Unexpected: The Disruptive Power of Low-carbon Technology." Report by the Carbon Tracker Initiative and the Grantham Institute at Imperial College, London. February 2017. www.carbontracker.org/wp-content/uploads/2017/02/Expect-the-Unexpected_CTI_Imperial.pdf.

Fennell, Anne-Marie. "Mineral Resources: Mineral Volume, Value, and Revenue," U.S. Government Accountability Office, GAO-13-45R Mineral Resources, November 15, 2012.

Frank, Billy Jr. "The Life and Legacy of Billy Frank Jr." billyfrankjr.org.

Forest Firefighter: Salary Info, Job Duties and Requirements, study.com/articles/Forest_Firefighter_Salary_Info_Job_Duties_and_Requirements.html.

Gardner, Warner W. Memorandum to Secretary of Interior: Columbia River Dams or Salmon. Department of the Interior. March 6, 1947. Washington, DC, National Archives, RG-48. (photocopy)

Garton, Edward O. et al. "Greater Sage-Grouse Population Dynamics and Probability of Persistence." Final Report to Pew Charitable Trusts. March 18, 2015. www.pewtrusts.org/~/media/assets/2015/04/garton-et-al-2015-greater-sagegrouse-population-dynamics-and-persistence-31815.pdf.

Gillette, Edward. "Suggestions on the Conservation of Some of Our Resources." In *Proceedings of a Conference of Governors,* May 13–15, 1908, Washington, DC: Government Printing Office, 1909, 395.

Goble, Dale D. and Paul W. Hirt eds. *Northwest Lands, Northwest Peoples: Readings in Environmental History*. Seattle: University of Washington Press, 1999.

Godman, John D. *American Natural History.* Vol. 2. 2nd ed. Philadelphia: Stoddart and Atherton, 1831. Reprint Google Books, n.d.

Goode, Erica. "Polar Bears' Path to Decline Runs Through Alaskan Village." *New York Times*, December 19, 2016.

Graves, Henry S. *Protection of Forests from Fire.* U.S. Department of Agriculture, Forest Service, Bulletin 82. Washington, DC: Government Printing Office, 1910. Reprint, Delhi, India: Facsimile Publisher, 2015.

Graves, Henry S. "Report of the Forester for 1913." In *Annual Reports of the Department of Agriculture for the Year ended June 30, 1913.* Washington, DC: Government Printing Office, 1914.

Hanable, William S. "Leffingwell: Prudhoe's Pioneer Scientist." *Our Public Lands* 23, no. 3 (1973): 18–21. Department of Interior, Bureau of Land Management, U.S. Government Printing Office, Washington, DC.

Handwerk, Brian. "Why Tens of Thousands of Toxic Mines Litter the U.S. West: The spill in Colorado's Animas River highlights the problem of wastewater building up in abandoned mines." smithsonian.com August 13, 2015.

Hardin, Garrett. "The Tragedy of the Commons." *Science* 162, no. 3859 (1968): 1243–1248, December 13, 1968.

Harrison, John. "Dams: Impacts on Salmon and Steelhead," Northwest Power and Conservation Council, October 31, 2008. www.nwcouncil.org/history/DamsImpacts.

Henshaw, Henry W. "Report of Chief of Bureau of Biological Survey," U.S. Department of Agriculture. Washington, DC, August 31, 1916.

Heter, Elmo W. "Transplanting Beavers by Airplane and Parachute." *Journal of Wildlife Management* 14, no. 2 (1950): 143–47.

Hey, Donald L., et al. *Flood Damage Reduction in the Upper Mississippi River Basin: An Ecological Alternative.* The Wetlands Initiative, Chicago, 2004. www.academia.edu/5261508.

Hill, Barry T. "Fire Management: Lessons Learned From the Cerro Grande (Los Alamos) Fire." In U.S. General Accounting Office, GAO/TRCED-00-257 Cerro Grande Fire, July 20, 2000.

Hurley, Mark and Pete Zager, "Influence of Predators on Mule Deer Populations Study." Idaho Department of Fish and Game. Boise, September 2007.

Idaho Department of Fish and Game. "Director's Annual Report to the Commission, FY2015." idfg.idaho.gov/sites/default/files/directors-annual-report-2015.pdf.

———. Bighorn Sheep Management Plan, Appendix B: Translocation, Table 1. July 30, 2010. idfg.idaho.gov/old-web/docs/wildlife/planBighorn.pdf.

James, Ronald. "General Mining Act of 1872." Online Nevada Encyclopedia. Nevada Humanities. November 3, 2010. www.onlinenevada.org/articles/national-mining-act-1872.

Jamison, Michael. "Timber in Transition: Subdivisions in Remote Areas Increase Cost County Services," *Missoulian* (Missoula, MT), February 6, 2007.

———. "Tracking Science: Biologist's Findings Show Forest Diversity, Health Influenced by Wolves." *Missoulian* (Missoula, MT). October 25, 2009.

Kaye, Roger. *The Last Great Wilderness: The Campaign to Establish the Arctic National Wildlife Refuge.* Fairbanks: University of Alaska Press, 2006.

Kuipers, Jim. "Putting a Price on Pollution: Financial Assurance for Mine Reclamation and Closure." Mineral Policy Center, Issue Paper No.4, March 2003. www.earthwork.org/files/publications/PuttingAPriceOnPollution.pdf.

Leffingwell, Ernest K. *The Canning River Region Northern Alaska.* Washington, DC: U.S. Government Printing Office, 1919.

Leopold, Aldo. *A Sand County Almanac, and Sketches Here and There.* Commemorative edition. New York: Oxford University Press, 1989.

———. "Grass, Brush, Timber, and Fire in Southern Arizona," *Journal of Forestry* 22, no. 6 (1924): 1–10.

Lewis, Meriwether and William Clark, et al. *The Journals of the Lewis and Clark Expedition.* Lincoln, NE: University of Nebraska Press, online edition at lewisandclarkjournals. unl.edu.

Lichatowich, Jim. *Salmon Without Rivers: A History of the Pacific Salmon Crisis.* Washington, DC: Island Press, 1999.

Lopez, Barry H. *Of Wolves and Men.* New York: Charles Scribner's Sons, 1978.

Lowdermilk, W.C. *Conquest of the Land Through 7,000 Years.* Agriculture Information Bulletin No. 99. U.S. Department of Agriculture, Soil conservation Service. Reprint 1989.

Maffly, Brian. "Barrett Walking Away from West Tavaputs Gas Field." *Salt Lake Tribune,* October 30, 2013.

Manning, Richard. *Grassland: The History, Biology, Politics, and Promise of the American Prairie.* New York: Viking Penguin, 1995.

Marshall, George. Introduction to *Alaska Wilderness: Exploring the Central Brooks Range,* 2nd ed., by Robert Marshall. Berkeley: University of California Press, 1970.

Matthiessen, Peter. *Wildlife in America.* Rev. ed. New York: Elisabeth Sifton Books, Viking, 1987.

———. "In the Great Country." In Banerjee, *Arctic National Wildlife Refuge.*

McClure, Robert. "Pegasus Gold: From Boom to Bankruptcy." In "The Mining of the West: Profit and Pollution on Public Lands." *Seattle Post-Intelligencer* reprint, June 11-14, 2001.

McGee, W. J., ed. *Proceedings of a Conference of Governors.* Washington, DC: Government Printing Office, 1909.

McGrane, Sally. "German Forest Ranger Finds that Trees Have Social Networks, Too." *New York Times.* January 29, 2016.

Mikkelsen, Ejnar. *Conquering the Arctic Ice.* London: William Heinemann, 1909. Reprint, Whitefish, MT: Kessinger Publishing, 2010.

Mineral Lands Leasing Act of 1920. 30 U.S.C. 191 Sec 17.

Mining Law of 1872. Forty-Second Congress. Sess. II Ch. 149, 152. 1872.

Mitchell, John G. *Losing Ground.* San Francisco: Sierra Club Books, 1975.

Mittal, Anu K. "Abandoned Mines: Information on the Number of Hardrock Mines, Cost of Cleanup, and Value of Financial Assurances." U.S. Government Accountability Office, GAO-11-834T, Abandoned mines, Washington, DC, July 14, 2011.

Montana Bureau of Mines and Geology. "Environmental Studies Berkeley Pit and BMF Operable." April 11, 2015. www.mbmg.mtech.edu/env/env-berkeley.asp.

Morison, Samuel Eliot. *The European Discovery of America: The Northern Voyages A.D. 500–1600.* New York: Oxford University Press, 1971.

Mozingo, Hugh N. *Shrubs of the Great Basin: A Natural History.* Reno: University of Nevada Press, 1987.

Murie, Adolph. *A Naturalist in Alaska.* New York: The Devin-Adair Company, 1961.

Murie, Olaus J. *Journeys to the Far North*. Palo Alto, CA: The Wilderness Society and American West Publishing Co., 1973.

Murkowski, Sen. Frank. "It's Not Oil vs. Beauty in the Arctic." Op-Ed. *New York Times*, October 9, 2000.

Murray, David. "State Conservation Team Approves $1.5 Million for Sage Grouse." *Great Falls (MT) Tribune*. November 21, 2016.

Nash, Roderick Frazier. *Wilderness and the American Mind*. 5th ed. New Haven: Yale University Press, 2014.

National Agricultural Statistics Service. www.nass.usda.gov.

National Historic Preservation Act of 1966, 16 U.S.C. 470 Section 106.

National Fire Plan, "Managing the Impact of Wildfires on Communities and the Environment: A Report to the President in Response to the Wildfires of 2000," U.S. Departments of Agriculture and Interior, September 2000. www.forestsandrange lands.gov/documents/resources/reports/2001/8-20-en.pdf.

National Interagency Fire Center website www.nifc.gov/fireInfo/fireInfo_stats_histSig-Fires.htm.

National Park Service, *Natural Resources Report Number 11*, 1978. (In author's possession.)

Natural Resources Defense Council and Defenders of Wildlife. "Petition to Prepare a Recovery Plan Under the Endangered Species Act for the Gray Wolf." February 20, 2008. www.nrdc.org/sites/default/files/wil_08022001a.pdf.

Nazzaro, Robin M. "Hardrock Mining: Information on State Royalties and the Number of Abandoned Mine Sites and Hazards." U.S. Government Accountability Office, GAO-09-854T, Hardrock mining, Washington, DC, July 14, 2009.

Newman, Peter C. *Company of Adventurers: The Story of the Hudson Bay Company*. Vol. 1. New York: Viking Penguin, 1985.

Nixon, President Richard M. State of the Union Message to Congress, February 15, 1973.

NOAA Fisheries. Proposed ESA Recovery Plan for Snake River Sockeye Salmon (*Oncorhynchus nerka*) June 30, 2014. www.westcoast.fisheries.noaa.gov/publications/ recovery_planning/salmon_steelhead/domains/interior_columbia/snake/snake_ river_sockeye_salmon_recovery_plan.pdf.

Nokkentved, Niels S. (N. S.).

———. "Agreement Resuscitates Mine Cleanup Project," *Daily Herald* (Provo, UT), September 8, 2005.

———. "Ancient Art vs. Natural Gas: A Canyon of Controversy," *Daily Herald* (Provo, UT), October 23, 2005.

———. "Bankable Resource: Value of Grazing Permits Raises Many Questions," *Times-News* (Twin Falls, ID), September 22, 1997.

———. "Birth of a Hotspot: Canyonlands Have a Violent Past," *Times-News* (Twin Falls, ID), *April 22, 2001*.

———. "Cattle Foul Mountain Lakes: Trout Listing May Help Resolve Issue," *Times-News* (Twin Falls, ID), September 19, 1999.

———. "Cattle Keep Ranchers in Trouble Over Sensitive Frog Lake Area," *Times-News* (Twin Falls, ID), July 12, 2000.

———. "Controversy Looms Over Archeologist's 'Conflict of Interest,'" *Daily Herald* (Provo, UT), October 5, 2003.

———. *Desert Wings: Controversy in the Idaho Desert.* Pullman: Washington State University Press. 2001.

———. "Feds OK the Killing of Wolves," *Times-News* (Twin Falls, ID), September 7, 2000.

———. *A Forest of Wormwood: Sagebrush, Water and Idaho's Twin Falls Canal Company.* Twin Falls, ID: Twin Falls Canal Company, 2008.

———. "Funds Approved for American Fork Canyon Mine Cleanup," *Daily Herald* (Provo, UT), November 9, 2005.

———. "Gold in Them Hills: Pegasus Launches Black Pine Mine Project," *Times-News* (Twin Falls, ID), September 4, 1992.

———. "Indians, Trappers and More Mark Owyhee History," *Times-News* (Twin Falls, ID), April 22, 2001.

———. "Mating Rituals Among Grouse Similar to Those in Other Species," *Times-News* (Twin Falls, ID), April 22, 1991.

———. "Mining Legacy Lives On: BLM Considers Canyon Claims Active," *Times-News* (Twin Falls, ID), December 3, 2000.

———. "More Protection? Owyhee Dispute Simmers," *Times-News* (Twin Falls, ID), April 22, 2001.

———. "Night Moves on the Lek," *Times-News* (Twin Falls, ID), April 22, 1991.

———. "Ranchers Bank on Furry Engineers to Save Streams," *Times-News* (Twin Falls, ID), September 28, 1992.

———. "Relating to Beast and People: New Wolf Manager Brings Experience, Expertise to Job," *Times-News* (Twin Falls, ID), September 3, 2000.

———. "Salmon Hatchery Changes Recommended," *Olympian* (Olympia, WA), February 20, 2002.

———. "Saving Idaho's Outback: Conservationists Push Monument Proposal," *Times-News* (Twin Falls, ID), November 12, 2000.

———. "Thorn Creek, Indian Spring Fires Contained," *Times-News* (Twin Falls, ID), August 12, 1990.

———. "A Walk on the Range: Critic, Rancher Meet to Talk Grazing," *Times-News* (Twin Falls, ID), September 30, 2000.

———. "Wolves Face Long History of Persecution." *Times-News* (Twin Falls, ID), March 18, 2001.

———. "Wolf Trapping Ends; Road Reopens," *Times-News* (Twin Falls, ID), August 11, 2000.

"137 Years Later." Editorial. *New York Times*, July 20, 2009. www.nytimes.com/2009/07/21/opinion/21tue3.html.

Osborn, Fairfield. *Our Plundered Planet.* Boston: Little Brown and Company, 1948.

Otter, C. L. "Governor Otter, Legislature Sue Feds Over Flawed Process Behind Sage-Grouse Decision." News release, September 25, 2015.

Outwater, Alice. *Water: A Natural History.* New York: Basic Books, 1996.

Pellant, Mike. "Cheatgrass: The Invader That Won the West." Report prepared for the Interior Columbia Basin Ecosystem Management Project, 1996.

Pérez-Peña, Richard. "Study Faults E.P.A. for Toxic Wastewater Spill in Colorado Rockies," *New York Times,* October 22, 2015.

Petersen, Keith. *River of Life Channel of Death: Fish and Dams on the Lower Snake.* Lewiston, ID: Confluence Press, 1995.

Pew Campaign for Responsible Mining. "Reforming the U.S. Hardrock Mining Law of 1872: The Price of Inaction." January 27, 2009. www.pewtrusts.org/en/research-and-analysis/reports/2009/01/27/reforming-the-us-hardrock-mining-law-of-1872-the-price-of-inaction.

Pinchot, Gifford. *Breaking New Ground.* New York: Harcourt, Brace and Company, 1947.

Pissot, Jim. "Timber Troubles: The Spotted Owl is Not the Cause of the Northwest Forest Crisis." *Washington Post.* Op-Ed. April 2, 1993.

Public Land Order 2214, Department of Interior, December 6, 1960.

Pyle, Robert Michael. *Wintergreen: Rambles in a Ravaged Land.* Seattle: Sasquatch Books, 2001.

Pyne, Stephen J. *Fire in America: A Cultural History of Wildland and Rural Fire.* Seattle: University of Washington Press, 1997.

Read, Wolf. "The 1962 Columbus Day Storm," www.climate.washington.edu/storm king/October1962.html.

Reed, John C., Cdr., USNR. *Exploration of Naval Petroleum Reserve No. 4 and Adjacent Areas, Northern Alaska, 1944-53, Part 1, History of the Exploration.* U.S. Geological Survey, Government Printing Office, Washington, DC, 1958. pubs.usgs.gov/pp/0301/report.pdf.

Ribe, Tom. *Inferno by Committee: A History of the Cerro Grande (Los Alamos) Fire.* Victoria, BC: Trafford Publishing, 2010.

Ribe, Tom and Timothy Ingalsbee. *Smoke Signals: The Need for Public Tolerance and Regulatory Relief for Wildland Smoke Emissions.* Firefighters United for Safety, Ethics, and Ecology (FUSEE), August 2011. www.fusee.org/resources/Documents/FUSEE_SmokeSignals5_print.pdf.

Ridler, Keith. "Jewell Orders Firefighting Strategy That Protects Habitat," *The Associated Press,* January 6, 2015.

Ripple, William J. and Beschta, Robert L. "Trophic Cascades in Yellowstone: The First 15 Years after Wolf Reintroduction." *Biological Conservation* 145, no. 1 (January 2012). www.sciencedirect.com/science/article/pii/S0006320711004046.

Rivers and Harbors Act 1945, Public Law 79-14, Ch. 19, S.35.

Salvo, Mark. *Western Wildlife Under Hoof: Public Lands Livestock Grazing Threatens Iconic Species.* Report, WildEarth Guardians, April 2009.

Schaffer, Paul. "Beaver on Trial." *Oregon Fish and Wildlife Magazine.* December 22, 1941.

Schamberger, M. L., M. J. Hay, and R. L. Johnson. "Economic analysis of critical habitat designation effects for the northern spotted owl." U.S. Fish and Wildlife Service, Washington, DC 1992. pubs.er.usgs.gov/publication/70127880.

Shanks, Bernard. *This Land is Your Land: The Struggle to Save America's Public Lands.* San Francisco: Sierra Club Books, 1984.

Smith, Bruce D. *The Emergence of Agriculture.* New York: Scientific American Library, 1998.

Smith, Douglas, et al. "Yellowstone after Wolves." *BioScience* 53, no. 4 (April 2003).

Smith, Michael and Elizabeth S. Merritt. Letter to BLM officials in Utah "Re: Disagreement with BLM's 'Finding of No Adverse Effect' Stone Cabin Seismic Exploration

Project Utah-70-2003-15." National Trust for Historic Preservation. September 29, 2003.

Smurthwaite, Don. "Sage Grouse: A Part of Idaho's High Desert Heritage." Idaho Department of Fish and Game and Bureau of Land Management. May 1998.

Southern Utah Wilderness Alliance et al. "BLM's Approval of 25 Natural Gas Wells in Utah's Nine Mile Canyon Region Sparks Lawsuit." News release, August 7, 2008.

Spokesman Review (Spokane, WA). "Future of Area's Salmon at Stake: Whether to Sacrifice Industry for Dams up for Decision." June 25, 1947.

Swan, James G. *The Northwest Coast, Or Three Years' Residence in Washington Territory*, 5th ed. Seattle: University of Washington Press, 1992.

Taylor Grazing Act of 1934, 43 USC 315.

Taylor, Joseph E. III. *Making Salmon: An Environmental History of the Northwest Fisheries Crisis*. Seattle: University of Washington Press, 1999.

Trimble, Stephen. *The Sagebrush Ocean: A Natural History of the Great Basin*. 10th anniversary ed. Las Vegas: University of Nevada Press, 1999.

Trueblood, Jack. "Driving Guide to the Mud Flat Road." *Idaho Wildlife* 16, no. 2 (Spring 1996). Idaho Department of Fish and Game, Boise.

Turkewitz, Julie. "Colorado Spill Heightens Debate Over Future of Old Mines," *New York Times*, August 16, 2015.

U.S. Constitution, Article IV, Section 3.

U.S. Court of Appeals, District of Columbia Circuit. 880 F.2d 432. July 14, 1989.

U.S. Court of Appeals for The Ninth Circuit. No. 14-35811 D.C. No. 4:13-cv-00018-RRB.

U.S. Department of Agriculture. "Forest Service Large Fire Suppression Costs." *Audit Report*, Office of Inspector General, Western Region. Report No. 08601-44-SF, November 2006. www.usda.gov/oig/webdocs/08601-44-SF.pdf.

U.S. Departments of Agriculture and Interior. "Managing the Impact of Wildfires on Communities and the Environment: A Report to the President in Response to the Wildfires of 2000." September 2000.

U.S. Department of Interior, Bureau of Land Management, and USDA Forest Service. "Rangeland Reform '94; A Proposal to Improve Management of Rangeland Ecosystems and the Administration of Livestock Grazing on Public Lands," August 1993.

U.S. Department of Interior. *Study of Fees for Grazing Livestock on Federal Lands: A Report from the Secretary of the Interior and the Secretary of Agriculture*. Washington, DC: U.S. Government Printing Office, 1977. Reprint, Google Books.

U.S. Energy Information Administration. "Short Term Energy Outlook," *Analysis and Projections*. March 2017. www.eia.gov/outlooks/steo/report/global_oil.cfm.

———. "How Much Petroleum Does the United States Import and Export?" www.eia.gov/tools/faqs/faq.php?id=727&t=6.

U.S. Environmental Protection Agency. *Abandoned Mine Site Characterization and Cleanup Handbook. August 2000*. www.epa.gov/sites/production/files/2015-09/documents/2000_08_pdfs_amscch.pdf.

———. *Polluted Runoff: Nonpoint Source (NPS) Pollution*. www.epa.gov/nps

———. *Superfund Policy, Guidance and Law*. February 10, 2017. www.epa.gov/superfund/superfund-policy-guidance-and-laws.

U.S. Fish and Wildlife Service. Arctic National Wildlife Refuge, Alaska. "About the Refuge." www.fws.gov/refuge/Arctic/about.html.

————. "Designation of Revised Critical Habitat for Northern Spotted Owl." *Federal Register* 77, no. 233 (December 4, 2013): 71876–72068.

————. "Endangered and Threatened Wildlife and Plants; 12-Month Finding on a Petition To List Greater Sage-Grouse (*Centrocercus urophasianus*) as an Endangered or Threatened Species," *Federal Register* 80, no. 191 (October 2, 2015): 59858–59942.

————. "Interior Expands Common-Sense Efforts to Conserve Sage-Grouse Habitat in the West." News release, March 5, 2010. www.fws.gov/mountain-prairie/pressrel/dc02.html.

————. "Memorandum Regarding a Viable Wolf Population in the Northern Rocky Mountains." In *The Reintroduction of Gray Wolves to Yellowstone National Park and Central Idaho,* Final Environmental Impact Statement, Appendix 9. April 14, 1994.

————. *Public Land Order 2214,* December 6, 1960. www.fws.gov/uploadedFiles/Region_7/NWRS/Zone_1/Arctic/PDF/ANWR_plo.pdf.

————. "Reclassification of the Gray Wolf in the United States and Mexico, with Determination of Critical Habitat in Michigan and Minnesota." *Federal Register* 43, no. 47 (March 9, 1978): 9607–9615.

————. "Table 5b: Northern Rocky Mountain Confirmed Wolf Depredations by State, 1987–2012." *Northern Rocky Mountain Wolf Recovery Program 2012 Interagency Annual Report.* April 17, 2013. www.fws.gov/mountain-prairie/es/species/mammals/wolf/annualrpt12/index.html.

————. "2011 National Survey of Fishing, Hunting, and Wildlife-Related Recreation." digitalmedia.fws.gov/digital/collection/document/id/859.

U.S. General Accounting Office. *Chandler Lake Land Exchange Not in the Government's Best Interests.* Report to the Chairman, Subcommittee on Water and Power Resources, Committee on Interior and Insular Affairs, House of Representatives. GAO/RCED-90-5. October 1989.

U.S. Geological Survey. "How Does the 2017 National Petroleum Reserve-Alaska Assessment Compare to Other Assessments USGS Has Done?" www.usgs.gov/faqs/how-does-2017-national-petroleum-reserve-alaska-assessment-compare-other-assessments-usgs-has?qt-news_science_products=0#qt-news_science_products.

U.S. Government Accountability Office. *Energy Policy Act of 2005: Greater Clarity Needed to Address Concerns with Categorical Exclusions for Oil and Gas Development under Section 390 of the Act.* GAO-09-872 Section 390 Categorical Exclusions, September 2009.

————. *Livestock Grazing: Federal Expenditures and Receipts Vary, Depending on the Agency and the Purpose of the Fee Charged.* GAO-05-869 Livestock Grazing, September 2005.

Volz, Matt. "Thousands of Geese Deaths Put Focus on Toxic Pit that Concerns Montana City, EPA," *Idaho Statesman,* January 29, 2017.

Warren, David. "Texas Oil, Gas Discovery Biggest Ever in U.S." *Idaho Statesman.* November 17, 2016.

Washington Department of Fish and Wildlife. *Conservation.* "Hatcheries: Salmon Hatchery Overview." 2014. wdfw.wa.gov/hatcheries/overview.html.

Welch, Julia Conway. *Gold Town to Ghost Town: The Story of Silver City, Idaho.* Moscow: University of Idaho Press, 1982.

Western Watersheds v. Schneider. Complaint. Case 1:16-cv-83 filed February 25, 2016, in The United States District Court for The District Of Idaho.

Whitney, David. "Seeking Statehood—Stevens Bent Rules To Bring Alaska Into the Union." *Anchorage Daily News*, August 10, 1994.

Wildlife Services Data Reports, 2014. USDA Animal and Plant Health Inspection Service, www.aphis.usda.gov/aphis/home.

Williams, Richard N. ed. *Return to the River: Restoring Salmon to the Columbia River*. San Diego: Elsevier Academic Press, 2006.

Wilson, Edward O. "The Global Solution to Extinction." Opinion. *New York Times*. March 13, 2016.

Wohlleben, Peter. *The Hidden Life of Trees: What They Feel, How They Communicate*. Berkeley: Greystone Books, 2016.

Wolf, Eric R. *Europe and the People Without History*. Berkeley: University of California Press, 1997.

Worster, Donald. *A River Running West: The Life of John Wesley Powell*. New York: Oxford University Press, 2002.

Wright, Sam. Declaration in support of plaintiff's motion for preliminary injunction, Case No. CV03-0687Z in U.S. District Court Western Washington, Seattle. March 2003.

Wulf, Andrea. *The Invention of Nature: Alexander von Humboldt's New World*. New York: Alfred A. Knopf, 2015.

Wuerthner, George. "Sage Grouse Funding Priorities are Misplaced." *The Wildlife News*. November 22, 2016. *www.thewildlifenews.com*.

———. "Sage Grouse, Livestock Grazing, and the Bovine Curtain." *The Wildlife News*. August 3, 2013. www.thewildlifenews.com/2013/08/03.

———. "Burning Questions." Counter Punch. June 12, 2009. www.counterpunch. org/2009/06/12/burning-questions.

Wuerthner, George, ed. *The Wildfire Reader: A Century of Failed Forest Policy*. Washington, DC: Island Press, 2006.

Wuerthner, George, and Mollie Matteson, eds. *Welfare Ranching: The Subsidized Destruction of the American West*. Washington, DC: Island Press, 2002.

Yergin, Daniel. *The Prize: The Epic Quest for Oil, Money and Power*. New York: Simon & Schuster, 1991.

Zager, Peter, Craig White, and George Pauley. "Elk Ecology Study IV: Factors Influencing Elk Calf Recruitment July 1, 2005 to June 30, 2006." Idaho Department of Fish and Game, Boise: September 2007. collaboration.idfg.idaho.gov/WildlifeTechnical Reports/W-160-R-33-31%20Completion.pdf.

Zager, Peter and Michael W. Gratson. "Elk Ecology Study IV: Factors Influencing Elk Calf Recruitment July 1, 2000 to June 30, 2001." Idaho Department of Fish and Game. Boise, ID, April 2002. collaboration.idfg.idaho.gov/WildlifeTechnical Reports/Elk%20Ecology%20SIV%20PR01.pdf.

Index

About the Author

A native of Copenhagen, Denmark, Niels S. Nokkentved immigrated to Canada with his parents in 1957, and three years later to Illinois where he became a U.S. citizen in 1966. He served a hitch in the U.S. Navy aboard a destroyer in the Pacific during the Vietnam War. After the military he traveled extensively for a time before attending Western Washington University.

In nearly two decades as a newspaper journalist, Nokkentved reported on natural resources, nuclear energy and waste, water quality, water rights, fire, and public lands, receiving awards for his work from the Society of Professional Journalists, the Associated Press, and the Idaho Press Club, along with a C.B. Blethen award for investigative reporting. From 2005 to 2013, he served as a public information specialist with the Idaho Department of Fish and Game.

Photo by Sue Nass

Nokkentved is the author of three books: *Back Road Daydreams: Reflections on the Great Outdoors* (2010); *A Forest of Wormwood: Sagebrush, Water and Idaho's Twin Falls Canal Company* (Twin Falls Canal Company, 2008), and *Desert Wings: Controversy in the Idaho Desert* (WSU Press, 2001). He holds degrees in journalism and environmental studies from Western Washington University and currently lives in Boise.